D0424974

AFRICA IN THE MODERN WORLD

Edited by GWENDOLEN M. CARTER
Director, Program of African Studies
Northwestern University

The Cameroon Federal Republic
by Victor T. Le Vine

Ethiopia: The Modernization of Autocracy
by Robert L. Hess

Liberia: The Evolution of Privilege
by J. Gus Liebenow

West Africa's Council of the Entente
by Virginia Thompson

The Entente states

WEST AFRICA'S
Council of the Entente

VIRGINIA THOMPSON

UNIVERSITY OF CALIFORNIA, BERKELEY

Cornell University Press

ITHACA AND LONDON

320.966
T47w

Copyright © 1972 by Cornell University

All rights reserved. Except for brief quotations in a review, this book, or parts thereof, must not be reproduced in any form without permission in writing from the publisher. For information address Cornell University Press, 124 Roberts Place, Ithaca, New York 14850.

First published 1972 by Cornell University Press.
Published in the United Kingdom by Cornell University Press Ltd.,
2-4 Brook Street, London W1Y 1AA.

International Standard Book Number 0-8014-0683-8
Library of Congress Catalog Card Number 70-171935

PRINTED IN THE UNITED STATES OF AMERICA
BY VAIL-BALLOU PRESS, INC.

Librarians: Library of Congress cataloging information
appears on the last page of the book.

To R. A.

UNIVERSITY LIBRARIES
CARNEGIE-MELLON UNIVERSITY
PITTSBURGH, PENNSYLVANIA 15213

Foreword

Before 1958, the map of West Africa was vastly simpler than it is today. Stretching from Dakar on the Atlantic Ocean to the borders of French Equatorial Africa nearly half across the continent, French West Africa included eight units that were contiguous along substantial borders although separated at the coast by three members of the British Commonwealth and Empire: Nigeria, Ghana, and Sierra Leone. The dominant question for the future of West Africa and for the relation of the francophone African states to France itself was whether the inexorable movement of African states to independence would maintain the federal structure of French West Africa but transfer its control to African leadership, or whether the process of fissure would reduce French West Africa to a conglomeration of separate and relatively weak states. If the movement for unity succeeded, an independent Federation of Francophone West Africa would be strong enough to negotiate on more or less equal terms with the Federation of Nigeria, Africa's most populous state, and with France itself. If it failed—and it did fail—each of the separate units that had constituted the former federation would be left to make what arrangements it could, politically, economically, educationally, and militarily, with its own neighbors and the former metropole.

One paradox of African development is that Ivory Coast, under its crafty but far-sighted leader, Félix Houphouët-Boigny, which in 1958 threw its decisive influence against maintaining the federation of West Africa, has subsequently been the moving force in developing cooperative relations between francophone African states, through both what is now known as the Organisation Commune Africaine et Malgache (OCAM), and its nucleus, the Council of the Entente. Neither of these organizations has been particularly cohesive, but their continued existence is in itself significant; other efforts within the same group of states to establish yet closer relationships have been transitory—notably the Mali Federation between Senegal and the Soudan (subsequently renamed Mali) which lasted for only eighteen months during 1959 and 1960.

Since a subsequent volume in this series will be devoted to an analysis of Ivory Coast, the most prosperous and successful of the francophone states, the present study deals with Ivory Coast only to the degree necessary to explain its leading role within the Council of the Entente. This self-restraint has provided the author with the space to deal comprehensively with the other members of the Entente— Niger, Dahomey, Upper Volta, and Togo—as well as with the association itself. One of the smaller states of the Entente, Dahomey, will also be the subject of a book in this series.

Americans, on the whole, know much less about francophone Africa than they do about those countries like Nigeria, Ghana, Kenya, or South Africa which present no language barrier and on which a wider range of publications is available. Thus, there is a particular satisfaction in presenting such rich resources for the understanding of these French-speaking states: this work on the Council of the Entente, the recently published volume by Victor Le Vine on the Cameroon Republic, and the two projected books on the Ivory Coast and Dahomey. Together they illuminate the internal structures and developments of an especially interesting group of states and also, through this volume, the international interactions among five of them.

The Council of the Entente and the British Commonwealth of Nations offer some tantalizing similarities as well as differences. Each of these groupings includes one dominant state: the United Kingdom within the Commonwealth, and Ivory Coast within the Entente. Both countries have shown remarkable restraint in exploiting their superior resources, a fact which has made self-interest a powerful, perhaps the most powerful, bond of these associations. Admittedly, there are fundamental differences between the historical evolution and the international significance of the Commonwealth and those of the Council of the Entente. Moreover, the latter could scarcely have existed without the geographical contiguity of its member states, which contrasts sharply with the wide dispersion of the territories of the Commonwealth. But the postwar Commonwealth, like the Entente, has had to adjust to some profound transformations, including army rule, within certain of its member states, and its ability to survive in the face of internal and external strains has been one of its chief distinctions. "Better to keep an association in being than to destroy it," said Pandit Nehru, Prime Minister of independent India, when he was challenged on why he kept that country within the Commonwealth of Nations. The Council of the Entente is an insignificant grouping in comparison with the Commonwealth, but in its own small way it provides a tenuous bridge linking five very different francophone West African states. It is worth while finding out how and why it continues to do so.

GWENDOLEN M. CARTER

Northwestern University
June 1971

Acknowledgments

The material for this book was largely gathered during four study-trips to the Entente states between 1953 and 1969. I would like to express my warm gratitude to the many officials, politicians, and laymen who were most helpful in providing otherwise unobtainable documents and granting me informative interviews. A special word of thanks for his kindness and cooperation is owed to M. Paul Kaya, the able secretary-general of the Council of the Entente.

Dahomey Information Service has supplied photographs 2, 3, 4, and 5; Documentation Française, photographs 6, 10, and 11; *Europe-France-Outremer* and Associated Press Ltd., photograph 14; Info-Niger, photograph 8; Ivory Coast Information Service, photograph 1; Togo Information Service, photographs 15 and 16; and Voltaic Information Service, photograph 9.

VIRGINIA THOMPSON

Eze Bord-de-Mer, France
June 1971

Contents

Illustrations

Tables

Introduction

Of all the successive reforms enacted by the French Parliament for Overseas France after World War II, the *loi-cadre* (framework law) of 1956 left the deepest imprint on the internal political evolution of francophone Black Africa. The reforms of 1946 had ended some of the worst abuses of the colonial regime, initiated the Africans into the processes of elected representative government, and had given to a few of their elite experience in Metropole and world affairs. They had also been accompanied by the injection of massive amounts of French public funds into developing the economies of the federations of French West and French Equatorial Africa. The referendum of September 1958 on the constitution of the Fifth Republic offered Africans *inter alia* the choice between independence without further French aid and membership in an amorphous Franco-African Community. It did not, however, settle their future relationship with France, as intended, nor did it attempt to determine the interrelationships of the newly semiautonomous African states.

It was the *loi-cadre,* however, that broke up the two federations that had theretofore given a certain cohesion to their members' economic and political structures. Moreover, the law granted the individual countries the larger measure of self-government that led inexorably to their achievement of independence within a relatively short time. At the same time, the *loi-cadre* divided the francophone units into two groups that cut across existing territorial and party lines.

On the one hand were the "federalists," who sought to create African unity through new organizational forms, and on the other the "autonomists," who wanted only direct relations between France and the individual territories as established by bilateral agreements. Late in 1958, soon after the constitutional referendum, Ghana and Guinea, the first two states to become independent in West Africa after World War II, created the earliest of a series of unions and federations whose origins, motivation, and organization were diverse, although they all stemmed from the desire for some form of African unity. Some of the groups were ideologically oriented, others owed their formation to events outside the area, and still others resulted from their leaders' personal ambitions or from purely practical considerations. In most cases all those factors were present. The creation of one group inspired the founding of still another, either emulating or opposing it.

The Ghana-Guinea Union, which started this chain reaction in November 1958, died of inaction; the Mali Federation, founded in January 1959, broke up noisily a year and a half later; and the Union of African States, formed in December 1960, was absorbed into the Casablanca bloc the following month. The latter bloc and the competing Monrovia group, born in May 1961, were already moribund before they were formally dissolved following the creation of the Organization of African Unity in May 1963. One of the most durable of such groups has been the organization of moderate French-speaking African states, known successively as the Brazzaville bloc, the Union Africaine et Malgache (UAM), the Union Africaine et Malgache de Coopération Economique (UAMCE), and the Organisation Commune Africaine et Malgache (OCAM), whose nucleus was and still is the Council of the Entente.

The founder and prime mover of the Entente is Félix Houphouët-Boigny, president of Ivory Coast, who also organized the Rassemblement Démocratique Africain (RDA), first interterritorial political movement in French Black Africa. The RDA was formed in 1946 under the aegis of the French Communist Party, which gave it organizational form and encouraged its opposition to the colonial regime, though not to the point of demanding independence. By 1949, the RDA's rapid growth and electoral successes had alarmed the colonial administration, especially in Ivory Coast, into using forceful methods which disrupted the RDA's organization and reduced its effectiveness. At the same time, the French Communist Party's preoccupation with revolution in Europe and its ebbing strength in the Paris government convinced Houphouët that its affiliation with the RDA had become more of a liability than an asset. As a result, late in 1950 he accepted the offer of collaboration made by the then Minister of Overseas France. Although most RDA members followed Houphouët's lead, his drastic change of course inevitably alienated its more radical fringe, which broke away to form splinter parties, notably in Senegal, Cameroun, and Niger.

Two years before this break occurred, a second interterritorial French Black African party, the Indépendants d'Outre-Mer (IOM), was created under the leadership of Léopold Senghor, Senegal's outstanding intellectual and later its president. The IOM offered an alternative organization to Houphouët's movement for those Africans seeking a middle course between the now conservative RDA and its communist-oriented dissidents. In the 1951 elections to the French National Assembly, the IOM gained seats at the RDA's expense, and thereafter employed its parliamentary strength to win legislative reforms from successive French governments, such as the Overseas Labor Code of 1952 and the Municipal Reform Bill of 1955. Moreover, it drew up a platform in 1953 that advocated the transformation of the French Republic into a federation composed of France and its largely autonomous overseas territories.

Despite its legislative successes and its formulation of what was then a bold African policy, the IOM lacked mass support in Africa and remained essentially a pressure group based in Paris. The RDA, on the other hand, was assiduously cultivating good relations with local French administrators and businessmen. By mending its political fences at home, the RDA staged a spectacular electoral comeback in 1956, despite its failure to devise a new ideological base. Indeed Houphouët, by his very pragmatism and policy of economic liberalism, inspired the confidence of foreign investors, with the result that Ivory Coast became the most prosperous of the West African territories, rapidly outdistancing its old rival, Senegal. His electoral and financial successes restored Houphouët to his former eminence as leader of French Black Africa and won for him the first full ministerial post ever accorded an African in any French government.

As a minister in the Mollet government, Houphouët coauthored the *loi-cadre,* in which he gave legislative form to his new policy of close political and economic collaboration with France. This collaboration was to be spelled out in bilateral agreements that would leave each territory free to dispose of its own resources and eliminate the contributions it had formerly made to the federal government at Dakar or the one at Brazzaville. The eclipse of the two French-dominated, top-heavy, and costly federations met with widespread approval. At the same time these developments aroused African fears of a "balkanization" of French

Black Africa, and also of the new financial burden placed on the meager resources of each territory by the necessity of establishing separate administrative services in place of those formerly provided by the federal governments. Thus although the *loi-cadre* prepared the way for the territories' political independence, it also threatened to increase their economic dependence on France. Moreover, because it destroyed whatever formal unity had existed among the territories, the *loi-cadre* drew sharp criticism from such respected moderate leaders as Senghor, as well as from Marxists like Sékou Touré.

In West Africa, the rapid political evolution of the Gold Coast and of the United Nations trust territories of Cameroun and Togo was fanning aspirations for independence and African unity in the neighboring French territories. By remaining in Paris as minister in successive French governments during the late 1950's, Houphouët became identified with France's repression of the Algerian revolt and lost touch with the fast-changing African scene. It was not until the RDA held its party congress at Bamako in September 1957 that Houphouët fully realized that he was no longer in control of its territorial branches in Black Africa. At that meeting it became apparent that he could command the loyalty of only the conservative minority, whereas the more radical elements, under the leadership of Sékou Touré of Guinea, were gravitating to the federalist camp headed by Senghor.

Six months later, the division of francophone Black Africans into federalists and autonomists was institutionalized when the former group formed the Parti du Regroupement Africain (PRA) at Dakar, with territorial branches throughout the two federations. The federalists themselves were soon split, however, by the referendum on the constitution of the Fifth French Republic held the following September, although the question of African unity was not then directly involved. Sizeable groups in Senegal, Soudan, and Niger advocated a negative vote in the referendum, but only Guinea opted for total independence. Abruptly cut off from ties with France and isolated from the other French-speaking territories, Guinea quickly accepted Ghana's invitation to form a union that rescued it from imminent bankruptcy and laid the foundations for what those two countries' leaders—Sékou Touré and Kwame Nkrumah—hoped to make into a wider organization.

The formation of the Ghana-Guinea Union was one of three significant setbacks for Houphouët's policies during the last months of 1958. In October, riots by Ivorian youths in Abidjan directed against the Dahomeans and Togolese employed there resulted in a large-scale exodus of those aliens and created tensions between their governments and that of Ivory Coast. Then, in December, it was announced that the premiers of Dahomey and Upper Volta would attend the meeting at Bamako called by Senghor and Modibo Keita of Soudan to form a primary federation. This seemed to foreshadow a reconstitution of the old West African Federation and the restoration of Dakar to its status of federal capital, thus making it once again a formidable competitor with Abidjan. If Houphouët were not to lose permanently his leadership position in French Black Africa, it had become imperative for him not only to restore good relations with his French-speaking neighbors, but also to prevent them from gravitating into the Senegal-Soudan orbit. Still another danger for Houphouët loomed on his eastern horizon, where Nigeria with its economic potential and huge population constituted an almost irresistible pole of attraction for Niger, Dahomey, and Upper Volta.

Houphouët realized, albeit belatedly, that to offset these centrifugal forces he must offer those countries stronger counterattractions. The high price that he would have to pay was the sacrifice of much of the financial resources that he had tried to safeguard for Ivory Coast's own use through the *loi-cadre*. Houphouët's realism and pragmatism were demonstrated by his willingness once again to change course drastically as he had in 1950, and to pursue a policy diametrically opposed to his previous position. In early December 1958, he made a statement upon returning from Paris which indicated the new trend in his thinking. While still adamantly opposed to any reconstitution of the old French West African Federation, he declared his support for inter-African "ties of solidarity in the domains of justice, civil service, labor, public health, and tariffs in a *conseil d'entente*." [1] This vague and general statement of intent was hardly tempting enough to deter Premiers Maurice Yameogo of Upper Volta and Sourou-Migan Apithy of Dahomey from attending the federalist congress scheduled for the end of that month in Bamako. Houphouët then realized that he must rapidly and appreciably raise the stakes if he were to exert effective pressure on the Voltaic and Dahomean leaders. In so doing he had the support of General de Gaulle, who had been jolted by the failure of his policy to isolate Guinea and who was prone, in any case, to back fully the loyal Ivorian president.

Before the end of 1958, Upper Volta, Dahomey, and Niger had all voted to become autonomous republics and member states of the Franco-African Community, but this did not preclude their joining an African primary federation of the kind Houphouët opposed. In his view, the main drawbacks to such a federation as Senghor and Modibo Keita were

[1] *Le Monde,* Dec. 6, 1958.

trying to create would be the inevitable curtailment of its members' national sovereignty and the subordination of their relations with France to those with other African countries. His Council of the Entente, on the other hand, was to have no rigid supranational structures and would leave each member country free to shape its own political and economic policies in all respects other than the few specific ones on which they unanimously agreed to collaborate.

In setting up the Entente, Niger presented the fewest problems for Houphouët, for its premier, Hamani Diori, was one of his most devoted followers. Dahomey and Upper Volta proved to be far more difficult, since both had specific grievances against Ivory Coast and their leaders were not bound to Houphouët by longstanding ties of loyalty. Moreover, each of those countries had a federalist party, was beset by internal divisions, and was preoccupied with drafting its constitution, and not one of their heads of government was secure in his tenure of power.

In these unstable conditions Houphouët had to operate with great discretion, for by openly throwing the weight of his influence on one side or the other he risked arousing an adverse political reaction. Only in the economic sphere could he safely contribute to those countries' stability and, at the same time, exploit motives of self-interest to induce their leaders to join his Council of the Entente. Poverty in varying degrees was common to all three, and the imminent breakup of the French West African Federation would further impoverish them by cutting off their federal subsidies. In central West Africa, Ivory Coast was the only country whose leader was politically unassailable in his home territory and whose economy was prosperous. Houphouët was therefore in a unique position to exert a preponderant influence on all his French-speaking neighbors except Guinea.

But he had to move swiftly because the four delegations which met at Bamako at the end of December were to hold another conference within two weeks at which the Mali Federation would be constituted. Although it was not yet clear how the new federation would shape up, it was already apparent that the Senegalese and Soudanese leaders were eager to give the widest possible territorial base to their prospective organization.

Houphouët began a series of behind-the-scenes negotiations with Maurice Yameogo and Sourou-Migan Apithy designed to detach Upper Volta and Dahomey from association in the Mali Federation. He enlisted the services of Hamani Diori of Niger to help stabilize the position of Apithy in Dahomey, and also later to persuade Hubert Maga to join the Entente. Houphouët himself undertook to negotiate with Yameogo, for of the three countries most directly concerned, Upper Volta had the greatest importance for Ivory Coast. Upper Volta was the West African territory with which Ivory Coast had the longest and closest ties, its manpower was indispensable for the Ivorian economy, and it constituted a geographical link with Dahomey and Niger. But in choosing to come to terms first with Upper Volta, Houphouët was handicapped by his lack of political leverage with Yameogo, who had only recently joined the RDA, and by the Voltaics' longstanding resentment of the role that Ivory Coast had played in their history. Thus it took all his skill as well as financial inducements to bring Upper Volta and Dahomey into the Entente under Ivory Coast leadership. How this was done and what the Entente embodied are best followed through a study of its member countries and of the course of events in each of them.

WEST AFRICA'S
Council of the Entente

CHAPTER 1

Ivory Coast's
Junior Partners

Upper Volta

For more than eight centuries the internal history of Upper Volta was dominated by that of its major tribal group, the Mossi. Established in the east and center of the territory, the Mossi were divided into the four kingdoms of Ouagadougou, Yatenga, Tenkodogo, and Fada N'Gourma. Each was headed by a *naba,* or chief, all of whom initially owed allegiance to the Moro Naba[1] of Ouagadougou. Although Fada N'Gourma soon broke away to form an independent kingdom, it retained a political and social structure analogous to that of Ouagadougou. After a period of military aggressiveness, which included the conquest of Timbuktu in the fourteenth century, the Mossi contented themselves with defending their existing boundaries against the encroachments of Muslim invaders.

In the late nineteenth century, French army officers began systematically exploring this area of the West African hinterland. In the west they found a scattering of small tribes in varying stages of evolution, but in the east they were surprised to come upon the populous and cohesive states ruled by the animist Mossi *nabas.* Although these states possessed remarkably well-developed administrations headed by the *nabas* and their courts, rigidly hierarchized social orders, and relatively prosperous economies, they were beginning to

[1] Moro is the singular of Mossi.

disintegrate. Consequently the *nabas* agreed in 1896 to accept a French protectorate centered at Ouagadougou. The
western tribes in the Bobo-Dioulasso region offered longer
resistance to French rule, but by 1904 the whole area had
become part of the colony then known as Haut Sénégal–
Niger.

After World War I, when the French authorities considered revising this colony's administration, they disagreed
as to what course to follow. Some of them maintained that
because the Mossi formed a distinct ethnic group, the region
in which they lived should have a separate administration,
while others insisted that because the Mossi country was
linked by geography and trade to neighboring French colonies, it should either be divided among them or handed over
as a whole to Ivory Coast. The former view prevailed, and in
1919 Upper Volta was constituted as a separate colony, to
the discontent of the French in Ivory Coast.

The Ivorian administration backed the contention of its
French planters, foresters, and merchants that the cost of
providing a separate administration for Upper Volta was too
great for such a poor region to support. Actually, what they
feared was a curtailment in the number of Mossi immigrants,
on whose labor they had come to depend. The Dakar federal
government, however, turned a deaf ear to their pleas until
the world depression of the early 1930's gave greater cogency
to arguments in favor of economy measures. So little effort
had been made by France to develop the country's resources
or to check the exodus of its manpower to the coast that Upper
Volta was far from being economically viable. Consequently,
in 1932 Upper Volta was dismembered, and its territory and
populations were divided among the neighboring colonies of
Niger, Soudan, and Ivory Coast.

The Mossi were the main victims of this radical and

arbitrary surgery. Not only was their region isolated and their capital city, Ouagadougou, destituted of such administrative and economic equipment as it possessed, but they were governed from distant Abidjan, where their problems and needs were ignored. Although in 1937 the French authorities in Abidjan made some amends by reconstituting the Mossi area as a separate administrative unit, this did not arrest Ouagadougou's decline. Furthermore, its western rival, Bobo-Dioulasso, was growing in importance as a commercial crossroads and as the northern terminus of the Abidjan-Niger railroad.

By the end of World War II, the Mossi were psychologically eager for a change. However, it was certainly an exaggeration to describe this upsurge of solidarity and apartness as a "Voltaic risorgimento," [2] as did agents of the RDA who, operating from Abidjan, took the initiative in making the peoples of Upper Volta politically conscious. Soon after that movement was formed in 1946, it sent emissaries to the territory to enlist as members the Mossi, and later the Bobo and Lobi tribes in the west. The preoccupation with ethnic interests that the RDA encountered among the Mossi precluded their usefulness to the political organization that Houphouët was then trying to build up. When Houphouët asked the Moro Naba to collaborate in naming an Ivorian candidate for election to the French constituent assembly, the *naba* chose a loyal servitor who proceeded to campaign successfully and exclusively on the issue of reconstituting a Mossi state.[3] The only immediate result of this evidence of the Mossi's desire to be separated from Ivory Coast was a

[2] Gabriel d'Arboussier, speaking in the French Union Assembly, June 24, 1949.

[3] F. J. Amon d'Aby, *La Côte d'Ivoire dans la Cité Africaine* (Paris, 1951), p. 55.

large increase in the Moro Naba's official emoluments, but this did not deter that paramount chief from continuing to exert pressure on the Paris government.

France finally acceded to his plea and on September 4, 1947, Upper Volta once again became a territory in its own right, not because it was any better equipped than before to maintain its own administration but in the hope that it might curtail the RDA's expansion in that area. Several more years were to pass, however, before the long-promised extension of the Abidjan-Niger railroad to Ouagadougou was completed and before Upper Volta was provided with representative elected institutions and a budget that would give reality to what had been until then merely an academic recognition of its separate status. This long delay hampered Upper Volta's political as well as its economic evolution.

Foiled in the Mossi region, the RDA turned to more promising fields in western Upper Volta. There that movement was able to make headway among the smaller and more subdivided tribes—the Bobo, Gourounsi, Lobi, and Peul (Fulani)—who were apprehensive about the prospective reconstitution of a territory in which they would be at a disadvantage vis-à-vis the more populous and cohesive Mossi. Because the RDA made such rapid progress among the western tribes, Bobo-Dioulasso was chosen as the site for its second congress in 1948. The RDA high command, however, had not reckoned with the forceful opposition of the local French administration, which not only forbade the holding of the congress but jailed some members of the movement's territorial branch, the Entente Voltaïque. By encouraging the proliferation of regional opposition parties, the governor prevented the election of most RDA candidates to the French Parliament and to the territorial assembly during the following years.

The eclipse of the Entente Voltaïque between 1948 and 1956 resulted also in part from the threat which the early RDA's communistic orientation seemed to hold for native vested interests, as represented mainly by the Mossi chieftaincy. Of all the regional parties sponsored by the administration to offset the RDA, the most important was the all-Mossi Union Voltaïque, under the leadership of Dr. Joseph Conombo, who was elected in 1951 to the French National Assembly, where he joined the IOM. In local political terms, this party comprised two increasingly divergent elements—the traditional chiefs and the young Mossi elite who were reportedly backed by the regionally powerful Catholic mission. By 1953, when the IOM—then at the peak of its influence—held its all-African congress at Bobo-Dioulasso, rifts in the Union Voltaïque were already apparent. Friction existed not only between the two generations of Mossi but also between individual leaders representing the rival regional interests of Ouahigouya and Ouagadougou, encouraged respectively by the Yatenga Naba and the Moro Naba. The Union Voltaïque was formally dissolved in 1955, and to replace it Dr. Conombo and the Christian trade-union leader, Joseph Ouedraogo, organized the Parti Social d'Education des Masses Africaines (PSEMA), with Catholic-mission backing. Although the PSEMA enjoyed an immediate success, both in the size of its membership and at the polls, it vainly tried to embrace all elements of Mossi opinion and, like its predecessor, soon disintegrated.

This breakdown in Mossi solidarity opened the way for groups in and around Bobo-Dioulasso to strengthen their political influence throughout the territory. For some time, Nazi Boni, the western area's deputy to the National Assembly and founder of the Mouvement Populaire de la Révolution Africaine (MPA), had been demanding a division of

Upper Volta into two territories. The MPA's platform and rapid growth indicated that regional issues, aggravated by personality conflicts, were fast becoming paramount in Upper Volta. They were reflected in the growing rivalry between Ouagadougou, the administrative capital, where the Mossi formed an overwhelming majority and the chieftaincies were strongest, and Upper Volta's economic capital, Bobo-Dioulasso, where smaller tribal groups opposed Mossi domination but lacked the cohesion and organization required to match Mossi strength. Signs of restiveness among Bobo-Dioulasso's cosmopolitan floating population augured a revival there of RDA strength based on labor organizations. However, the Union Démocratique Voltaïque (UDV), as the Entente Voltaïque was now called, lacked competent local leadership, and so its resurgence was slower than that of the other RDA territorial branches.

In January 1956, the UDV's failure to elect a deputy to the French National Assembly awakened Houphouët to its need for outside help, so later that year he sent his ablest and most trusted lieutenant, Ouezzin Coulibaly, to reorganize the party. Although Coulibaly's political career had been in Ivory Coast, he was a native Voltaic, and this—together with Houphouët's strong backing—greatly facilitated his task of unification. Coulibaly was able so rapidly to effect a merger between the UDV and the PSEMA that candidates of the newly united party—named the Parti Démocratique Unifié (PDU)—were elected mayor in both Ouagadougou and Bobo-Dioulasso in November 1956. The PDU became the first party in Upper Volta to represent Mossi as well as non-Mossi, and its instant and remarkable success made Upper Volta's political future look bright. Yet almost at once the horizon clouded when the PDU elected the Moro Naba as its honorary president. This move revived the opposition of the

MPA in the west and also prompted three anti-Moro Naba
elements in the Ouahigouya region to coalesce and organize
still another party, the Mouvement Démocratique Voltaïque
(MDV).[4]

Coulibaly worked valiantly to heal these rifts in the
Voltaic body politic and to such good avail that in the ter-
ritorial-assembly elections of March 1957 the PDU won
control of that body and consequently of Upper Volta's first
government council. Coulibaly's majority in the assembly
was very slender, however; hence he tried to neutralize his
opposition by distributing the council portfolios among the
anti-Moro Naba forces. His coalition government might have
achieved stability had Coulibaly not so soon shown his determination to bring Upper Volta formally back into the
RDA fold by insisting that the PDU revert to the name of
UDV. To be sure, this step had been taken through an agreement sponsored by Houphouët, under which exclusive zones
of political influence had been assigned to each of the major
Voltaic parties, but in three by-elections held late in 1957
Coulibaly was accused of trespassing on the areas assigned to
the parties of Joseph Conombo, Nazi Boni, and Gérard
Kanga Ouedraogo.

Forthwith those three men organized a Solidarity Group
whose combined strength enabled its members to pass a vote
in the assembly censuring the Coulibaly government. Coulibaly refused to resign, however, and within a few weeks
succeeded in winning over enough assemblymen to annul
the no-confidence vote. At this sharp reversal of the assembly's previous stand, the angry MDV members all resigned

[4] These elements were led by the Yatenga Naba; Gérard Ouedraogo,
Ouahigouyan deputy to the French National Assembly; and Captain
Michel Dorange, a former administrator in Upper Volta who had
great influence over the region's war veterans.

from the council, except for the young trade-union leader Maurice Yameogo, who was rewarded by being named Minister of the Interior in Coulibaly's new government, formed late in January 1958.

This shift in Voltaic party politics coincided with the new alignments that were shaping up throughout French West Africa over the primary-federation issue. While all Upper Volta's politicians continued to insist that theirs was a purely Voltaic dispute, the conflicts between them soon hardened along the lines prevailing elsewhere in French Black Africa —that is, the orthodox RDA against a common front composed of all its opponents. Coulibaly, as Houphouët's faithful executive officer, naturally opposed a primary federation. His Voltaic opponents just as automatically favored it, and in the spring of 1958 they formed themselves into the territorial branch of the PRA. This formal division of Voltaic politicians into pro- and antifederalists, however, was only nominal, for the assemblymen never discussed the issue in abstract terms and soon reverted to in-fighting and local-politics-as-usual. Indeed, the term "party" could not be properly applied to the cliques that formed and reformed around outstanding personalities. Not even the referendum of September 1958 aroused much discussion, and in fact it had the paradoxical effect of uniting all the Voltaic leaders in favor of an affirmative vote. Out of about 1.5 million registered voters, fewer than 12,000 favored independence from France.

Just before and just after the referendum, two local events occurred that profoundly affected Upper Volta's political evolution. The death of Ouezzin Coulibaly a few days prior to the referendum deprived the RDA in general and Upper Volta in particular of an irreplaceable leader. Almost at once the unity that he had been at pains to build in the territory was destroyed by the resurgence of rivalries be-

tween local factions, and by the Moro Naba's surprising bid
for political recognition. In 1957 a new Moro Naba, trained
in French schools, had succeeded to the throne at Ouagadougou, and soon his unconventional behavior caused a
flurry in the traditionalist Mossi dovecotes. He married a
young Mossi commoner who had been educated in Paris,
modified the rigid protocol of his court, and began touring
the country to expound his ideas on how Upper Volta should
evolve as a modern country. His actions shocked the Mossi
elders and also frightened the young progressives, who were
opposed in principle to the traditional chieftaincy, resented
his moral authority over his fellow-tribesmen, and feared he
might try to set himself up as a constitutional monarch for
the whole territory.

Coulibaly's death seemed to provide the Moro Naba a rare
opportunity to assume leadership in Upper Volta by playing
arbiter between the RDA and its PRA opponents. But the
tactics he employed (and the encouragement reportedly
given him by some French officers) proved to be as unfortu-
nate for his cause as they were bizarre. On October 15, 1958,
he sent a message to the assembly urging it to elect a government of national union. Two days later, when the election
was to take place, he staged an extraordinary show of force.
Early in the morning, some 3,000 Mossi on horseback, armed
with bows and arrows, took their stand in front of the assembly hall, and the Moro Naba and his courtiers appeared,
dressed in traditional war attire. No untoward incidents
occurred, however, and in a few hours his strange troops disbanded upon order of the Minister of Interior. The Moro
Naba's demonstration was a success insofar as it showed his
hold over the uneducated Mossi people, but for that very
reason it spelled defeat for his plans. His fellow chiefs met
hastily and disavowed his action, and rival politicians were

thrown into each other's arms by their common fear of a resurgent Mossi chieftaincy. Within a few days, the PRA pledged its support for a provisional RDA-UDV-dominated government under the premiership of Maurice Yameogo.

As the threat represented by the Moro Naba's intervention receded, the PRA leaders reconsidered their political truce with the UDV and stayed away from a meeting scheduled for late November at which a government of national union was to be formed. Moreover, a new element of discord had entered Upper Volta's troubled atmosphere, in the form of an invitation to the territory to attend the federalist congress to be held in Bamako at the end of December. This invitation widened the opposition between the RDA-UDV and the PRA, and at the same time split the former party into pro- and antifederalist groups. To compound its difficulties, a schism developed between the supporters and the opponents of Yameogo as party leader. Some of the old militants, who distrusted him as a newcomer to the RDA ranks, preferred Joseph Ouedraogo. In this they were joined by that faction of the UDV which favored a primary federation and resented Yameogo's equivocal attitude in regard to it. The cause of federalism was drawing the Ouahigouya PRA-MDV into cooperating with a strange assortment of UDV leaders, including those who voiced the western region's desire for closer ties with adjacent Soudan and two left-wing ministers in the government, one a Soudanese and the other a Frenchman.

After a hurried trip to Abidjan to consult Houphouët, Yameogo dismissed the two profederalist ministers on the ground that he would have no foreigners in his government. This aroused the wrath of the Voltaic federalists and prompted Modibo Keita of Soudan to make a quick trip to Ouagadougou, where he pleaded the cause of federalism.

Early in December, the Moro Naba caused another furore by coming out in favor of a primary federation, and, as had happened before, his action proved catalytic and rallied wider support for the UDV-PRA coalition government headed by Yameogo. The new cabinet included the widow of Ouezzin Coulibaly, who thus became the first woman minister in any French West African government.

On December 11, the assembly voted to become a member of the Franco-African Community (composed of France and the African territories that had voted affirmatively in the 1958 referendum) as an autonomous republic, and a few days later it passed by two votes a resolution leaving the way open for Upper Volta to join a primary federation. Both the closeness of the vote and the resolution's ambiguous wording served Yameogo's purposes well, for he had not yet made up his mind which way to jump. On the one hand, Upper Volta could not afford to be left out of any large-scale grouping of West African states, but, on the other hand, Yameogo was afraid to cut his country's close political and economic ties with France and Ivory Coast. In consequence he made moves in both directions. Since he was not yet fully accepted as head of the Voltaic branch of the RDA, Yameogo first dispatched missions to reassure Houphouët and General de Gaulle, but a few days later he went to the Bamako conference, accompanied by a group of Voltaic federalists. He also attended the constituent congress of the Mali Federation held at Dakar in January 1959. At neither meeting, however, was it clear whether the Voltaics present were their country's official delegates or merely observers.

While Yameogo was absent at Dakar, an event occurred which temporarily tipped the scales in favor of Upper Volta's joining the Mali Federation. The French government, perhaps to show its displeasure at Yameogo's profederalist moves, abruptly and without consulting him named a new high commissioner to Upper Volta. Not only did the Voltaics regard this as an affront to their country's now-autonomous status, but the new high commissioner was none other than an official who had been closely associated with the prosecution of the Voltaic RDA in the late 1940's. At once Yameogo reacted to this appointment by warmly praising the Mali Federation and, with his approval, the assembly on January 28, 1959, adopted the federal constitution that had been drafted at Dakar. Profiting by the widespread enthusiasm generated by Yameogo's spirited response to France's apparently deliberate provocation, the assembly at once granted him the full powers he asked for.

This vote proved to be a turning point in Yameogo's political career, although for some time thereafter he felt he must move with great caution. Legally, he now had a free hand to consolidate his authority and to determine Upper Volta's foreign policy. But he still had to cope with formidable opponents, among them some powerful Ouahigouyan politicians who began to suspect that Yameogo's sudden conversion to federalism had been only a ruse to win the assembly's consent to his assumption of dictatorial powers. An even more influential opponent was the Moro Naba, who now suddenly reversed his previous stand in favor of a primary federation. This abrupt turnabout was attributed variously to pressures upon the Moro Naba by the French military commander at Ouagadougou and to financial inducements from Houphouët. Then, early in February, the Moro Naba's anti-Mali position was reinforced by the visit of a delegation of three prominent chiefs from Niger. Reportedly, they proposed that he accept the leadership of a new Mossi federation, which would comprise his own subjects and those of certain chieftaincies in western Niger.[5]

[5] G. Dugué, *Vers les Etats-Unis d'Afrique* (Dakar, 1960), pp. 98ff.

Although the Moro Naba did not commit himself, the possibility that he might later accept the proposal and break away from Upper Volta, and also the rising opposition in Ouahigouya, reawakened Yameogo's doubts as to the wisdom of the course he had recently chosen. The Mossi, after all, were by far the most important tribe in Upper Volta, and the very name of the new federation recalled to their minds the bitter wars between the Mossi *nabas* and the empire of Mali. Moreover, Islam, whose encroachments the Mossi had long resisted, was the dominant faith in Senegal and Soudan —a drawback that was further underscored by the announcement of Dahomey's decision to withdraw from the Mali Federation late in January. A federation with Senegal and Soudan had few temptations for Upper Volta compared with the material inducements proffered by France and Ivory Coast. Furthermore, on the personal level at which Yameogo consistently operated, Upper Volta's membership in the Mali Federation might lead to a revival of Senghor's friendship with Joseph Ouedraogo and of Modibo Keita's ties with the western Voltaic leaders—both of which could be dangerous for Yameogo's position.

By late February 1959, the disadvantages of membership in the Mali Federation had come to outweigh the advantages in Yameogo's mind, and he decided to withdraw from it. The compelling factor in his decision was his determination to safeguard his own power and to maintain Upper Volta's territorial ingrity. To be sure, if he reneged on his commitments at Bamako and Dakar, he risked retaliation from the federalists both at home and abroad. Thus he had to find some means of minimizing this danger as well as the dangers that would be involved if Upper Volta remained isolated. The obvious alternative to joining the Mali Federation was membership in the Council of the Entente that Houphouët was in the process of forming, but achieving it required dif-

ficult and delicate maneuvering. To overcome the Voltaics'
resentment of the dominant political and economic role
which Ivory Coast had long played in relation to their
country, Yameogo had to win from Houphouët immediate
and appreciable advantages for Upper Volta in return for
its membership in the Entente. Weeks of hard bargaining
were spent by the Voltaic and Ivorian leaders in reaching an
agreement, and it was not until early April that Yameogo
formally announced that Upper Volta had joined the Entente.

On April 7 the terms of the protocol signed by Yameogo
and Houphouët were published. They were of an economic
nature and gave no indication of any secret political commitments. The two countries were to form a customs union
in which the duties collected on imports and exports at Abidjan port would be equitably divided between them, and a
common court of appeal would judge all disputes that might
arise in this connection. Both that port and the railroad from
Abidjan to Ouagadougou would be managed by commissions
on which the two countries would have equal representation.
A common policy for road transport would be laid down
which later could be extended to their post and telegraph
communications. Most important of all, a solidarity fund
financed by an equal percentage of each country's national
revenue would be created, to be used for their mutual benefit. Upper Volta thus achieved a position of apparent equality in the joint organs with the Ivory Coast which went far
to allay its earlier suspicions and fears of Ivorian domination.

Dahomey

All of the West African countries owe their present boundaries to rivalry between European powers in the nineteenth
century. Dahomey, however, is one of those with the most

artificial frontiers and most clearcut regional divisions. Even after the mutually isolated kingdoms in the north and in the south were brought under a single administration by France in 1902, Dahomey's diverse and individualistic tribes were never fused into one people. These centrifugal forces and inequalities, expressed in regional rather than ethnic terms, remain Dahomey's greatest handicap to the achievement of nationhood.

In the late nineteenth century, the French were so pre-occupied in the south, first with outmaneuvering their European rivals and then with conquering the local kingdoms, that they did not attempt to penetrate the hinterland. Not until the 1890's did they extend their protectorate over the north by means of treaties negotiated with the region's many tribal chiefs. Of the mosaic of small northern "kingdoms," the most important was Nikki, which was ruled by Bariba princes. Wars with neighboring principalities and conflicts among contenders for the throne were their main occupation, for wide-ranging slave raids provided them with the manpower needed to cultivate the crops and tend the herds on which their economy depended.

The French protectorate put an end to this chronic warfare but brought few other changes to the north. Except for the paramount rulers of Nikki, Parakou, Kandi, and Djougou, no chief controlled an area larger than his village's boundaries, and these diverse tribes vegetated on their ancestral lands. The extension of the railroad from the seaport of Cotonou to Parakou in 1908 gradually drew the economies of northern and southern Dahomey closer together, but this did not appreciably increase contacts between their populations. Indeed, when the colonial administration at Porto Novo assigned southern Dahomeans as chiefs of the newly created northern cantons, the gap between north and

south actually widened. The southerners regarded their
assignments in the north as exile to a primitive land and
did not try to disguise their feeling of superiority to their
more backward northern "compatriots." Inevitably this increased the northerners' consciousness that they were isolated
and neglected, although it also developed in them a common
sense of collective grievance against the more developed
south, thus uniting tribes theretofore divided ethnically and
culturally.

The kingdoms of southern Dahomey had already attained
a remarkable degree of sophistication and cohesion by the
time European traders and missionaries reached the region
in the seventeenth century. Chiefs of the dominant Fon tribe
had established strong centralized governments, cultivated
the arts, and traded in slaves, merchandise, and oil-palm
products with merchants of various European nationalities.
Unlike the northern Dahomeans, the southerners were aggressive in their dealings with the Europeans, and they
offered prolonged armed resistance to the French conquest.
Subsequently, the most refractory of the kings were either
deposed or deported by the French, and the more amenable
were named chiefs of the cantons into which the old kingdoms were divided. Yet even under the colonial administration, the old regional rivalry between Abomey and Porto
Novo persisted, and despite their loss of political power the
southern chiefs continued to demand tribute and services
from their erstwhile subjects.

Years of contact with Europeans, the presence of many
African immigrants and of the "Portuguese creoles" (also
known as Brazilians), and the early establishment of mission
schools combined to place the southern Dahomeans among
West Africa's best educated, least docile, and most enter-
prising populations. Although the French developed the

south far more than the north, the country had few resources and its economy could not provide jobs for so numerous an educated elite. The surplus therefore was sent to fill administrative posts in France's other African colonies. (An indication of the competence of Dahomey's surplus elite is the number of distinguished Dahomeans now serving in international organizations. Outstanding among them are Olympe Bhély-Quénum (UNESCO), Dr. Alfred Quénum (WHO), Louis Ignacio Pinto (World Court), and Albert Tevoedjre (ILO). This, however, did not dispose of all of the exceptionally intelligent and qualified southern Dahomeans, whose restiveness manifested itself in active resistance to the chiefs' exactions and a series of strikes and riots in the 1920's against the colonial administration. The disorders were sparked by outspokenly critical journalists organized into *sociétés de presse* which, in 1945, formed the electoral committees that, in turn, provided the framework for Dahomey's first political party.

When elective political institutions were introduced after World War II, Dahomey was still a wretchedly poor country without experience in self-government; it was divided economically and psychologically, and it had an overabundant intelligentsia in the south. The elite there, however, were so strongly influenced by the Catholic mission that they resisted attempts of the radical RDA to establish a foothold in the country. On the other hand, religious affiliation has never been the key to the electoral successes or failures of Dahomey's politicians, for virtually all of them are Christians and a large majority are Catholics. Their support has come from three regional (and, by extension, tribal) constituencies of approximately equal numerical strength. Dahomey's perennial deputies in the French National Assembly, Sourou-Migan Apithy and Hubert Maga, respectively represented

the populations of the south and of the north, and throughout the first postwar decade this basic division was the hall-
mark of Dahomean politics despite frequent changes in the
names of the "parties" and in their alliances in the French
Parliament.

In Dahomey's political history, as in that of the other
territories of French West Africa, the mid-1950's marked
a turning point. The accelerated progress toward self-government in nearby Togo and Ghana could not but strengthen
the Dahomeans' aspirations for greater autonomy. Passage
of the *loi-cadre* in 1956 had an even more immediate impact, for it introduced the federalist issue into territorial
politics, theretofore almost wholly dominated by personal and
parochial rivalries, and it inadvertently strengthened the
regional character of Dahomean parties. In 1955, Justin
Ahomadegbe had formed the Union Démocratique Dahoméenne as a "third force," and he affiliated it with the
interterritorial RDA. To make it a truly national party,
however, he succeeded in attracting to its membership the
most important segment of Dahomey's organized labor.

As a descendant of the kings of Abomey, Ahomadegbe
commanded the loyalty of the south-central region, but he
drew his most significant support from the trade unions of
Cotonou—a fast-growing town which had long resented its
subordination to the administrative capital of Porto Novo.
The introduction of this new element into the electoral
scene did not enable Ahomadegbe to create a party that
transcended regional boundaries, but he was able to challenge Apithy's long hold on the southern constituency and
also to pave the way for organized labor to play a decisive
role. Although Dahomey's wage earners formed only a
small percentage of the country's active population, their
concentration at specific points in the south and especially

at the commercial nerve-center of Cotonou facilitated their organization into unions and gave additional leverage to their leaders' demands. The strikes of late 1957 and early 1958, organized by the UDD-backed unions and initially motivated by labor's grievances, degenerated into violence, paralyzed Cotonou's services, and took a political turn that eventually toppled the government council headed by Apithy.

In the increasingly bitter political contests that marked the late 1950's, the basic issues were still largely Dahomean, both personal and regional, but they had become aggravated by ideological concepts just as the country was being gradually and reluctantly drawn into the mainstream of West African politics. In 1957, Ahomadegbe's recent successes at the polls and as a labor leader earned for him a place on the interterritorial RDA's coordinating committee, but he found the price set in local terms for the UDD's integration into that movement unduly high. He and other UDD leaders resented interference by Houphouët's emissaries in their party's internal disputes and even more in their labor policy, and as time went on the UDD pursued an increasingly independent course.

As for Apithy, although in the French National Assembly he successively joined various parties, including the IOM, he in fact conducted himself there as an independent. Even in March 1957, after he was elected head of Dahomey's first government council, he was still proud that he could depend solely upon local support and could keep Dahomey free of entangling interterritorial alliances. By the spring of 1958, however, Apithy's position had been so weakened by the UDD's electoral inroads and by the defection of some of his main supporters, such as Dr. Emile Zinsou and Ignacio Pinto, who had become ardent federalists, that he altered his isolationist attitude and attended the Dakar meeting at which the PRA was formed. Upon returning home, Apithy founded a territorial branch of that movement and enlarged his cabinet to include Maga and some federalists. This coalition government was invested by the assembly only a few weeks before the PRA's constituent congress was held at Cotonou in July.

At that congress, which called for immediate independence and African unity, neither Apithy nor Maga—albeit delegates—played an outstanding role. As always, they were far more preoccupied with local politics than with French-speaking Africa's future relations with France or interterritorial unity. Since there was no question in their minds as to impoverished Dahomey's continuing need of France's financial support, acceptance of de Gaulle's constitution was not made a local party issue, and Apithy, Maga, and Ahomadegbe united in appealing for an affirmative vote in the referendum of September 28, 1958. Of the Dahomean voters who went to the polls, 97 per cent voted to join the Franco-African Community, which the assembly formally did on December 4, at the same time that it proclaimed Dahomey an autonomous republic.

Inevitably the question of federalism now came to the fore. It was to be expected that Apithy, as an outspoken opponent in the National Assembly of the balkanization of West Africa and as a founder-member of the PRA, should attend the Bamako conference and agree there to join the Mali Federation. Yet only a few weeks later, at the end of January 1959, Apithy resigned from the PRA and announced his strong opposition to Dahomey's participation in the proposed federation. He explained that its over-rigid structure would inhibit the development of Dahomey's own personality and economy, and he added that his country's interests would be better served by creating a union with its Benin Gulf neighbors than by joining up with distant Senegal and Soudan.

In reality, Apithy's sudden volte-face was motivated by complex political and economic considerations. Following the anti-Dahomean (and anti-Togolese) riots at Abidjan in October 1958, thousands of Dahomeans employed in Ivory Coast had precipitately returned home, where their presence worsened an already bad economic situation. They swelled the ranks of Cotonou's unemployed and, he feared, might well enhance the political potential of the labor unions controlled by the UDD. Consequently Apithy realized that he must take steps to conciliate Ahomadegbe and to improve the economy. As regards the latter objective, he succeeded in wresting from France a long-solicited pledge to build a deepwater port at Cotonou and from Houphouët a promise of financial aid, both given on condition that Dahomey decline to join the Mali Federation.

These successes tided Apithy over his immediate budgetary difficulties and also assured him of the support of Maga, whose northern constituents were far more interested in the future development of their region than in the academic issue of federalism. Furthermore, even if Apithy's withdrawal from the Mali Federation soon after signing the "proclamation" of its foundation meant alienating influential Dahomean federalists, this would be more than offset by its making possible a rapprochement with Ahomadegbe, who on this issue echoed Houphouët's opposition to a primary federation. In any case, the federalists had no mass support, whereas the UDD leaders were far more dangerous and determined adversaries because they split the southern vote. As a further gesture to Ahomadegbe, Apithy set a date for holding elections to the assembly, which had long been demanded by the UDD. On February 14, therefore, in a rare vote of unanimity, the assembly rejected Dahomey's membership in the Mali Federation and accepted the constitution submitted to it by Apithy.

For the next few weeks it seemed likely that Apithy's gamble would succeed. He reached a firm agreement with Maga whereby in the forthcoming elections he would present no candidates in the north, in return for Maga's pledge to reciprocate in the south. Apithy, however, was unable to come to terms with the UDD, and in a desperate effort to circumvent its opposition he resorted to gerrymandering tactics. By a revision of the electoral law, he altered the boundaries of the southern electoral circumscriptions so as to assure his party a majority in the future assembly. So patently fraudulent was the official count of the votes cast on April 2 that the UDD lodged strong protests, which took such a violent turn that French troops had to be flown in to keep order.

Still unable to reach a modus vivendi with Ahomadegbe and faced with the prospect of a civil war, Apithy finally resigned as head of the government, but this did not resolve the impasse. Inasmuch as the southern electorate's support continued to be about evenly divided between Ahomadegbe and Apithy, the only compromise candidate acceptable was the northerner, Maga. Before accepting the assembly's investiture on May 21, 1959, Maga prudently negotiated for Apithy's support, which was reluctantly given in return for a cabinet post. A few days later, however, when Apithy found that he had been named only a minister without portfolio, he turned against Maga. With a view to overthrowing Maga's government, he began a series of political maneuvers that augured ill for Dahomey's future stability.

During this politically turbulent period, Houphouët was busy behind the Dahomean scene. His emissaries vainly tried to dissuade Ahomadegbe from trying to oust Apithy as premier. In view of Apithy's past vacillations, Houphouët could hardly have regarded him as a reliable partner. Nevertheless, in view of his promising negotiations with Apithy as regards Dahomey's membership in the Entente, Houphouët wanted him to stay in power. When this attempt failed, Houphouët with Hamani Diori's help tried to reconcile Dahomey's feuding parties, with the aim of obtaining a joint commitment by the principal Dahomean leaders to join the Entente. But he found both Apithy and Ahomadegbe unresponsive and even hostile to his appeal, for they regarded it, as well as his efforts at conciliation, as undue interference in Dahomey's internal affairs. Indeed, their persistent refusal to accept Houphouët's leadership probably accounted for the support that Houphouët subsequently gave Maga, although Maga during his years in the National Assembly had been a loyal member of the IOM. Nevertheless, in the spring of 1959, it was not clear whether Maga's sympathies lay with the Mali Federation or with the Council of the Entente, for he had never publicly committed himself on the federalist issue. Now, however, he recognized the weakness of his position as a compromise premier who, as a northerner, was automatically unpopular in southern Dahomey. At the time of his investiture, Maga thought he had neutralized Apithy, but there remained Ahomadegbe, whose strength in Cotonou made him a formidable opponent. To deprive Ahomadegbe of Houphouët's support, Maga now proposed that his own party join the RDA. Houphouët, who was then courting Maga, had no qualms about dropping the recalcitrant Ahomadegbe, and he welcomed Maga's proposal in the hope that it would be the first step toward Dahomey's joining the Entente.

If unabashed self-interest had induced Apithy and Maga successively to seek a rapprochement with Houphouët, the same could be said of the Ivorian leader. Houphouët was under no illusions as to their motivation. With equal realism he chose to support Maga in preference to his rivals because, under the circumstances, he believed that Maga alone could give Dahomey the governmental stability it required. Small and poor as Dahomey was (and is), its geographical position gave it importance in Houphouët's eyes. Its very poverty and proximity to Nigeria made Dahomey highly susceptible to external pressures, and especially to the attraction exerted by its powerful eastern neighbor. If Houphouët were to prevent Dahomey from gravitating into Nigeria's orbit and instead persuade it to join the Entente, he had to provide Dahomey with the means of surviving as a national entity.

Maga proved to be a hard bargainer, especially as he had been ignored in the negotiations which Houphouët had been conducting with Apithy in the weeks before the latter fell from power. After some hesitation, the new Dahomean premier did agree to accept Houphouët's invitation to attend the first formal meeting of the Entente held at Abidjan a few days after his investiture. It was noteworthy that Maga, on the way to Ivory Coast, made a point of stopping off at Lomé to consult with the Togolese premier, Sylvanus Olympio. Perhaps as a result of the prudent Olympio's advice, Maga refused at Abidjan to commit Dahomey to join the Entente, pleading that he must first weigh the pros and cons involved, which were much the same as those that had influenced Apithy.

Dahomey was not dependent on the port of Abidjan as

was Upper Volta, Maga felt no ties of personal loyalty to Houphouët as did Hamani Diori, and he risked adding the Dahomean federalists to the ranks of his political adversaries if he joined the Entente. Furthermore, public opinion in Dahomey was hostile to any alliance with a country whose nationals, only a few months before, had done physical violence to the Dahomeans living in their midst, and which had added to Dahomey's economic troubles by forcing them to return home. Yet the marked deterioration in Dahomey's economy, due in large measure to this sudden increase in the ranks of the unemployed, was in itself an argument in favor of joining the Entente, whose solidarity fund promised substantial financial aid in meeting Dahomey's growing budget deficit. Additional pressure was exerted on Maga by Hamani Diori, who came to Cotonou expressly to add the weight of his influence to that of Houphouët. Niger was the only territory in the Entente of vital importance to Dahomey, for much of the former's foreign trade passed through Cotonou's port and many Dahomeans were employed in the Nigérien administration. Diori's intervention was a compelling factor in Maga's ultimate decision to join the Council of the Entente. Their friendship, dating from student days at the Ponty School in Dakar, influenced Maga's decision, and this episode well illustrates how important are personal relationships in African policy making.

Niger

Niger is the largest and least densely populated member of the Entente. Like Upper Volta it is landlocked, has highly permeable frontiers, and is dependent on a southern seaport for its foreign trade. Unlike Upper Volta, however, it has an immense desert area, two major Negro tribes, and a sizeable nomadic population. Furthermore, a longer military campaign was necessary to pacify Niger than was the case of its southwestern neighbor, and it did not become a colony and a member of the French West Africa Federation until 1922. Consequently, while the French ruled the south directly, in the northern regions they confined themselves to maintaining order and delegated administrative duties to the traditional authorities under the military's overall supervision. Thus the great chiefs of the Touareg, Hausa, and Djerma tribes retained more of their traditional powers than did the chiefs in the coastal colonies. France's administration of Niger, preservation of its established social order, and failure to develop the country's economy were characteristic of its policy in governing the poor, underdeveloped Saharan borderland areas.

The perpetuation of chiefly rule throughout most of the colony and the stagnation of its economy at least enabled Niger to enjoy a long period of peace between 1922 and 1946. In the latter year, the Parti Progressiste Nigérien (PPN) was founded as the territorial branch of the RDA by three men who were among its charter members— Hamani Diori, Boubou Hama, and Djibo Bakary. This triumvirate of leaders dominated the Nigérien political scene for the next thirteen years; The first two are still in power. Hamani Diori was elected to the French National Assembly and Boubou Hama to the French Union Assembly, and Djibo Bakary became a member of the territorial assembly, the party's secretary-general, and the organizer of Niamey's federation of labor unions, which were affiliated with the French communist Confédération Générale du Travail (CGT). All three were Muslims and members of the Djerma-Songhai tribe, although Djibo was a Hausa on his mother's side. They were all schoolteachers and graduates of the Ponty School at Dakar. Despite a marked age differential—Diori was ten years younger than Boubou Hama and five years older than Djibo—they worked closely together during the RDA's radical period. But in 1950, when Houphouët altered the RDA's policy to one of cooperation with the French administration, the PPN leadership was split asunder. Djibo broke away to form a radical splinter party of his own, whereas Diori and Boubou Hama accepted Houphouët's lead and remained in the orthodox RDA fold. Djibo's defection so weakened the PPN that Diori was defeated for reelection to the French National Assembly in 1951, and the party went into eclipse during the next five years.

In Niger, as elsewhere in French West Africa, the RDA staged a comeback in the legislative elections of January 2, 1956, and Diori once again became his territory's deputy in Paris. Yet he was almost defeated in this election by Djibo, who suddenly reappeared in Niger after several years' absence in eastern European countries which he had visited under the auspices of the CGT. This evidence of Djibo's continuing appeal for the Nigérien electorate was but the first of a series of surprises that followed rapidly. After publicly endorsing the *loi-cadre* in June 1956, in what may well have been an unsuccessful bid for readmission to the RDA, Djibo joined the African Socialist Movement, was elected mayor of Niamey the following November, and four months later won the election that made him the African head of Niger's first government council.

During the next two years, Djibo extended the field of his operations and successes beyond the confines of Niger. He rose rapidly to the top rank in the hierarchies of the radical labor federation, the Union Générale des Travailleurs de l'Afrique Noire (UGTAN), and of the African Socialist Movement. Then, at the PRA constituent congress in July 1958, Djibo was such an eloquent advocate of immediate independence from France and the creation of a primary federation in West Africa that he was forthwith elected secretary-general of that interterritorial movement. Upon returning to Niamey, he renamed his old political organization the Sawaba, or Freedom, Party, and made it a territorial branch of the PRA. He then announced that he would campaign for a negative vote in the referendum on the constitution of the Fifth French Republic to be held in September 1958. Djibo announced this stand one day before a similar decision was reached by Sékou Touré, to whom Djibo—as a Marxist-nationalist —was much closer than he was to the Senegalese socialist leaders of the PRA.

Although Djibo had vacillated in regard to the *loi-cadre* and had not been above courting the traditional chieftaincy in order to regain political power, he could not compare with such opportunistic politicians as Apithy and Maga of Dahomey. To be sure, Djibo operated more often than not as a political freelance and was therefore somewhat suspect to his more disciplined and moderate colleagues in the PRA and socialist movements. Yet he was a sincere nationalist as well as a charismatic mass leader and on both counts was able to inspire and keep the loyalty of his youthful followers. It was at first Djibo's authoritarian character, impatience, and intransigence and, later, his acceptance of alien African support that made him commit errors of which his less talented and dynamic rivals were able to take advantage.

After having formed an electoral alliance with the traditional chiefs who had been estranged from the PPN during the RDA's radical period, he proceeded to alienate them without first having given his own party a solid organizational base throughout the country. No sooner had he been elected head of the government council, through the chiefs' support, than he brusquely removed seven of them from their posts. Almost at the same time he offended his left-wing followers by clamping down on a strike by schoolteachers at Niamey. Djibo's cardinal mistake, however, was to propose an independence that would entail alliance with the English-speaking West African territories. During a visit Djibo made to Accra in the early summer of 1958, he reportedly received verbal and financial encouragement from Nkrumah to vote "no" in the referendum, but it was Djibo's contention that close ties with Nigeria would be more beneficial to Niger than membership in the Franco-African Community that was the main cause of his undoing.

Djibo could offer his compatriots no firm assurance that Nigeria, after it became independent in 1960, would provide as much aid as France had pledged if Niger voted affirmatively in the referendum. Furthermore, none of Niger's chiefs—particularly the Touareg, the Djerma and even the Hausa chiefs—relished the prospect of dependency on the powerful black emirs of northern Nigeria, despite the close ties of trade and kinship that existed between the tribes of Niger and those of Nigeria. Even though, in the past, Niger's chiefs had actively resisted French rule, they at least knew what to expect and therefore felt that continuing links with France offered the best guaranty of maintaining their privileged position. Consequently, on the eve of the referendum, they and other members of the Sawaba deserted that party and joined with Diori's PPN and the French administration to defeat Djibo.

Djibo had good reason to assert that fraud and pressure from the French governor of Niger had falsified the vote count in the referendum,[6] which in any case was marked by the abstention of nearly one-third of the registered electorate and by negative votes cast by one-fifth of those who actually went to the polls. Moreover, he refused to resign as premier because he still controlled a majority in the assembly, and in this he was supported by other top PRA leaders, who carried his case to Paris. Djibo's refusal, however, to accept the compromise they worked out with the French authorities, and then the failure of a general strike which he called in Niger, left him with no alternative but to resign late in October 1958. This enabled the governor to dissolve the assembly, call for new elections, and institute judicial proceedings against Djibo and his erstwhile ministers despite renewed protests on the part of the PRA high command.

In the legislative elections of December 14, 1958, which were again marked by large-scale abstentionism, the PPN was officially announced to have won a decisive victory, although both Diori and Djibo were defeated in their own constituencies. Nevertheless, Diori, as head of the victorious party, replaced Djibo as prime minister of Niger, and a few days later the assembly, now controlled by the PPN, voted to make Niger an autonomous republic and member state in the Community. Furthermore, on January 21, 1959, the assembly granted Diori full powers for a six-month period (which were renewed the following August for another half year), and on February 25 it accepted the constitution which he had submitted to it.

As soon as he had constituted his first government,

[6] See G. Chaffard, *Les Carnets Secrets de la Décolonisation* (Paris, 1967), pp. 269–332.

Diori moved on both the domestic and foreign fronts. First, in a series of steps, he liquidated the Sawaba and its supporting organizations. Then, as regards external relations, Diori eagerly agreed to join the Entente as proposed by his old friend and mentor, Houphouët. Indeed, following the death of Ouezzin Coulibaly, Diori had rapidly come to the fore as the Ivorian leader's main collaborator and emissary. Houphouët could count on Diori's loyalty, and also on the latter's spontaneous support for his policies. Like Houphouët, though for very different reasons, Diori had long resented the government-general at Dakar because of its neglect of Niger in both the economic and cultural spheres. So sincerely did he believe that any attempt to form a primary federation in West Africa would mean a revival of the former federal government that he refused to have Niger represented at the Bamako federalist congress. When Djibo urged that Niger join the Mali Federation when it was formed in January 1959, Diori had an additional reason for opposing it. Obviously Niger's poverty and geographical location would not permit it to remain isolated, and the Entente seemed to meet the country's major requirements. Early in April 1959, therefore, Diori joined the Entente and also helped Houphouët in his efforts to persuade Dahomey to become a member.

CHAPTER 2

Independence

In the months preceding the formal inauguration of the
Entente on May 29, 1959, important changes were made
in its organization, the range and methods of its proposed
activities, and even in its nomenclature—but not in its
basic objectives. Houphouët persevered in his grand design
to recapture the leadership of the greatest possible number
of West African states, and he fashioned the Entente in
conformity with the principles he had expressed in drafting
the *loi-cadre*. From the outset he opposed setting up any
supranational organization, insisted on maintaining the
autonomy of each member state, and stressed close relations
with France within the framework of the Franco-African
Community. His hope of eventually enlarging the Entente's
membership was reflected in his early discarding, as too
restrictive, its original name of Union Sahel-Bénin.

The organizational form which Houphouët gave to the
Entente was accepted without reservations by all its members.[1] The council was to be composed of the premiers of
each state, the presidents and vice-presidents of their legislatures, and those ministers whose special competence was
required for discussion of specific items on the agenda.
Presidency of the council was to rotate among the premiers,
and the capital of the president's country would be the host
town for its meetings. Ordinary sessions of the council were
to be held twice yearly and behind closed doors, but extraordinary meetings could be called at the request of two mem-

[1] "Création du Conseil de l'Entente," *Afriques-Magazine,* July 1959.

32

ber states. The Entente was to form a customs union, and policies on financial affairs, labor, the civil service, health, public works and telecommunications were to be harmonized. Decisions had to be unanimous and were automatically operative; cases of conflict between member states could be carried before the arbitration court of the Community. Time was to prove the solidity of this organization, for it underwent few changes. The customs union never materialized, however, and it became increasingly difficult to formulate common policies even in the technical domain. Moreover, interstate conflicts were never brought before the Community court for the good reason that it never met. Then, too, the timing and number of sessions held by the council was a barometer of the Entente's current importance as a group to its founder, for he preferred to arbitrate disputes between its members on a personal basis rather than to have them settled by the round-table method.

The negotiations which Houphouët conducted with Upper Volta, Dahomey, and Niger during the early months of 1959 convinced him that his initial proposal of collaboration in economic and social affairs was not a sufficient inducement to those countries which had been inclined to join the Mali Federation. Furthermore, he came to know the depths of their economic needs, the scope of their leaders' personal ambitions, the range of their problems related to tribalism and regionalism, and, above all, the strength of their nationalist sentiments. In view of the instability of the governments with which he was dealing and the difficulty of finding a "valid interlocutor" with whom to negotiate, Houphouët threw the weight of his influence behind whichever leader seemed to have the widest popular support and was most receptive to his proposals. He soon learned, however, the limits of his intervention, especially in Upper Volta and Dahomey, where his behind-the-scenes activities were resented even by those politicians who were nominally members of his RDA, and where public opinion was already adverse to Ivory Coast. Houphouët found that the most he could do was to shore up the incumbent leaders by providing their governments with a firmer financial base. In brief, not only did Houphouët have to tread softly but he had to carry a big money bag.

Lack of capital and technical skills were the obvious handicaps to the attainment by those countries of the modern economic development they craved. Inasmuch as they had joined the Franco-African Community, they could expect France to continue subsidizing their budgets and supplying them with some technical aid, but if they were to be firmly bound to Ivory Coast, additional financial inducements were required. This conviction lay behind Houphouët's decision to create a solidarity fund that would provide loans for their development projects and outright gifts in emergencies. The very name of the fund showed Houphouët's new-found concern not to offend the sensibilities of his partners. Although each member state was to donate 10 per cent of its annual revenues to the solidarity fund, the combined contributions of Upper Volta, Niger and Dahomey would not amount to more than a fraction of Ivory Coast's. Soon after it was launched on July 1, 1959, the solidarity fund justified the sacrifices and expectations of its sponsor. Maga was frank to admit that it was thanks to the financial advantages offered by the Entente that his hesitations about joining it had been overcome.[2] Indeed, the fund proved to be not only Houphouët's trump card in forming the Entente, but the magnet that has been chiefly responsible for holding it together.

[2] *Le Monde,* June 3, 1959.

In Black Africa, generally speaking, the formation of the Entente and its fund did counter some of the criticism by Houphouët's adversaries who had earlier accused him of territorial egotism and of balkanizing Africa. But if criticism became muted, the Entente did not win any new members. The same, however, could also be said of the Mali Federation and of the Ghana-Guinea Union, whose leaders hoped their respective groups would become nuclei for the wider African unity they had long advocated. Mauritania, far from joining the Mali Federation, accused its leaders of encouraging a secessionist movement in the Senegal River valley, and Sékou Touré and Nkrumah failed to persuade President Tubman that Liberia should join forces with them. This stalemate seemed to justify Houphouët's publicly expressed skepticism about both those groups. The Ghana-Guinea Union's hope of creating a Pan-African ensemble moved him to comment that "the sum total of misery does not make for abundance," [3] and "knowing Sékou Touré and Nkrumah as I do, I cannot believe that either one wants to play second fiddle to the other." [4] Of the Mali Federation, he was quoted as saying, "I have no confidence in its survival or its efficacy." [5]

The years were to prove Houphouët right about both groups. In the meantime, however, the evolution of the Ghana-Guinea Union and especially of the Mali Federation had a profound influence on the Entente and on the Community as well. During 1959, successive meetings of the Community's executive council revealed the Africans' growing dissatisfaction with the cumbersomeness of its machinery, its slowness in reaching decisions on matters they considered of urgent concern, and France's domination of the proceedings. Modibo Keita of Soudan, goaded by the

[3] *Ibid.,* April 9, 1959.   [4] *Marchés Tropicaux,* June 13, 1959.
[5] *Dakar-Matin,* March 25, 1959.

left wing of his party—which had wanted him to follow Guinea's lead in the September 1958 referendum—now exerted pressure on Senghor to demand immediate independence for the Federation from France. Threatened with the alternative of holding a plebiscite on the issue in Senegal and Soudan, Senghor acquiesced, as did General de Gaulle later. The French president announced this decision dramatically on December 13, 1959, adding that France would continue to grant aid to the sovereign Mali Federation.

This sharp reversal of French policy only fifteen months after the 1958 referendum was a double blow to Houphouët, who felt aggrieved that his loyalty to France had been poorly rewarded. He also realized that an independent Mali Federation continuing to enjoy French aid would undermine the cohesion of his Entente. If Houphouët was disillusioned, his Voltaic and Nigérien colleagues were even more embittered, Diori was especially indignant because he felt that de Gaulle, by his concessions, had indirectly confirmed the theses of Djibo Bakary. Indeed, so strident were the criticisms of France expressed at the Entente meeting in Niamey at the end of December that Houphouët had to warn those uttering them to moderate their tone and stop voicing individual complaints, for "the Entente must speak with one voice." [6]

As to asking France for a status as favorable as that accorded to the Mali Federation, the Entente leaders were fully agreed. But early in 1960, the harmony of interstate relations was marred by a dispute between Upper Volta and Ivory Coast, which militated against the achievement of common fiscal and labor policies. The Voltaics had long resented what they considered to be the unfair treatment

[6] *Le Monde,* Dec. 25, 1959.

of Mossi laborers working in Ivory Coast and the still in-
equitable division of customs duties on the foreign trade
of the two countries at Abidjan port. Late in January
1960, fuel was added to the flame by Ivory Coast's sudden and
unilateral abolition of its head tax, a step which, under
the Entente's policy of fiscal uniformity, would become
automatically effective also in Upper Volta. Inasmuch as the
head tax in Ivory Coast was difficult to collect and represented only 4 per cent of its annual revenues, the government
there could well afford a gesture that would enhance the
popularity of the Parti Démocratique de la Côte d'Ivoire
(PDCI), the territorial branch of the RDA. Upper Volta's
head tax, however, brought in one-quarter of its budgetary
income. In retaliation, Upper Volta abolished the organization which had been set up by Ivorian planters in 1952 for
the annual recruitment of 18,000 to 30,000 Mossi laborers,
and announced that henceforth its government would control
their emigration.

Houphouët moved hastily to patch up this quarrel, and
after he had concluded a new labor agreement on terms
acceptable to Upper Volta, Yameogo denied a rumor that
he was going to take his country out of the Entente. There
were, however, so many unresolved questions between them
that gradually the project of adhering to a common fiscal
policy was abandoned. To avoid such conflicts in the future, it was decided to hold more frequent council meetings, increase the exchange of information between the
states, and install an embryonic secretariat at Niamey,
following Diori's election as council president for 1960.[7]

The first months of that year also brought changes in
the Entente's West African relations, as evidenced by the

[7] Conseil de l'Entente, "Conférence de Bobo-Dioulasso, 8–10 mars,
1960," mimeo.

exchange of missions between it and the Mali Federation. Houphouët's decision to negotiate in Paris for the Entente's independence at the same time that Madagascar and Mali were negotiating for theirs further facilitated the Entente's rapprochement with the Mali Federation. The improvement in their relations was promoted also by the apprehensions awakened in Houphouët as a result of the aggressive policies being followed by Ghana and Guinea. To both Sékou Touré and Nkrumah, the Entente represented an obstacle to the kind of Pan-African unity they wanted to build, and Ivory Coast's continued dependence on France and its economic liberalism were anathema to their Marxist creed—the more galling because the Ivory Coast was so prosperous. According to their analysis of the situation, "Ivory Coast must be detached from the states to the north by infiltrating them with the proper ideology." [8] For good measure, Nkrumah was also encouraging a government-in-exile formed by Ivorian dissidents at Accra, which was promoting a secessionist movement headed by the "king" of Sanwi in the Aboisso district adjacent to Ghana.

Houphouët reacted vigorously to this threat by arming Ivorian military veterans along Ivory Coast's frontier with Ghana and broadcasting a warning against any illusions that Nkrumah might cherish that he has "either the right or the means to claim, and thus hope to annex, the least portion of the Ivory Coast state." [9] Nkrumah pulled in his horns and conciliatory missions were exchanged between Accra and Abidjan, but the setback to the Ghana-Guinea Union's expansionism in that part of West Africa did not allay Houphouët's fears of its activities in the international sphere. In mid-March 1960, Houphouët told

[8] *The Economist,* June 25, 1960.   [9] *West Africa,* Feb. 13, 1960.

the Ivorian legislature that Nkrumah and Sékou Touré had "opened Africa for the first time to communist influence, for the Russians are in Guinea and the Chinese there along with them. Their presence in West Africa constitutes a threat on the ideological level, and a much more serious economic one." [10]

Guinea's efforts to undermine the Ivory Coast government antedated by almost six months Nkrumah's attempts to break up the Entente. The personal and political character of the relations between Houphouët and Sékou Touré determined those between their two countries. A sharp blow to the father-son and teacher-disciple attitude of Houphouët toward the younger man, who was formerly one of the brightest stars in his RDA, had been dealt by Sékou Touré's vote for independence in September 1958 and, even more, by the subsequent union of Guinea with Ghana. Nevertheless, for some time thereafter, Houphouët entertained hopes of a reconciliation, and apparently he did not realize the intensity of Sékou Touré's hostility to him until the summer of 1959, when the Guinean leader tried to create difficulties for the Ivorian government in its relations with organized labor.

In so doing, Sékou Touré utilized the UGTAN, the radical labor organization he had organized in 1957, whose headquarters had been transferred to Conakry early in 1959. Not only did Sékou Touré wield a preponderant influence in directing the activities of its territorial branches, but the situation then in Abidjan made the time propitious for him to fish in Ivory Coast's troubled labor waters. Although the riots of October 1958 had eliminated much of the competition for jobs from the domiciled Dahomeans and Togolese, many unemployed and usually unskilled native youths remained in the Ivorian capital. Official efforts to check the

[10] *Le Monde,* March 12, 1960.

rural exodus and to institute a form of forced labor related
to compulsory military service had not solved the problem.
So the PDCI government, realizing that labor leaders might
use this potentially dangerous force for political purposes,
tried to create a single union that would be apolitical and
independent of the UGTAN.

This move, which split the Ivorian UGTAN, prompted
Sékou Touré to send to Abidjan the labor leader Ngo Blaise
to take charge of the orthodox UGTAN section and transform it into a weapon against the government's policies. The
ensuing trial of strength, which focused on control of the
Ivorian civil servants' union, culminated in the expulsion of
Sékou Touré's emissary and the strengthening of Houphouët's control over the local labor movement. Furthermore, while spelling defeat for Sékou Touré's attempt to
foment subversion in Houphouët's territory, this episode also
indirectly influenced the Entente.

At one point during that conflict, each of the rival forces
set up its own labor organization for the whole Entente. In
August 1959, Ngo Blaise chose Abidjan as his headquarters
because the "orthodox" UGTAN was rooted there and
offered the best prospects for disrupting the Entente by
boring from within. Similarly, Houphouët utilized the more
tractable "autonomous" section of the Ivorian UGTAN as
the nucleus for his Entente labor organization, but to attract
the unions of the other Entente states he based it at Niamey.
At the latter's first conference in mid-August, it was obvious
that neither the Voltaic nor the Dahomean labor movement
would rise to the bait; the conference was attended only
by the Ivorian and Nigérien union delegates.[11] After Ngo
Blaise's forced departure from Abidjan the following October, his Entente labor movement disintegrated and, partly

[11] *Marchés Tropicaux*, Aug. 22, 1959.

as a consequence and partly because of the indifference of all the unions concerned, that of Houphouët never met again. (Eleven years were to pass before another effort was made to form a labor organization for the Entente, and this time the initiative was taken not by any member government but by the Union Nationale des Travailleurs Dahoméens. Representatives of the main Entente labor unions met to define the role, rights, and duties of organized labor, and in November 1970 they organized themselves into an association with a permanent secretariat at Cotonou.)

Although Sékou Touré's attempt to weaken Houphouët's power in Ivory Coast failed, it did produce one dividend for him, for it demonstrated Houphouët's inability to give organizational form to one of the Entente's original tenets—that of formulating and carrying out a uniform labor policy.

The anxiety inspired in Houphouët by the Ghanaian and Guinean leaders' "opening to the East" and their sponsoring of dissident movements in the conservative West African countries was gradually to become an obsession. Its immediate effect was to cause him to try to erect a barrier against them through renewed efforts to enlarge the membership of the Entente. With this in view, he asked Diori to visit French Equatorial Africa early in March 1960, in the hope of persuading its leaders to join the Entente. Diori, however, received only verbal assurances of cooperation, for the equatorial countries were then in the process of forming their own economic union. Throughout the spring of 1960, the Entente's only diplomatic success on the African scene was the conclusion of a customs agreement with newly independent Togo.

With Togo's accession to independence in April 1960 and the scheduling of independence for the Mali Federation two months later, restlessness was ·becoming evident in the En-

tente territories. Their elites did not relish the prospect of
remaining, along with Mauritania, the only dependent territories in West Africa and thus possibly being ineligible for
membership in the United Nations. Consequently Houphouët, to keep them in line and himself at their head, felt
impelled to outbid Mali and the equatorial countries in the
negotiations he was then conducting in Paris on behalf of
the Entente. France was more than willing to grant the
Entente territories independence on the same terms as it had
to its other African dependencies, but was unprepared for
Houphouët's insistence that sovereignty and admission to
the United Nations must precede any commitment to remain
in the Franco-African Community. In the Paris National Assembly debates of June 9 and 20, 1960, the French government expressed its surprise and displeasure at the "original
path" to independence that Houphouët had chosen. Nevertheless, it wanted to avoid at all costs a referendum on the
issue in all the Entente states, which Houphouët proposed
as the alternative to meeting his terms.

On July 25, therefore, by a vote of 386 to 65, the National
Assembly granted what Houphouët had asked, in the expec-
tation that the Entente would later reenter the Community.
Early in August all four states officially became independent,
and the following month, with France's sponsorship, they
were admitted to the United Nations. The atmosphere engendered by these events was so euphoric that Sékou Touré
was invited to attend the independence celebrations at Abidjan and Ouagadougou. To some optimists a reconstitution
of the old French West African Federation now appeared to
be within the realm of possibility, and in any case the path to
a wider African unity than yet existed seemed to have been
cleared.

Independence brought a new unity as well as new problems to the Council of the Entente. After its four premiers met at Abidjan in mid-August, they declared that they would draft identical constitutions, form the same administrative and electoral regimes, organize national armies on a uniform pattern with coordination at the summit, strengthen their economic ties, and formulate a common foreign policy. As to the Entente's international relations, they showed great prudence, simply stating that Africa should not serve as a bone of contention between the eastern and western blocs, and that they themselves would wait until after admission to the United Nations before committing their organization to a position on specific questions such as the current conflict in the ex-Belgian Congo.[12]

Within a few days of this meeting, the mounting discord between Senegal and Soudan came to a head, and the Mali Federation broke up spectacularly on August 20. Despite rumors that Houphouët would be asked to mediate between Senghor and Modibo Keita, he was careful to steer clear, pleading that he was fully occupied in consolidating the Entente and in preparing to negotiate cooperation agreements between it and France. Nevertheless, the brusque elimination of a federation that had been the Entente's most formidable rival naturally raised the question of whether the Entente would disappear with the organization to whose creation it owed its birth, or would undergo a radical transformation. It was clear that Houphouët intended to give the Entente a more political orientation, but already the commissions of experts trying to work out common policies were encountering regional opposition, notably in regard to the size and role of the national armies,[13] and unanimity in foreign policy would be even more difficult to reach. Actu-

12 *Le Monde,* Aug. 13, 1960.
13 *The New York Times,* Aug. 24, 1960.

ally, agreement in this domain could be realized only on such matters as the general principle that African disputes should be settled by negotiation rather than by the use of force and the question of representation of the Entente—whether by one of its members or by France—in foreign countries.

The breakup of the Mali Federation had created a fluid situation which encouraged the centrifugal tendencies latent in all the Entente states and at the same time offered Houphouët a wider field of maneuver. By the late summer of 1960, he had come to realize that the machinery of the Entente would never work smoothly and that his unstable partners would cooperate with him only when and where it suited their personal or national interests. What he needed was a larger organization which would perhaps be more responsive to his leadership and would certainly carry more weight in the United Nations, where he felt it was urgent for all the recently admitted French-speaking African countries to adopt the same stand on such burning issues as Algeria and the ex-Belgian Congo. To explore the possibilities in this domain, Houphouët convened a conference at Abidjan in October 1960, to which he invited the states whose lingua franca and institutions inherited from the French colonial regime gave them at least a common point of departure.

Obviously Guinea and the North African countries favorable to the Algerian rebels would not attend a meeting called by the francophile Ivorian leader, and Togo probably would not abandon its traditional policy of aloofness from West African political alignments. On the other hand, the outlook was propitious for attracting Senegal, where Senghor was now on bad terms with both Modibo Keita and Sékou Touré; Mauritania, which needed Black African support against Morocco's irredentism; Cameroun and Madagascar, whose leaders had become concerned about their countries' isolation; and the equatorial states, which were increasingly worried about developments across the Congo River. These countries did in fact attend, and despite the absentees, the conference justified Houphouët's initiative. Two months later, twelve of the countries represented at Abidjan formed the Brazzaville bloc, which took organizational form as the Union Africaine et Malgache (UAM) in March 1961.

In sponsoring the UAM, Houphouët applied the lessons learned from the failure of the Mali Federation and from his own experience with the Entente. He avoided the rigid structure that had been a main cause of Mali's undoing, and brought into being a loose organization of sovereign states similar to that of the Entente. Furthermore, he was careful to remain in the background and give far wider latitude to his more disparate and powerful UAM partners, and to place even greater emphasis on areas of agreement. By persevering in this policy, Houphouët prevented the Entente and the UAM from falling apart and retained his paramount position in both, but at the cost of changes in the two organizations which altered the orientation he had originally tried to impose on them.

Successive changes altered the character of the Entente more rapidly than that of the UAM. Within a few weeks of the Entente's accession to independence, the project of identical constitutions had to be dropped in favor of a model constitution—in which the Entente was not mentioned—that the member states were free to modify. However, they all adopted, with only minor variations, constitutions of the presidential type, in which a strong executive was backed by a legislature composed largely or wholly of members of the governing party.[14] On November 27, 1960, Houphouët, Diori, Yameogo, and Maga were duly elected presidents of

[14] See D.-G. Lavroff and G. Peiser, *Les Constitutions Africaines* (Paris, 1961); and *Africa Report* (monthly), Feb. 1961.

their respective republics. Only the Ivorian president, however, felt strong enough to risk legislative elections, and the
other three simply prolonged the mandates of the incumbent
assemblymen. An even more drastic transformation of the
Entente was to result from the cooperation agreements
reached with France early in 1961. Nevertheless, neither the
compromises that Houphouët felt compelled to make, nor
the success of the UAM, caused him to abandon an organization that he had built up at great cost. Even after the Entente
was incorporated into larger groups and became progressively less useful to him, Houphouët took pains to preserve
its separate identity so that it could serve as his regional base
of operations.

Late in December 1960, the four Entente presidents
reached agreement on the general principles that should determine their countries' future relations with France. They
authorized Houphouët to conduct the negotiations on behalf of the Entente, but they did not give him a wholly free
hand. Because of his prestige, diplomatic skill, and experience, he was unquestionably the most qualified of the four
to get the best terms possible from the French government,
but at the same time they feared he would contrive to win
special privileges for Ivory Coast that would not be shared
with other members of the Entente. This mistrust on the
part of his colleagues added to his difficulties in reaching
an agreement with France, and the negotiations which he
opened at Paris in January 1961 proved to be exceptionally
stormy and prolonged.

The French government was shocked, first by the Entente's
refusal to reenter the Community and then by the conditions it posed for accepting France's cooperation. On the one
hand, the Entente's members insisted on being treated as
fully sovereign states, while on the other hand the group

sought substantially increased aid from France. Specifically, the Entente wanted bilateral defense agreements, the grant of a global sum (spanning a five-year period) over which it would have full control, and a free hand in its foreign relations. In other words, the Entente demanded treaties of the sort that France would negotiate with a foreign state but wanted at the same time a most-favored-nation status. In return for more privileges than France had accorded any of its other former African dependencies, the Entente would give only the assurance of its good will and friendly sentiments.

Inevitably the French government's reaction was one of hurt surprise. It had not contemplated this type of relationship, nor did it expect Houphouët, France's most faithful African ally, to be the spokesman for such demands. Houphouët, however, was now primarily solicitous of his position in Africa and the world and far less concerned than before with Franco-African relations. General de Gaulle, for his part, was preoccupied with ending the Algerian war while maintaining France's influence in Africa and, in this respect, he also had to take into account the trend of French public opinion.

Developments generally throughout west and central Africa were hardly reassuring as regards the safeguarding of French interests in those areas. The Union of African States, created by Ghana, Guinea, and the Mali Republic in December 1960, was absorbed into the Casablanca bloc, formed a month later by the revolutionary African states which were anything but friendly to France. At about the same time, Nigeria broke off its diplomatic relations with Paris as a protest against the French nuclear tests in the Sahara. The Entente's refusal to accept a regional defense pact might induce the equatorial states to follow suit, thus depriving France of the military leverage that would be needed should the Algerian war expand southward into the desert and the current disorders in the former Belgian Congo spill over that country's western frontiers. To be sure, the recently formed Brazzaville bloc seemed friendly to France, but it had been organized by Houphouët and so, like the Entente, might move out of the French orbit. In short, the Entente's defection from the Community might provoke a mass exodus from that organization, for its advantages to the remaining members would then be reduced to the vanishing point.

In France itself, the thesis defended by Raymond Cartier —that the funds spent in Africa were wasted and would be better used to modernize the French economy—was gaining ground.[15] If the Entente were given a blank check for funds over which France would have no control, French taxpayers might rebel and the Parliament refuse to vote further financial grants to Africa. Despite its recognition of all those risks, the most serious of which in de Gaulle's eyes was the destruction of the Community, the French government decided to accept the Entente's basic terms. On a few points, however, compromises were worked out. The funds would be granted on an annual schedule over a five-year period, France would exercise supervisory powers over the Entente's utilization of them, and those states which signed bilateral defense agreements would permit France to station troops in their territory as well as to train and equip their armies.

Curiously enough, Houphouët was encountering difficulties with his partners on the very same issues of defense and financial aid. When, during one of the stalemates in the Paris negotiations, Houphouët withdrew to Switzerland for a rest, Yameogo, Diori, and Maga met at Ouagadougou in such secrecy as to suggest that disagreements had developed between them and the Ivorian leader. It soon became apparent

[15] "En France Noire," *Paris-Match,* Aug. 11, 18, 1956.

that at least two of his partners believed that Houphouët intended to control the distribution of France's financial aid in such a way as to "reduce Upper Volta, Niger, and Dahomey to the status of Ivorian provinces." [16] This reaction prompted Houphouët to make a hurried trip to Niamey, where he denied ever having entertained such an idea, but he made no mention of the trouble then brewing between Ivory Coast and Upper Volta, which was probably the root cause of his difficulties with Yameogo. Although Yameogo had been elected president of the Entente for 1961 and in a press interview had praised that organization for its "realistic approach and democratic institutions," [17] the new ties he was developing with Ghana and the Mali Republic indicated that he was considering leaving the Entente.

The current flareup between Ouagadougou and Abidjan was a recrudescence of their old conflict over the division of their common customs revenues. In January 1961, it was precipitated by a decision of the Ivorian Finance Minister to replace the rebate on Voltaic imports, which dated from the days of the French West African Federation, by a flat sum which Yameogo felt was far less than his country's just due.[18] In December 1960, Ghana and the Mali Republic began cultivating Yameogo's friendship by sending missions to Ouagadougou. Upper Volta had become an important transit area for Mali's merchandise after Modibo Keita closed the frontier with Senegal. For Ghana, Upper Volta was a main source of laborers and livestock, and an alliance with Yameogo also fitted in with Nkrumah's projects to undermine Houphouët's position. When Nkrumah offered Upper Volta

[16] *Afrique Nouvelle,* Feb. 22, 1961.

[17] A. Blanchet, "La Haute-Volta," *Nice-Matin,* Jan. 12, 1961.

[18] I. M. Wallerstein, "Background to Paga," *West Africa,* July 28, Aug. 5, 1961.

the same economic advantages as Ivory Coast, and on more advantageous terms, Yameogo was receptive for reasons of internal politics. He was still politically vulnerable to pressures from the western Voltaics, who had long clamored for closer ties with their fellow tribesmen in Mali, from local nationalists and young radicals who disapproved of Upper Volta's "subordination" to Ivory Coast and its conservative president, and from the large contingent of Mossi military veterans who wanted Upper Volta to have a strong national army and rid itself of the French officers who were prone to intervene in domestic politics.

To placate these restive elements by a show of independence vis-à-vis Houphouët and France, Yameogo instituted a tariff barrier against Ivory Coast, refused to sign a defense treaty with the French government, and also asked France to withdraw its troops from Upper Volta. Inasmuch as France, only a few weeks before, had vacated its bases in Mali and then had only two small garrisons stationed at Ouagadougou and Bobo-Dioulasso, General de Gaulle immediately complied. To obviate a strongly adverse reaction to these moves on the part of the French government and Houphouët, which might entail their cutting off further aid to Upper Volta, Yameogo made gestures of appeasement to both. He voiced his approval of the French nuclear tests in the Sahara, praised Houphouët by calling him "notre général à nous," and endorsed all the economic and cultural agreements negotiated between the Entente and France.

At long last, on April 24, 1961, the various agreements of cooperation were signed. They were a testimonial to France's willingness to compromise, as well as proof of Houphouët's diplomatic skill. France's friendship and aid had been pledged on terms that fell far short of General de Gaulle's initial hopes, and at the same time Houphouët had disproved his opponents' contention that he was a French stooge and the Entente a French satellite. Nevertheless, Yameogo's refusal to sign a defense agreement, as well as the minor variations in the different cultural agreements, breached the principle of unanimity in decisions that had been basic to the Entente's organization, and also diminished Houphouët's personal prestige. Although, from the inception of the Entente, Houphouët had stressed the member states' autonomy, he had also expected them to accept his guidance in essential matters that affected the group as a whole. Developments in Africa external to the Entente had forced him to demand, first, independence for its members and then that they be granted full sovereign status. To his consternation, these new rights were promptly invoked not only in their dealings with France but also in their relations with Ivory Coast. Nevertheless, just as France had preferred to accept what it considered less than satisfactory cooperation agreements rather than risk a total rupture with the Entente, so Houphouët progressively renounced political control over his partners lest they break up that organization.

Within a few weeks the sincerity of his acceptance of this new relationship was put to a severe test, for in June 1961 Yameogo announced with considerable fanfare that Upper Volta had formed a customs union with Ghana. Houphouët not only did not protest this move but supported Yameogo's right to make it, and he was rewarded by Yameogo's publicly expressed protestations of "unshakeable attachment" to the Entente.[19] Two more years were to pass, however, before the wisdom of Houphouët's policy would receive a resounding endorsement. After the Ghana-Upper Volta frontier was closed, because of a quarrel between Yameogo and Nkrumah, the chastened Voltaic leader became one of Houphouët's most faithful followers.

On a much smaller scale, Maga's concurrent and brief

[19] *Afrique,* Sept. 1961.

flirtation with Ghana had a similar effect upon Dahomey's relations with Ivory Coast. Although, economically, Dahomey was far less important to Ghana than was Upper Volta, Nkrumah saw in Maga's ambivalent attitude toward Ivory Coast another opportunity to undermine the Entente. In February 1961 he began courting Maga, and he persuaded the Dahomean president to come to Accra four months later. There the two leaders signed a trade agreement and issued a communiqué in which they inevitably denounced white colonialism in Angola and Southwest Africa. This led to Dahomey's takeover of the tiny Portuguese enclave at Ouidah, but not to much more. The commercial agreement of June 1961 simply gave official sanction to a trade current between the two countries that had previously escaped all governmental controls. Maga's responsiveness to Nkrumah's overtures had been, like Yameogo's, partly due to his compatriots' long-standing resentment against Ivory Coast, but it was also motivated by Dahomey's desire to constitute a Benin Union that would include Ghana as well as Togo and Nigeria. However, the growing tension between Sylvanus Olympio and Nkrumah not only dashed hopes for such a union but made impolitic ties with Ghana lest they jeopardize Dahomey's far more important relationship with Togo.

These episodes were shortlived and mainly significant for the light they threw on inter-Entente relations. If the outcome to some extent proved Houphouët's ability to handle his two skittish partners, this was mainly because of Yameogo's and Maga's realization that the alternatives to continued membership in the Entente were less advantageous. Political events in 1963 would show how strong were the centrifugal tendencies in Upper Volta and Dahomey and how tenuous was Houphouët's hold over their leaders.

CHAPTER 3

Plots, Conflicts,
and Coups d'Etat

For several years after the cooperation agreements with France were signed, such changes as occurred in the Entente countries were those of degree rather than of kind. The trend was increasingly toward one-man, one-party rule, and the heads of state who had been elected at the time of independence consolidated their positions by banning or absorbing the most dangerous opposition forces and by establishing diplomatic and commercial relations with many foreign countries and international bodies. To all appearances, a certain degree of internal economic stability had been reached, thanks in part to the solidarity fund but far more to continuing French aid in the form of subsidies and special privileges in the French market for some of the Entente's exports. Indeed, the Entente was functioning so smoothly during 1962 that its council met less frequently than before, and by the end of that year Ivory Coast decided to eliminate the post of minister in charge of relations with the other Entente states. At the time, Houphouët was preoccupied far more with widening the foreign relations of the UAM than with the development of the Entente, for it was the era when all the African nations, regardless of their leaders' ideologies, were tending toward unity on a continental scale.

The only episode that marred the generally tranquil scene in the "moderate" French-speaking Black African states in 1962 was a conflict in October between Gabon and Congo-

Brazzaville, and this involved primarily the UAM and only indirectly the Entente. It was the upsurge of an old quarrel between two of the equatorial territories, and though the Congolese were the main target of the xenophobic emotions released in Gabon, several hundred Dahomeans working at Pointe Noire felt its backlash. On a much smaller scale, their situation resembled in many ways that of their compatriots during the Abidjan riots exactly four years earlier. As Houphouët had done in 1958, the Congolese president expressed his government's regret and promised to pay damages, but the Cotonou authorities remained deeply worried lest this fresh evidence of the strength of territorial nationalism develop into a pattern endangering the many thousands of Dahomeans employed in other African countries. With remarkable prescience, Maga urged that this problem be viewed by the UAM in an all-African context rather than mediated as an isolated conflict. When the UAM leaders turned a deaf ear to his plea, Maga refused to have Dahomey represented at the Yaoundé round-table conference which, early in November, succeeded in settling the Gabon-Congo dispute. His lone stand, however, did not become an issue in inter-Entente relations, as was to be the case several months later in regard to the upheaval in Togo.

The assassination of the Togolese president, Sylvanus Olympio, on January 13, 1963, opened an era of plots and coups d'état in Black Africa, which eventually brought military governments to power in two of the Entente states and in Togo. This crime may have had some affinity to the first of two serious plots that were uncovered in Ivory Coast during 1963, in one of which military officers were reportedly involved. In any case, Olympio's murder revived the Entente's fears of subversion, particularly in Ivory Coast and Niger, where Ghana's support for the Sanwi secessionists and for the Sawaba dissidents was already giving Houphouët and Diori cause for alarm.

This collective fear drew the Entente states closer together, and at an unusually important meeting of the council, held February 17–19, 1963, at Abidjan, the four heads of state condemned assassination as a political weapon and agreed to coordinate their defense against any threat of subversion that might lead to coups d'état in their respective states. Exactly what joint defense measures they planned to take was not then made known, but they were probably identical with those embraced in the project which Houphouët outlined to the UAM conference held at Ouagadougou one month later. There the Ivorian president, speaking in the name of the Entente, proposed that regular consultations between the member states' police services be instituted and that automatic extradition procedures be followed in the case of persons considered dangerous to the state's security.[1] The UAM, however, proved unresponsive to his suggestion, for Togo was too small and remote from the great majority of UAM members for their leaders to fear the contagion of violence as keenly as did the nearer-by Entente states.

Of all the Entente countries, Dahomey was the most directly affected by Olympio's assassination, not only because of its geographical proximity, but also because it had the closest ethnic, commercial, and personal ties with the Togolese. Moreover, Maga had reasons of his own for fearing that any drastic change in Togo's leadership would jeopardize the success of the Benin Union project that he was sponsoring. In mid-1962, his plans for that union had got off to a good start with the negotiation of a customs agreement with Nigeria, and in December a similar arrangement had been made with Olympio. In the power struggle that followed

1 *Afrique Nouvelle,* Feb. 28, March 21, 1963.

Olympio's death in Togo, it appeared to many of the Entente leaders that Ghana and Nigeria were intervening and giving their support to rival Togolese parties. To prevent this trend from developing further, Maga promptly attempted to promote agreement between Togo's warring politicians. Maga, having managed to remain on good terms with Olympio at the same time as he was providing a refuge for the Togolese president's predecessor and principal adversary, Nicolas Grunitsky, was well placed to play the role of honest broker. The provisional coalition government which Grunitsky managed to put together in March 1963, uneasy as it was, owed its establishment partly to Maga's diplomacy.

Despite his success in helping to stabilize Togo's political situation, Maga could not persuade the Entente council to give its official recognition to the Grunitsky regime. Houphouët and Yameogo, in particular, although they applauded Maga personally for his peacemaking efforts, were adamantly opposed to countenancing any government that had come to power by violence. Their stand was approved not only by the UAM heads of state when they met at Ouagadougou in March, but also by the great majority of African leaders who convened at Addis Ababa two months later to form the Organization of African Unity (OAU). However, the elections in Togo, held almost concurrently with that conference, gave legitimacy to the Grunitsky government, and it soon received widespread official recognition throughout Africa. Nevertheless, this did not serve to revive the Benin Union project, despite some support for it in Togo and Nigeria, and it was to be further set back by the overthrow of Maga's government in October 1963.

On the eve of Olympio's assassination, Maga to all appearances had good reason to feel satisfied with the accomplishments of his government during the preceding three and one-half years. Although he had become premier and then president of the Dahomey Republic only because of the rivalry between the two southern parties, he had managed to stay in office by playing their leaders off against each other and by detaching them from the most active elements of their respective power bases. By alternately allying himself with Ahomadegbe and Apithy, he had prevented their teaming up against him. Furthermore, by forcing all the wage earners to join a national labor federation, he had undermined Ahomadegbe's control over the Cotonou unions, and by taking some bright former student radicals into his government he had frustrated Apithy's bid for leadership of the left-wing opposition. Then, in reorganizing the judicial and administrative systems, he had reduced the salaries of the bureaucracy but not their number, thus diminishing the risk of the civil servants' re-forming a united front with the unemployed—a phenomenon that in the past had led to politically dangerous strikes and demonstrations. Consequently Apithy and his followers, as well as most of Ahomadegbe's, to save their political skins, had joined the single Parti Dahoméen de l'Unité (PDU) which Maga formed in December 1960. Although Ahomadegbe himself had held out, at the cost of serving a prison term on dubious charges of plotting against the security of the state, he was released in November 1962 after showing signs of repentance. Thus the outlook for a general political détente seemed promising.

In the field of foreign relations Maga had also registered outstanding successes, and even his failures ultimately proved beneficial to Dahomean national unity. His inability to form the Benin Union reassured those Dahomeans who had long resented the claims made by some Togolese to the mouth of the Mono River [2] and to a deepwater port of their

2 R. Grivot, *Réactions Dahoméennes,* Paris 1954, p. 167.

own at Lomé (rather than sharing that of Cotonou). It also
calmed those who had been alarmed by articles in the Lagos
press that promoted a scheme of uniting the Yoruba peoples
on both sides of the frontier by absorbing Dahomey as a
province of Nigeria.[3]

On the positive side, the breakup of the Mali Federation
and the Entente's accession to independence, in August
1960, had justified Maga's adherence to the latter organization—a step which also insured French financial backing for
building the Cotonou port on which the Dahomeans believed their economic future depended. Furthermore, by
joining various international organizations and making agreements with a number of non-African governments, Maga
had proved that membership in the Entente did not prevent
Dahomey from expanding its foreign relations. All these
developments cut the ground from under Maga's opponents,
who had criticized him for subservience to France and to
Houphouët. To be sure, Maga had been so absorbed in keeping his head above Dahomey's troubled political waters that
he had failed to improve his country's financial position, but
he could blame the deterioration of its economy on the
forced return of the thousands of Dahomeans formerly employed in the Dakar federal government and in other newly
independent African states. As regards Dahomey's long-term
prospects, he could point to the national-development plan
he had drafted, which, in conjunction with the Cotonou
port, should eventually increase the country's productivity
and exports: in the meantime, France was still meeting
Dahomey's growing budget deficits.

Successive postponements of the PDU national congress
during 1963 gave the first visible evidence of the trouble
that was brewing beneath the surface. When it was finally

[3] *Afrique Nouvelle,* March 2, 1960.

held in August, a rift developed between Maga and his Defense Minister, which affected the army. Then Apithy's resignation from its politburo, on the ground that Dahomey's educated youth was insufficiently represented in the government, showed that the party was now united in name only. Obviously the classical divisions between, on the one hand, Maga's traditionalist north, the youthful radicals and the Goun and Nagot (Yoruba) civil servants of Porto Novo who were Apithy's main support, and, on the other, the trade unions of Cotonou still loyal to Ahomadegbe, had been simply papered over. Indeed they had been deepened because the government had made wage earners the main target of the austerity measures imposed to meet Dahomey's growing budget deficits, for which, it was becoming clear, wasteful expenditures and embezzlement by Maga and his appointees were in great part responsible. These collective grievances, which had tribal and regional overtones, erupted on October 20 in week-long riots, triggered by the release from prison of a Nagot deputy from Sakété charged with murdering a Goun civil servant from Porto Novo.

Maga, returning hastily from abroad, tried vainly to pour oil on the troubled waters, first by promising reforms and then by offering the resignation of his cabinet. At the request of the student and labor leaders who had spearheaded the riots, the army under Colonel Christophe Soglo and Captain Alphonse Alley took over the government. These professional officers dissolved the assembly and the party, and reluctantly agreed to form a provisional government and a new single party, draft a constitution that would diverge from the 1960 Entente "model," and hold elections. After trying different combinations of politicians, Soglo found that Maga and the other northerners in his cabinet were no longer acceptable as members of the government, and indeed for their own protection they had to be placed under house arrest.

Early in 1964, Dahomey's third constitution received overwhelming support in a popular referendum, and Soglo retired from the political scene, after turning the government over to Apithy and Ahomadegbe following their elections respectively as president and vice president-prime minister of the second Dahomey republic. Thus what Dahomeans called their "October revolution" amounted to only a palace coup and not a social revolution, but the executive power was now divided between two mutually incompatible southern politicians who headed a government from which representatives of the north were excluded. To compound the difficulties, the new government was faced with a public debt which had risen under Maga's maladministration to a figure almost equal to Dahomey's total annual revenues (6.5 billion CFA [Colonies Françaises d'Afrique] francs compared with 7.1 billion), and which could be met only by an increased French subsidy. Furthermore, the student and labor organizations were demanding as their reward for overthrowing the previous administration the abrogation of the 10 per cent cut in the pay of wage-earners which Maga had instituted, and the severance of Dahomey's ties with France and the Entente. Unexpectedly and inadvertently, the latter step had become by then almost inevitable because of a new development in inter-Entente relations.

Late in December 1963, two weeks before the referendum on Dahomey's constitution was held, Diori discharged without warning all the Dahomean civil servants in his administration, and also occupied Lété Island in the Niger River that forms the boundary between the two countries. Diori later justified the expulsions as retaliation for the death of three Nigériens at Porto Novo during the October riots, and his occupation of Lété as being a move to forestall a similar one by Dahomey. Lété, despite its strategic location, was hardly worth fighting over, for it was a no-man's island used as pasture by herders on both river banks during the six months of the year when it was not inundated. The expulsions were the crux of the matter, and they happened probably in part because the government of Niger was afraid that the Dahomey expatriates might try to propagate locally the "revolutionary ideology" which Diori then believed had motivated the overthrow of Maga.[4] An even more likely reason for them was Diori's resentment of the hospitality that Dahomey had allegedly offered to his archenemy, Djibo Bakary. In any case, panic seized the whole Dahomean colony in Niger, and there was a mass exodus of its members, variously estimated at 3,000 to 16,000, who made their way to the frontier under deplorable conditions.

The Soglo government reacted vigorously, charging Niger with "inhumanly and brutally" expelling the Dahomeans so as to "frustrate the objectives of the October revolution," start a civil war in Dahomey, and upset its new government by forcing it suddenly to find housing, food, and jobs for 16,000 returnees.[5] Soglo sent troops to defend Lété Island, closed the frontier, impounded Nigérien merchandise in transit at Cotonou, and lodged a complaint against Niger with the United Nations. Offers of mediation poured in from all sides, and the UAM called a special meeting at Abidjan to arbitrate the conflict. Soglo, however, refused to attend any conference held in the Ivorian capital, for he believed that Houphouët was so resentful of Maga's overthrow that he would prevent Dahomey's present leaders

4 See E. Terray, "Les Révolutions Congolaise et Dahoméenne," *Revue Française de Science Politique,* Oct. 5, 1964.

5 Broadcast by Colonel Soglo, Cotonou radio, Dec. 28, 1963.

from receiving a fair deal at the hands of any organization in which he was influential. Indeed, for more than a year Dahomey refused to attend the Entente council meetings, and not until after its dispute with Niger was finally settled was it again represented there.

Diori, perhaps regretting his overhasty action, had expressed in March 1964 his willingness to pay damages to the Dahomean refugees, but he found it harder to forgive their government for the facilities it offered to the Sawaba commandos in staging raids in Niger the following October. Nevertheless, he yielded to Houphouët's pressure and agreed to conduct negotiations directly with the Dahomean leaders. After he revised the contract under which the two countries jointly managed the Cotonou port and railroad, the way was cleared for an overall settlement of their feud under Houphouët's supervision in January 1965. Apithy and Ahomadegbe, for their part, were less responsive to the efforts being made concurrently by France and Houphouët to reconcile them with Niger, for they had long wanted to move out of the French orbit, as well as to leave the Entente. It was only after their attempts to revive the Benin Union project in May 1964 proved abortive and the port of Cotonou neared completion that their attitude toward both began to mellow. Also partly responsible for this change of front was a succession of strikes organized by the turbulent Dahomean trade unions, as well as several plots hatched by Maga's disgruntled northern supporters, both of which were endangering the foundations of their authority. An even greater threat to the survival of their government was their growing discord over the division of executive power and the orientation of Dahomey's foreign policy, and these factors combined to induce both men to seek outside support to bolster their respective positions.

Houphouët realized that it was high time to reinforce his leadership position in West Africa, for if 1964 had been a bad year for the Entente it was an even worse one for the UAM. The government installed in Congo-Brazzaville since August 1963 was showing signs of disaffection toward the UAM's pro-Western foreign policy; France's military intervention in February 1964 in Gabon to restore Léon Mba as president of that republic had created a rift among UAM members; and fresh trouble was brewing in the former Belgian Congo, where Moïse Tshombe had come to power. Then, in April, a majority of the UAM heads of state had voted to transform the organization into a purely economic regional group called the Union Africaine et Malgache pour la Coopération Economique (UAMCE). Houphouët and his closest collaborators opposed this move because they feared that the UAMCE might revive the old rivalry between Dakar and Abidjan and, worse, that it would be ineffective in stemming the rising "revolutionary" tide in Africa. That same month, therefore, Houphouët manifested his dissatisfaction with the UAMCE by trying to reconstitute the old RDA., whose West African leaders he invited to a meeting in Ivory Coast. Sékou Touré, Modibo Keita, and Hamani Diori accepted his invitation but not his proposal. Sentimental ties might still exist between these men as individuals, but they were not strong enough to counteract the ideological divergencies that now separated the presidents of Guinea and Mali, on the one hand, from those of the Ivory Coast and Niger on the other.[6]

Houphouët had perforce to fall back on the Entente as

[6] Analogous differences of opinion were also to prevent the materialization of a project sponsored by President Tubman in August 1964 to create a free-trade zone comprising Liberia, Guinea, Sierra Leone, and Ivory Coast.

his organizational base, although for all practical purposes it was now reduced to three members. To strengthen the bonds uniting them, he played up the danger to the stability of their governments arising from Communist China's recent activities in Africa and from Nkrumah's encouragement of subversion in their states. Yameogo and Diori were highly responsive: although neither of them had diplomatic relations with the communist countries, both had specific grievances against Ghana. Dahomey, however, could hardly be expected to share Houphouët's anxieties in either respect, for in the summer of 1964 Apithy still hoped to persuade Ghana to join the Benin Union. Moreover, in August he had exchanged missions with the USSR, and in November he had agreed to establish diplomatic relations with the Peking government. Something more tangibly advantageous must be offered if Dahomey were ever again to become a working member of the Entente and if Togo's hesitations about joining it were to be overcome.

During a state visit in December to Upper Volta, with which Ivory Coast was now on the best of terms, Houphouët announced his proposal for a "dual nationality" among the citizens of the Entente states. There had never been any doubt that Diori would follow where Houphouët led, and from the speeches the latter made during his tour of Upper Volta it was obvious that he had also obtained Yameogo's approval of his project. At Koudougou, he was quoted as saying: "in my own name and in that of my brother, President Yameogo, I declare that the first six months of 1965 will not pass without our two assemblies voting simultaneously in favor of our mutual desire for dual nationality. This means that every Voltaic living in Ivory Coast will have the same rights and duties as an Ivorian national, and vice-versa." [7] A few days later, Diori spelled out Houphouët's

[7] Ouagadougou radio broadcast, Dec. 14, 1964.

statement in relation to Niger by saying over the Niamey radio on December 18 that "as long as Nigériens serve in the Ivorian bureaucracy they will enjoy equal rights with Ivory Coast nationals, but once they leave that country they become citizens of Niger back home." Aside from this amplification, the whole subject was apparently dropped for about a year, and Houphouët's optimistic timetable was not respected. As so often happened before and since, the Entente was relegated to the background whenever Houphouët found that he could operate more effectively in the wider African field offered him by the UAM.

To be sure, the Entente did not simply mark time during most of 1965, and certain developments made its future look more promising. In January, Niger and Dahomey buried the hatchet and, for the first time in fourteen months, the latter country was represented at an Entente conference. Early in February the Togolese legislature—probably alarmed by Nkrumah's encroachments—voted to join the Entente. Although Grunitsky promptly declared such a decision to be "premature," he began to attend the Entente council meetings regularly. In so doing he was frank to admit that he had been attracted by the dual-nationality proposal as an outlet for Togo's overabundant elite, and that he was also motivated by his need for support vis-à-vis Ghana.[8] Then, in Niger, the attempt in April by Sawaba partisans, believed to have been trained in Ghana and Communist China, to assassinate Diori reinforced his government's support for Houphouët's antisubversion campaign. Thus the growing sense of insecurity shared by the leaders of Niger, Dahomey, and Togo induced them to draw closer to France and to the Entente as their sturdiest bulwarks against their internal and external enemies. In July, Grunitsky's presence with the four heads of the Entente states at-

[8] Lomé radio, Feb. 4, 1965.

tending the inauguration of Cotonou's deepwater port indicated that the Council of the Entente was gaining more strength and unity.

Houphouët's failure during 1965 to develop further his original statement about dual nationality for the Entente states was probably motivated by his hope of enlarging the scope of his proposal to include all the members of a new organization which he was in the process of forming. That he had never fully accepted the transformation of the UAM into the UAMCE had been shown by the refusal of the Entente countries in 1964 to sign the latter's charter, but it did not become clear until early 1965 that he was also planning to revive the UAM under a new name. By that time Houphouët's main concern had become the checking of the spread of communism and subversion throughout Africa, and in so doing he could count on the support of Niger, Upper Volta, and Togo. Now he was also able to enlist the cooperation of other conservative presidents such as Tsiranana of Madagascar, Mba of Gabon, and possibly Ahidjo of Cameroun, for those leaders had become increasingly alarmed during 1964 by the real or imagined growth of revolutionary dissident movements in their countries. Although such fears were felt with varying degrees of intensity, they were shared by a sufficient number of the heads of state attending the UAMCE meeting at Nouakchott in February 1965 for them to accept his proposal to make marked changes in that organization.

After lively debates, those who wanted a predominantly political body and those favoring a wholly economic one reached a compromise: both activities would be combined in a new group called the Organisation Commune Africaine et Malgache (OCAM). The OCAM's common denominator was its members' intention to modernize their countries' economy and, even more, their determination to resist revolution and subversion through coordinate action. In their final communiqué, they did not mention Communist China by name, out of respect for those members having diplomatic relations with Peking, but they felt no such compunctions about Ghana, which was specified as the main target of their censure.

The transformation of the UAMCE into the OCAM and the denunciation of Ghana added up to a clearcut victory for Houphouët and his fellow conservatives, but in June they overreached themselves by railroading through the admission to the OCAM of President Tshombe of Congo-Léopoldville. Because of his role in the Katanga secession and his use of white mercenaries to put down the revolts of his Congolese compatriots, Tshombe was personally unpopular with all the OCAM members, although there were cogent arguments in favor of his candidacy. To be consistent about endorsing the principle of legitimacy, the OCAM was forced to support him as the duly elected head of his government.

The decision to admit Tshombe had several consequences that not only were disruptive of the unity of the newborn organization but also widened the existing divisions among the West African states. It provided Mauritania with an excuse to withdraw from a Black African organization on the ground that it no longer needed to resist the encroachments of Morocco, and that such an association would hamper its developing closer ties with the revolutionary states of North Africa. In francophone Africa, the move so angered Sékou Touré that he launched a series of broadcasts over Conakry radio attacking the OCAM, the Entente, and above all Houphouët. To these outbursts the Ivorian president made no immediate or direct reply, but Yameogo took up the cudgels in his defense and counterattacked Sékou Touré with equal violence and relish. This radio war, which lasted through the summer of 1965, became so vitriolic that it seemed likely to end any hope of a rapprochement between the former RDA leaders. Because this exchange of insults was largely restricted to the personal level, it did not involve the Entente directly as a group, but Houphouët's concurrent campaign against Ghana did give that organization a new role.

When the OCAM was formed, it had been assumed that the Entente would fit into its structure as unobtrusively as it had into that of the UAM. However, it was soon evident that the Entente states were the only members of the OCAM that felt keenly enough about the threat of subversion emanating from the dissidents backed by Nkrumah to take direct action. Shortly before Dahomey rejoined the Entente, Houphouët, Yameogo, and Diori had set up a unified military command expressly to help any one of their states combat subversive elements that threatened their governmental stability. The value of such a gesture of solidarity, however, was purely psychological, for none of their armies was sufficiently strong, disciplined, or well equipped to be an effective military force, let alone be moved from one country to another as rapidly as would be required. Equally fruitless in terms of practical results were the secret missions dispatched during 1964 by Houphouët and Yameogo to demand from Nkrumah the extradition of the Voltaic and Ivorian dissidents who were using Accra as their base.[9] Then, in April 1965, an attempt by Ghana-trained Nigériens to assassinate Diori hardened the attitude of all the Entente leaders toward Nkrumah into one of active hostility. But at the same time they realized that to bring effective pressure to bear on Nkrumah required the cooperation of nations far more powerful than those of the Entente. Nevertheless, the En-

[9] See *Afrique Nouvelle,* Dec. 30, 1964.

tente countries were so united on this issue that they could serve as the springboard for the diplomatic offensive launched by Houphouët against Ghana in the first half of 1965.

The choice of Accra as the site for the OAU's summit conference in October gave Houphouët what he believed was a focal point for rallying the moderate English- and French-speaking African leaders to his cause. Specifically, he hoped to induce them to express their disapproval of Nkrumah's subversive activities by refusing to go to Accra. The Entente emissaries he sent to persuade them, however, met with either indifference or outright refusal. Even those African presidents who had reason to be suspicious of Nkrumah believed that Houphouët's accusations against him were exaggerated and, in any case, they did not want to jeopardize the OAU's unity.

Nkrumah himself, however, became alarmed to such a point of Houphouët's moves to sabotage the Accra conference that he undertook a diplomatic counteroffensive. In mid-March, after consulting with Sékou Touré and Modibo Keita, he extended the olive branch to Yameogo by unilaterally reopening Ghana's frontier with Upper Volta, which he had closed some time before. Then, after the *attentat* against Diori, he not only denied that Ghana was in any way implicated but had the temerity to send belated congratulations to the Nigérien president on his escape. After his overtures were rebuffed, however, Nkrumah turned savagely on the Entente and in a press interview he described the "antics of Ivory Coast, Upper Volta and Niger" as part of a "carefully worked out imperialist plot directly related to the Congo situation." Because "the Council of the Entente desperately needs foreign economic and military assistance, imperialism has chosen it to act as its instrument in support of Tshombe's policy." [10]

[10] *West Africa,* May 22, 1965.

As the time neared for the Accra conference, Nkrumah once more became conciliatory, as did the Entente leaders, who now had to acknowledge the ineffectiveness of their "peace offensive." Through intermediaries a meeting was arranged, at which Nkrumah promised to "send away" the alien dissidents he had been harboring and to guarantee personally the security of the Entente heads of state who would attend the Accra conference. But because he refused to let accredited Entente representatives come to Accra to verify the list of dissidents he claimed to have expelled, the Entente presidents found his concessions inadequate and persisted in their refusal to attend the October OAU conference. Their boycott was followed only by Gabon, Chad, Madagascar, and Togo, for the other African states felt ideologically committed to support the OAU, or Nkrumah's revolutionary principles, or both. Indeed some of them expressed their overall disapproval of the Entente, as well as of the OCAM, because they were "inward-looking groups, overly insistent upon deepening the divisions between English- and French-speaking Africa." [11] Probably Nkrumah's most effective propaganda weapon in saving the Accra conference was his charge that the Entente was deliberately trying to undermine African unity, even though the Entente leaders retorted that they would attend the conference if it were held anywhere other than Ghana.

Houphouët's inability to prevent a majority of African heads of state from going to Accra harmed his prestige and showed that once again he had miscalculated the temper of the times. Furthermore, his failure to quarantine Ghana had boomeranged by isolating the Entente and undermining its self-confidence and solidarity as a group. During the last months of 1965, the Entente's unity suffered another blow

[11] Lagos radio, April 23, 1965.

1. Félix Houphouët-Boigny, president of Ivory Coast and founder of the Council of the Entente.

2. Hubert Maga, president of the first Dahomean Republic, 1960–1963. He became chairman of the presidential council in May 1970.

3. Justin Ahomadegbe, descendant of the kings of Abomey, premier of Dahomey, 1964–1965 and slated to become chairman of the presidential council in 1972.

4. Sourou-Migan Apithy, vice-president of the Dahomean government council, 1958–1959, head of state, 1964–1965, and member of the presidential council, May 1970.

5. General Christophe Soglo, formerly a French army commissioned officer. He headed Dahomey's first military government, 1965–1967.

6. Hamani Diori, a charter member of the RDA and the founder of the PPN, president of the Republic of Niger since 1960.

7. Djibo Bakary, organizer of Niamey's radical trade unions. He has led the opposition to Diori and has been in exile since 1959.

8. General Sangoulé Lamizana, a career army officer. He has been head of state of the Republic of Upper Volta since the coup d'état of January 1966.

9. Maurice Yameogo, president of the Upper Volta Republic from 1960 until overthrown in 1966. He was under house arrest until freed by Lamizana in August 1970.

10. The Moro Naba, "Emperor" of the Mossi tribe of Upper Volta, and the outstanding paramount chief of francophone Black Africa.

11. Joseph Ki Zerbo, Upper Volta's leading intellectual, and secretary-general of the MLN.

12. Cardinal Paul Zoungrana, West Africa's first cardinal. He is the outspoken head of the Catholic hierarchy of Upper Volta.

13. General Etienne Eyadema, who played a key role in Togo's two coups d'état. He has been head of state since April 1967.

14. Nicolas Grunitsky, backed by the administration to lead successive anti-Ewe parties during the French trusteeship in Togo. He was president of the Togo Republic, 1963–1967, and died in Dahomey in 1969.

15. Sylvanus Olympio, a British-trained businessman, leader of the Ewe tribe in Togo, and president of the Togo Republic until his assassination in January 1963.

16. Great Chief of the Cabrais, the traditional head of northern Togo's most dynamic tribe.

when Dahomey experienced its second coup d'état within two years of the first. In November, the long-simmering power conflict between Apithy and Ahomadegbe came to a head, compounded by their government's failure to cope with dissent in the north and a steadily worsening economic situation. A pay cut, even more drastic than that imposed by Maga's government, revived agitation among Cotonou's restive labor unions that culminated in hostile demonstrations. Once more Soglo stepped in to restore order, ousted Apithy and Ahomadegbe, promised to hold elections soon, and tried vainly to form an acceptable provisional civilian government. The scenario, which up to this point repeated that of 1963, was changed abruptly by Soglo's decision on December 22 to stay in power.

This fresh proof of Dahomey's governmental instability at first disconcerted its Entente partners, for it seemed likely to nullify the long, painful, and ultimately successful efforts of Houphouët, Yameogo, and Diori to reach a working agreement with Apithy and Ahomadegbe. Almost at once, however, they were reassured by the orderliness of the military takeover and heartened by Soglo's policy declarations. Not only did the population remain passive, but there were no reprisals, and Apithy and Ahomadegbe were allowed to leave the country. (Eventually they joined Maga in Paris, where all three lived in exile if not in harmony.) Then Soglo set up an administration dominated by civilian technicians, broke off the diplomatic relations which Apithy had established with Communist China, and, best of all, reaffirmed Dahomey's membership in the Entente and the OCAM as well as its loyalty to France.

No sooner did the situation in Dahomey appear to have been settled to the satisfaction of its population and the Entente leadership than another coup d'état took place at

Ouagadougou during the first days of 1966. Basically, the circumstances leading to Yameogo's downfall resembled those that in Dahomey had resulted in Maga's overthrow, but subsequent developments in Upper Volta compressed Dahomey's timetable by bringing to power much earlier a military government at Ouagadougou. As in Dahomey, the austerity measures imposed by a corrupt and wasteful government aroused active hostility on the part, not of its desperately impoverished peasantry, but of the labor unions and students who were the least underprivileged strata of its population. Unable themselves to form a government, the student and union leaders soon called in the army under Colonel Sangoulé Lamizana to restore order—but not to stay in power, which it did.

In certain significant aspects, it should be noted, the precoup situation in Upper Volta had differed from that in Dahomey. Yameogo's personality was more dictatorial and his government more arbitrary than Maga's, and he was far harsher toward opposition forces in general and the traditional chieftaincy in particular. In 1960 he had forced Nazi Boni, the federalist leader of western Upper Volta, into exile at Dakar, then like an angry schoolteacher he disciplined the Voltaic students who disapproved of his conservative foreign policy, and finally he declared a vendetta against the influential Mossi chiefs, especially the Moro Naba.[12] Moreover, his nepotism brought his predatory relatives to high office, notably his unpopular and brutal cousin Denis, to whom he gave the key Interior portfolio. His own expenditures became increasingly sumptuary, including the building of palatial residences at Koudougou and Abidjan and the purchase of property in France. To cap it all, late in 1965 he divorced his wife of long standing and took a young bride

[12] See Ch. 7.

on a lavish wedding trip to Brazil, thereby simultaneously offending his Voltaic women supporters and the Catholic hierarchy, which had until then been a bulwark of his government. On returning to Ouagadougou in early December, he arranged to be reelected president of the republic by an overwhelming majority, and then, in order to refill the public coffers which had been emptied by his own and his family's extravagance, he got the assembly to vote a 20 per cent cut in the pay and family allowances of Voltaic wage earners.

Three days of hostile demonstrations against him convinced Yameogo that he must resign, but his refusal to accept exile in Ivory Coast showed that he had high hopes of staging a political comeback.[13] Despite the unions' clamor that Yameogo be brought immediately to public trial, Lamizana simply placed him under house arrest. Consequently Yameogo's relative accessibility facilitated later efforts by his friends and relations to restore him to power.

Yameogo's overthrow was far more traumatic for Houphouët and Diori than had been that of any of the Dahomean leaders. To be sure, Yameogo at the outset had been a volatile, peppery, and not wholly trustworthy partner, but with time he had developed into their close collaborator and, albeit not a charter member, had been accepted into the old RDA club. Although Lamizana, like Soglo before him, promptly reaffirmed Upper Volta's loyalty to France, the Entente, and the OCAM and gave his country a far more honest and stable government than had his predecessor, Houphouët still found it difficult to accept Yameogo's eclipse. In consequence, the Voltaics long suspected him of conspiring to restore Yameogo to power. Indeed, this suspicious attitude, together with the Voltaics' chronic resent-

---

[13] *Marchés Tropicaux,* Feb. 12, 1966.

ment of Ivory Coast's predominant economic and political influence in their country, largely explained their notable lack of enthusiasm for Houphouët's offer of dual nationality, which he had renewed on the eve of Yameogo's downfall.

CHAPTER 4

Togo, the Entente's Fifth Member

Houphouët's revival of his dual-nationality project was evidently timed to offset the damage done to his partners' morale by his failure to sabotage the OAU conference at Accra, as well as to strengthen Soglo's determination to adhere to the Entente. Equally important, in his view, was the likelihood that it would finally convince Togo of the economic advantages to be derived from a closer association with Ivory Coast, and of the political support which the Entente could give to Togo in its resistance to Ghana's encroachments. In all these respects he was successful, despite the chilly reception his proposal received in Upper Volta after Yameogo's overthrow. As regards Togo, which had informally agreed on December 29, 1965, to join the Entente, his timing could not have been better: if Nkrumah had been ousted in Ghana before the end of that year, Togo might never have become more than a *de facto* member of his organization.

Among the Entente countries, Togo holds a unique place. Its fifteen years as a German colony before World War I, its forty-year administration by France under the supervision of two successive international organizations, the post–World War II agitation for Ewe reunification in southern Togo, and the Togolese government's prolonged aloofness from francophone Africa's political parties and unity movements—all these factors make its evolution re-

semble that of Cameroun more than of any other West
African state. However, in some respects—the large-scale
emigration of its superabundant educated elite, the sharp
division and antagonism between the evolved southern region and the underdeveloped north, its high population
density in relation to its small area and meager natural resources, and its fear of absorption by richer and more powerful neighbors—Togo has greater similarities with Dahomey.
Nevertheless, it is differentiated from both Cameroun and
Dahomey by certain distinctive features. Among these are
the political repercussions of its Ewe tribal problem on its
recent history, France's encouragement of the north's "emancipation" from domination by the south, the predominance
of foreign-policy issues in the orientation of its parties, its
early attainment of autonomy, and, finally, the role played
since 1963 by its veterans and armed forces.

Since the end of World War I, Togo's German heritage
has evolved in three distinct phases. During the interwar
period, a small group of clerks, catechists, and planters who
had been trained under the German regime formed an association called the Togobund. Its members, encouraged by the
Nazis' success in Germany, petitioned the League of Nations
for the return of their former masters. The Togobund was
liquidated during World War II, but its brief existence
alarmed the French colonial administration into forming
among the anti-German elements in the south a Comité de
l'Unité Togolaise (CUT). Hitler's defeat in 1945 ended
French apprehensions about Germany's political claims to
Togo, but within a few years the reconstitution of German
Togoland was considered in connection with the issue of
Ewe tribal reunification. When that possibility was shelved
after Togo became independent in 1960, the German heritage entered a sentimental and economic phase. As the Bonn

government began to participate in the development of the Third World, the former German colonies in Africa became the objects of its special benevolence. Specifically as regards Togo, its most conspicuous manifestation has been West Germany's willingness to finance the construction of a deep-water port at Lomé.

After World War I, German Togoland was divided into two unequal parts, of which the larger and more populous was placed under French administration and the smaller under British rule, and both became mandates of the League of Nations. Thus the widely dispersed Ewe tribe, already separated by the preexisting colonial frontiers, was further divided between two very different types of colonial government.[1] Of a total of some 850,000 Ewes living along the Guinea Gulf coast, between 350,000 and 400,000 were in French Togo and 450,000 in the British-ruled Gold Coast and the mandated territory of British Togoland, and much smaller groups were in Nigeria and Dahomey. For administrative purposes, British Togoland was integrated with the Gold Coast, whereas French Togo was never fully integrated either with the French West African Federation or Dahomey. Only briefly and as an economy measure during the early 1930's, the two French territories shared a few of the same officials, and in 1945 together elected a joint deputy to the French constituent assemblies.

For many years the Ewes succeeded in ignoring these artificial colonial frontiers, and they circulated and traded freely across the frontiers of the two Togolands until World War II broke out. Then the defeat of France, followed by the division of French Africa into pro-Vichy and Gaullist administrations, effectively sealed off the boundary between them, creating far greater hardships and economic shortages in the

[1] R. Cornevin, *Histoire du Togo* (Paris, 1959), p. 215.

French than in the British area. The Ewes' first demands
for reunification, however, came from the British side where,
in 1944, they formed an All-Ewe Conference with the aim
of joining forces with their fellow-tribesmen in French Togo.

Two years later, Great Britain and France agreed to accept
United Nations' trusteeships over their respective Togolands, and thereafter the two administering powers found
themselves subjected to much closer international supervision than under the League of Nations. The All-Ewe Conference, with the active support of the CUT in French Togo,
carried the case for Ewe reunification before the United
Nations trusteeship council and, later, also to the United
Nations General Assembly's Fourth Committee. A majority
of the members of both those bodies were strongly anti-
colonialist, and they sent regular missions of inspection to
the two trust territories and welcomed the testimony of
aggrieved native petitioners from both areas. Although the
United Nations could only make recommendations to the
administering authorities, it acted as an effective pressure
group in support of Ewe reunification. For both political and
technical reasons, the French and British long resisted such
pressure, but they made minor concessions to ease the tensions.

The political situation of the Ewes, already confused by
their division among three territorial units, was further
complicated by the ambivalent juridical status of the Togolese in the French area. Under the French constitution of
1946, they were not citizens of the Fourth Republic but of
the French Union. Furthermore, by extension they were
given the same privileges as were the citizens of the two
French Black African federations of electing representatives
to the Paris Parliament and to their own territorial assembly.
Just as in the other French territories that had had no elec-

tive institutions before World War II, successive elections during the first postwar years stimulated political activity and the formation of parties. However, in Togo, the issue of Ewe reunification gave the new parties a precise focal point and a different orientation. In particular, the issue of tribal reunification transformed the CUT into a solidly Ewe political organization and separated it from the newer, pro-French Parti Togolais du Progrès (PTP).

Both those parties were formally constituted in southern Togo within a few days of each other in April 1946. Their members came from the small social stratum of Christianized, well-to-do bourgeoisie, dominated by a so-called Brazilian elite—the descendants of slaves who had returned from South America and whose origins, prosperity, and high cultural level were analogous to those of the Dahomean elite. Even the leaders of the two Togolese parties were closely related, for Dr. Pedro Olympio and Nicolas Grunitsky, president and secretary-general of the PTP, were respectively cousin and brother-in-law of Sylvanus Olympio, head of the CUT. At that time, the electorate itself was largely restricted to southern Togo and comprised only about 8,000 of a total territorial population numbering nearly one million. Thus Togo's political evolution intensified the ethnic and economic divisions between the north and the south, which had existed under German rule and had been perpetuated by the French administration. Both colonial powers had concentrated their efforts in the more evolved south, and even sent Ewes to administer the poorer and far less developed north, which was almost as densely populated but was inhabited by more heterogeneous tribes. Of these tribes, the most important in almost every respect were the Cabrais, animist farmers whose traditional chiefs enjoyed far more power than their counterparts in the south. For some years after

World War II, the northerners continued to be politically passive, and the representatives they elected to Togo's territorial assembly were members of no organized political group.

Between 1946 and 1951, the political situation in Togo remained remarkably stable, being dominated by the two southern parties, the PTP and the CUT. Because of its abler leadership and clear-cut program of Ewe reunification, the CUT captured Togo's seats in the French Parliament and a majority of those in the territorial assembly, of which the party's leader, Sylvanus Olympio, was elected president. In the early 1950's, however, this situation underwent a rapid change, as the result of a substantial enlargement of the electorate, the organization of the Juvento as a youth branch of the CUT, and, above all, the formation of a northern party, the Union des Chefs et des Populations du Nord (UCPN). In 1952, a split in the ranks of the PTP and, far more important, the active support of the French administration enabled the UCPN, now allied with Grunitsky's PTP, to forge ahead of its rivals. By that time France had come to look upon the CUT as a hostile, pro-British party whose influence must be drastically reduced. The French administration therefore saw to it that the political situation was completely reversed and that the UCPN would win all the local elections during the next six years.

In 1956, developments outside French Togo became more decisive in its political evolution. The first two, which took place in the spring, seemed only indirectly to concern that territory: in May British Togoland voted to unite with the Gold Coast, and in June the *loi-cadre* was passed, with a view to its application mainly in the two French Black African federations. However, the transformation of the Gold Coast into the sovereign state of Ghana, scheduled for

March 1957, greatly stimulated African aspirations for independence and enhanced the prestige of the Ghanaian leader, Kwame Nkrumah, among West Africans. To keep French Togo from gravitating into his orbit, France hastily organized a referendum there in October 1956, under certain blanket provisions of the *loi-cadre* but without formally consulting the United Nations. In that referendum the Togolese were offered the choice of autonomy in the French Union—but not independence—or of remaining a trust territory of the United Nations.

Officially, a majority of the Togolese electorate opted for an autonomous status but, in the absence of United Nations observers, the parties opposed to the UCPN boycotted the referendum and claimed that the vote had been rigged. The United Nations, for its part, refused to abrogate its trusteeship, and France finally had to accept a compromise whereby elections for a new legislative assembly would be held in April 1958 under that international body's supervision. Consequently, the CUT and its allies put up candidates for the first time since 1955, and they won twenty-nine of the forty-six seats at stake, compared with ten for the UCPN.

The northern party's crushing defeat was the price it had to pay for its long tenure of office under France's patronage, but, ironically enough, the CUT's success proved to be a Pyrrhic victory for the advocates of Ewe reunification. It opened the way for French Togo's accession to independence and hardened Olympio's resistance to Nkrumah's expansionist ambitions, which had been whetted by his incorporation of British Togoland after a plebiscite held there six months before the French referendum. The prospect of union with the Marxist and Pan-Africanist Nkrumah delighted the left-wing Juvento but alarmed Olympio, who did not relish the likelihood that his country would be absorbed by its more powerful western neighbor. Under his guidance, Togo chose to become a sovereign state in April 1960 and was duly admitted to the United Nations, and a year later Olympio was elected the first president of the Togolese Republic. A sequel to those developments was that Ewe reunification became a casualty of the independence won by Ghana and Togo thirteen years after the reunification issue had been born.

The CUT's victory in April 1958 was due in large measure to the united front it had formed with its former youth branch, the Juvento, which had gradually acquired the status of a virtually autonomous party. Olympio's first policy statement and the appointment of two Juvento ministers in his government were clearly inspired by his desire to maintain the solidarity of this southern alliance. Specifically, he promised amnesty for all political prisoners, Africanization of the administrative cadres, moves toward Ewe reunification within the framework of a widely based West African federation, and an end to the preceding government's financial dependence on France. This program, however, was hardly reassuring to the northerners, who, moreover, had been the main victims of a bloody settling of accounts by Juvento militants after the April 1958 elections. Despite the fact that the UCPN had the same number of deputies as the Juvento in the new legislature and also held two posts in Olympio's government, the northerners felt increasingly that they were being reduced to the status of second-class citizens. When Grunitsky left Togo after his electoral defeat, the UCPN rapidly disintegrated. In October 1959 it merged with the PTP to form what became a northern regional party, the Union Démocratique des Populations Togolaises (UDPT), of which the most dynamic leader was Antoine Meatchi, the deputy from Lama-Kara and a man with close ties to leaders in Ghana.

If the northerners' demoralization and virtually leaderless condition prevented their opposition to Olympio from crystallizing for some time, the same could not be said of the radical and intransigently nationalistic Juvento. Under the able leadership of another southern "Brazilian," Maître Anani Santos, the Juvento became increasingly impatient at Olympio's slowness in implementing his program, and indeed soon accused him of traducing its principles. The Juvento could not accept Olympio's explanation of his year-long delay in proclaiming Togo's independence as being due to the formalities required to lift United Nations' trusteeship and to the need to prepare the country carefully for a transfer of powers. They believed that the surprisingly cordial relations which Olympio rapidly established with the new Gaullist government in France and the latter's pledge of continued financial aid were a betrayal of his avowed policy of achieving total sovereignty. With good reason they suspected that Olympio had come to see in a close collaboration with France his best assurance of resisting Nkrumah's encroachments, and in May 1959 Maître Santos resigned from the government in protest.

What the Juvento wanted was a union with Ghana, not only to achieve Ewe reunification but also to help bring about a social and economic revolution in Togo and promote Nkrumah's Pan-African program. To be sure, Olympio tried to placate his left-wing opponents by certain minor concessions—such as a reform of local-government institutions, the establishment of trade relations with communist as well as Western countries, a refusal to sign cooperation agreements with France, and resistance to invitations to join any of the various groups formed by the moderate francophone African states—but these were not enough to satisfy his critics. Olympio's concept of independence was nonalignment with any foreign bloc but, at the same time, acceptance of aid and trade with all countries that would offer both without imposing political obligations. Because of his success as local manager for the Unilever company, he administered Togo as if it were a business enterprise. His competence, conservatism, and thrift won him the respect of the domiciled foreign community, but this policy alienated many of his own nationals.

Olympio was too closely bound to his own generation and by his ethnic and bourgeois social background to weld the Togolese into a united people. Within eighteen months of his party's electoral triumph in April 1958, he was faced with organized opposition from both the conservative northerners and the youthful radicals of the Juvento, whose strength he consistently underestimated. The north continued to be underdeveloped and its people neglected. Dissatisfaction existed in the south as well, when Olympio imposed a new tax on cocoa planters, frequently clashed with the Catholic archbishop of Lomé, and antagonized the educated youth of that region by failing to give them the government posts they wanted.[2] Furthermore, as a pragmatist he was so averse to committing his government to any ideology that it was almost a year after Togo became independent that the country acquired a constitution. Even then, it still had no development plan, and at the time Togo was the only country in francophone West Africa that had no formal alliances.

Largely responsible for Togo's isolation was its leaders' ingrained habit of looking for support to the United Nations, which many Togolese had come to regard as a national fetish or as a superpower. Olympio himself so profoundly believed that Togo's ills could be cured simply by

[2] R. Cornevin, "Les Militaires au Dahomey et au Togo," *Revue Française d'Etudes Politiques Africaines,* Dec. 1968.

throwing off the colonial yoke that not even Nkrumah's increasingly predatory attitude could convince him that for protection he should respond favorably to one of the many appeals he received to join the Mali Federation, or the Entente, or another bloc. Soon after Togo had declared its independence, Nkrumah suggested that it merge with Ghana, but he changed his tactics after Olympio firmly rejected this proposal. Nkrumah then began to harass the Ewe leaders of former British Togoland who still wanted reunification with their Togolese brethren, charged Olympio with conspiring to detach them from Ghana and also of harboring his enemies, and late in 1960 imposed restrictions on the frontier trade between the two countries.

In May 1961, Olympio retaliated by charging Nkrumah with plotting his downfall, and he arrested or forced into exile those Juvento leaders who still clamored for union with Ghana. Olympio was now empowered to take such strong steps against his internal enemies under the presidential-type constitution and single-party system which the Togolese legislature had reluctantly accepted on March 1, 1961, and this marked the beginning of the end of all democratic freedoms in Togo for the duration of his rule. That same year all parties in Togo except the CUT were banned, and the discovery of still another plot in December precipitated a new wave of persecutions. Santos was jailed, Meatchi escaped a similar fate by fleeing the country, and Grunitsky also prudently left Togo and eventually settled in Cotonou, where he started a transport enterprise. Although his principal enemies and rivals had been disposed of in one way or another, Olympio was the target of several conspiracies and one attempted assassination in 1962, but this neither changed his policy nor apparently shook his self-confidence. Except in the case of Nkrumah, who had become his seemingly implacable enemy, Olympio continued to enjoy wide-spread consideration abroad, where it was not realized how much of a police state he had created at home.

Despite the harshness of Olympio's authoritarian rule in Togo and his steadily worsening relations with Ghana, he was assassinated neither by his internal nor his external political foes but inadvertently, by a handful of disgruntled soldiers. As a trust territory, Togo had never had compulsory military service, and the hundreds of Togolese who served in the French army were volunteers almost exclusively from the impoverished villages of the north. After the Algerian war ended in 1962, they were demobilized and sent back to Togo, where they tried to enlist in the national army that had been formed when the country became independent. At this time Togo's armed forces comprised 700 members of the Garde Togolaise, 150 gendarmes, and 200 infantrymen, and the thrifty Olympio saw no need to enlarge it.[3] Not only did he turn a deaf ear to the demobilized veterans' pleas for employment, but he humiliated them by calling them useless mercenaries and *petits nordistes*.[4]

On January 13, 1963, a detachment of the most persistent veterans, commanded by Major Emmanuel Bodjollé, called on Olympio in his home and tried to force his hand. Under circumstances that have never been wholly clear, one of the soldiers, Sergeant Etienne Eyadema (who was named head of the army in 1965 and became president of the republic two years later) shot Olympio to death. No evidence was ever produced to substantiate the inevitable rumors that Nkrumah or some of Olympio's Togolese enemies were implicated in his murder. Indeed, it soon became evident that

[3] *Marchés Tropicaux,* Jan. 19, 1963.

[4] E. Milcent, "Tribalisme et Vie Politique dans les Etats du Bénin: Togo à l'Ombre d'Olympio," *Le Mois en Afrique,* June 1967.

some veterans of the French army from one of Africa's smallest countries had unwittingly triggered a series of military coups d'état with no motive other than that a few of them badly needed jobs. How politically naive and how unprepared they were to deal with the situation they had created was shown by their immediate release from jail of the ailing Santos, and their appeal to Grunitsky and Meatchi to return home and take over the government.

To appease the veterans and create a government of national union were difficult tasks which Grunitsky reluctantly assumed. After abrogating the constitution, dissolving the assembly, and promising to hold elections within a month, he promptly tripled the size of Togo's armed forces. He then managed to put together a provisional government, in which were represented the CUT, the Juvento, the UDPT, and the army. Grunitsky's next objective—to improve relations with Ghana—was facilitated by Nkrumah's immediate recognition of Grunitsky's government and his lifting of the embargo on frontier trade, despite Grunitsky's refusal to return to Accra the Ghanaian dissidents who had sought refuge in Togo. The new Togolese premier, however, was initially less successful with most of the moderate African heads of state, who had been shocked by his giving a cabinet post to Bodjollé, one of Olympio's alleged assassins. Nevertheless, they granted him official recognition after the Togolese in overwhelming numbers had, on May 5, 1963, voted their approval of his government and the constitution he had drafted.

By midsummer of 1963 Togo had also been admitted to the UAM and the OAU and had signed agreements of cooperation and defense with France. Grunitsky's regime effectively cultivated cordial and fruitful foreign relations particularly with those countries most able and willing to

promote Togo's economic development. The only flaw in
Togo's now generally satisfactory international position was
the renewal of its conflict with Ghana, following a series of
violent border incidents, and more than any other single
factor it was Grunitsky's fear of Nkrumah's aggressiveness
that induced him in 1965 to draw closer to the Entente. On
the whole, relations with Dahomey had been consistently
good, despite chronic disagreements over the Mono River
valley and a deepwater port.[5] The same could not be said,
however, with regard to Ivory Coast and Niger, from which
thousands of Togolese had had to be repatriated respectively
in 1958 and 1963. Nevertheless, their return had not created
such a formidable problem as had been the case in Dahomey,
and Houphouët's dual-nationality proposal seemed to clear
the way for their reemployment in Ivory Coast. After long
hesitation and some months of "trial marriage" in 1965,
Grunitsky decided to take the plunge, despite Meatchi's
opposition,[6] and Togo became a *de jure* member of the
Entente in June 1966.

On the domestic front, Grunitsky was less successful, notably in his role as national conciliator. Even before the elections of May 1963, disagreements had developed inside his
provisional government over the drafting of a presidential-
type constitution and also over the allocation of cabinet portfolios. Relations became tense between soldiers and civilians,
between the CUT (renamed the Parti de l'Unité Togolaise,
or PUT) and the Juvento on the one hand and Grunitsky
and the northerners on the other, and finally between the
leaders of the UDPT party itself. Although Grunitsky had
given the northerners their firs` substantial representation

[5] See Ch. 9.

[6] G. Comte, "Le Togo et le Conseil de l'Entente," *Europe-France-Outremer,* no. 432, Jan. 1966.

in any Togolese government, a large segment of the UDPT, led by vice-president Meatchi, was reluctant to have as president of the republic a mulatto from Atakpamé. As for the southerners, they were more united than the northerners by their opposition to a government which had been brought to power by Cabrais soldiers and was dominated by the northern adversaries of the PUT and the Juvento. In the absence of Maître Santos, forced by illness to leave Togo, the Juvento proved to be a less formidable opponent of Grunitsky than were the more intransigent leaders of the PUT. Outstanding among the latter were Noë Kutuklui, despite his position as a minister in Grunitsky's government; Olympio's son, Benito, who had fled to Accra; and Théophile Mally, former Minister of Interior who had sought refuge first in Nigeria and then in Ghana. Together these men plotted to overthrow the Grunitsky government, and after their efforts failed, they deliberately fomented trouble between Ghana and Togo by reopening the question of Ewe reunification.

By temperament Grunitsky was not cut out to be a dictator, and he showed weakness in dealing with his opponents by alternating repressive measures with overindulgence. His government of national union might not have broken down, however, had he had his own popular power base or, lacking that, had he and Meatchi been able to work harmoniously in tandem and retain the army's support. As was also the case in Dahomey, Togo's experiment with a dual executive proved disastrous because personal and regional rivalries between its president and vice-president prevented their maintaining a united front. Finally, in December 1966, Grunitsky alienated the north by demoting Meatchi from the vice-presidential post. Since this step followed shortly after an abortive putsch at Lomé, organized by some PUT extremists and involving elements of the army, it became apparent that the days of the government were numbered.

Despite Togo's chronic difficulties with Ghana and its membership in the Entente, foreign relations apparently played no part in motivating the successful coup d'état led by Eyadema on the fourth anniversary of Olympio's assassination. Given so many elements of internal dissension, what was surprising was not that Grunitsky's government was overthrown, but that it had survived for four years. Like Dahomey's defeated politicians, but with more dignity, Grunitsky almost thankfully surrendered the reins of power to a military government dominated by northerners. And like his military counterparts in Upper Volta and Dahomey, Eyadema lost no time in reassuring General de Gaulle of his loyalty to France, and Houphouët of his country's continued membership in the Entente and the OCAM.

CHAPTER 5

The Military Regimes

The military coups d'état that occurred in three of the Entente states give rise to several questions. What were the similarities and differences in the conditions that inspired them in Upper Volta, Togo, and Dahomey? In what ways were they distinguished from the situations in Ivory Coast and Niger, where the governments have been stable and remained in civilian hands? None of the coups was instigated by mass revolts or, aside from Olympio's murder, accompanied by bloodshed. All were palace revolutions by competitive segments of the elite, and outside intervention, if any, was negligible. Discontent with the economic situation and the country's leadership were the main causes of each of the coups. Although these factors were also present in Ivory Coast and Niger, the leaders and the single parties of those two states were stronger, and the malaise felt by their elites was apparently less intense, or they lacked the means of expressing it so effectively.

Niger's economy was certainly as poor as that of the Entente countries which experienced coups d'état, and its leaders lacked the charisma and authority of the Ivorian president. Nevertheless, the traditional chiefs were Diori's allies, his party was well organized, his only formidable opponent was in exile, and his government could not be accused of conspicuously wasteful expenditures. Moreover, his numerically weak opposition was too divided regionally and tribally to offer any united resistance to his regime. Niger— like Ivory Coast but unlike Togo and Dahomey—did not then have to cope with a plethoric and aggressive indigenous elite, whose numbers were swollen by the forced return of thousands of skilled and jobless expatriates.

A study of the conditions prevailing in Dahomey and Ivory Coast during the first years of independence may provide a clue to the incidence of military coups d'état in the Entente states, for those two countries best illustrate the political and economic extremes to be found in that organization. Ivory Coast, with few exceptions, has been a model of governmental stability and prosperity, whereas Dahomey has become the most conspicuous example of political instability and economic deterioration in West Africa.

During the early postwar years in French West Africa, Dahomey gave promise of rivaling Senegal's rapid political evolution. Its main asset was a relatively large and literate elite, exceptionally intelligent, adaptable, and proud of its special cultural heritage. Through the early development of a lively indigenous press and a single political party, the Union Progressiste Dahoméenne (UPD), formed in 1947, the urban population had achieved unusual political awareness and maturity. Even before World War II, the modern elite had undermined the temporal power of the chieftaincy, although the influence of religious leaders remained strong among both Christians and animists. By 1951, however, the UPD had broken asunder because its sole program—opposition to the colonial administration—did not prove cohesive enough to obviate disruptive personal ambitions. Soon these rivalries among its leaders crystallized into a regional pattern.

At the same time, Dahomey's economy, which in the early twentieth century had provided the federal budget with its largest territorial revenues, had declined to such a level that the masses' living standards had sunk below those in the prewar period. So preoccupied were Dahomey's politicians with seeking power that they neglected the country's economy, which continued to rest almost exclusively on shrinking sales of oil-palm products in a fluctuating world market. Mainly for these reasons none of them succeeded in politically uniting the country behind him. The single party that President Maga formed soon after independence in 1960 foundered because it was built on an unstable coalition of highly personalized "feudalities" and had no direct widespread popular support. Even Maga himself was the vassal of northern leaders such as the Bariba prince, Chabi Mama, and the Djougou merchant, Paul Darboux, who controlled regional blocks of votes, whereas his own following was confined to Natitingou and, to some extent, Parakou.

The French-trained Dahomean lawyer, Maurice Glélé, attributes his country's inability to attain nationhood and construct a viable economy primarily to his compatriots' acceptance of the colonial legacy and, secondarily, to their failure to produce a charismatic and forceful leader who could inspire the support of the masses and give it organizational form in a nationwide party.[1] Glélé believes that the restrictions imposed by Dahomey's inherited geographical boundaries are not fundamentally responsible for its present plight, because the Dahomeans have shown no desire for territorial aggrandizement. They are quite willing to work in other lands, provided they can earn good pay and retain their cultural identity and close ties with their home country. Rather, he holds as chiefly responsible for his country's main handicaps, the elite's adoption of alien institutions that are unsuited to Dahomean realities and its inability to erase the inequalities of all kinds bequeathed by the colonial regime.

To Glélé, the most significant of Dahomey's inherited in-

[1] See his *Naissance d'un Etat Noir* (Paris, 1969), p. 334.

equalities—and none of its governments has seriously tried to remedy them—are the underdevelopment and isolation of the north, which have perpetuated regional antagonisms and led to political instability. Another handicap is the elite's commitment to politics as the quickest and easiest means of upward mobility, with the result that all issues and problems are politicized. In turn this has led to a neglect of the economy, whose development is a prerequisite to gaining the material benefits of the Western civilization to which the Dahomeans aspire. The Dahomean peasant, Glélé claims, cherishes freedom more than equality, hence he is reluctant to work for others or even beyond the satisfaction of his immediate needs provided he can live as he pleases. As for the elite, it is the bureaucratic, military, and commercial bourgeoisie who are the heirs of their former French rulers, and Dahomey's chronic political instability derives from their refusal to share power with each other, let alone with the mass of the population.

Ivory Coast resembles Dahomey in some important respects. Among these are the unequal development of north and south in both countries, the heterogeneity of their ethnic composition, the subordinate role played by their traditional chiefs, and the elite's orientation to government employment. Their similarity is also apparent in their lack of known mineral resources and concentration on agricultural output, their dependence on foreign trade in uncertain world markets, and their proximity to more developed and dynamic Anglophone African countries. They are alike, too, in their peoples' sense of frustration regarding the control exercised over the national economy by foreign capitalists and merchants, in the wholesale adoption of alien institutions and a Western outlook, and in the masses' political passivity as well as their refusal to increase production by hard manual work. In addition, Ivory Coast, unlike Dahomey, has the problem of depending on an alien labor force, whose presence is increasingly resented by the native population. In Ivory Coast, however, these handicaps have been largely offset by assets that Dahomey does not possess. Of these, only one is physical—a larger geographical area and population. Virtually all the other factors accounting for Ivory Coast's preeminent position, not only in the Entente but in all West Africa, can be attributed to the qualities and personality of its president. Unlike Dahomey, Ivory Coast early produced a national leader who asserted his control throughout the country by organizing a strong party, directing his policy to promoting rapid economic development, maintaining public order and his authority but without brutality, and above all inspiring confidence and respect not only among the Ivorians but also foreign powers and investors by the stability of his government, his personal prestige, his experience and diplomatic skill, and his practice of economic liberalism.

Inevitably Houphouët's policies have evoked hostility at home and abroad. To African revolutionaries and extreme nationalists, his reliance on Western capitalists and advisers and his promotion of free enterprise are a betrayal of Africa's dignity and culture, no matter how successful are the results he has obtained. Although Ivory Coast's economy has not yet reached the "take-off" point, it is the most prosperous nation in West Africa, its regional and social inequalities are diminishing though by no means yet wholly eliminated, and a sizeable segment of the educated elite has already been brought into the government and is just beginning to exercise some control over the economy.

Houphouët's long career has naturally not been without its crises, some of them engendered abroad, notably in

Ghana and Guinea, but more of local origin. Thus far, however, he has kept the situation under control by changing his policy just in time to avert a catastrophe. So strong, in fact, has been his grip on Ivory Coast that his external enemies have not dared to make a frontal attack on him but have operated through indirect encouragement of his principal domestic opposition, the Ivorian students and wage earners.

During Ivory Coast's first two years of independence, Houphouët was able to cope easily with labor and student discontent, but 1963–1964 brought far more serious challenges not only from them but from within his own party, government, and army. This was due in small measure to a rejection of his basic policies by some youthful idealists, but much more to his failure to reorganize and rejuvenate the PDCI, which remained composed essentially of ethnic associations and which atrophied in the hands of long-entrenched party leaders. Some of the outstanding members of his government also resented the autocracy of his rule and, in some cases, the predominance of his fellow-Baoulé tribesmen in the administration. Resentment of Baoulé assendancy also accounted for the short-lived secessionist movements among the Agni and Bété.

The first serious plot against Houphouët's regime coincided with Olympio's assassination in January 1963 and similarly involved some members of the armed forces, as well as the ministers of education, health, and agriculture. Despite the ensuing drastic purge of the PDCI, the reorganization of government departments, and a reduction in and the dispersal of the army and creation of a militia to insure domestic order, a second plot was discovered eight months later. Once again, some of the most dynamic, educated, and highly placed young Ivorians, including five ministers, were implicated, and some were sentenced to death. Finally, in April 1964, Ernest Boka, president of the Supreme Court and a close friend of Houphouët, committed suicide in prison following his arrest for masterminding still another plot against the government.

The personal sorrow this caused Houphouët, and the disillusionment he felt at the defection of some of the elite he had raised to prominence, left him with confidence in the loyalty of only two of his oldest collaborators, August Denise and Philippe Yacé, although Houphouët refused to name either of these men his heir apparent. Houphouët's reaction may have been due to the fact that he subsequently learned that the 1963 plots were traceable, at least in part, to Bété tribal unrest and that the head of the Ivorian *sûreté* had exaggerated their importance in order to eliminate such ministers as J. B. Mockey, Jean Bani, and Charles Donwahl. This realization probably accounted for Houphouët's refusal to carry out the harsh sentences imposed on the plotters, whom he amnestied in 1967, and his perseverance in promoting younger men (such as Konan Bedié, Assouan Usher, and Mohamed Diawara) to important cabinet posts. Furthermore, he undertook important social reforms, such as the promulgation of a modern family code which attacked polygamy and the matriarchal system.

The crises of the mid-1960's did not alter Houphouët's fundamental political and economic policies, but they lessened his preoccupation with international affairs and made him more conscious of his party's weaknesses and more attentive to local protests. The most recent manifestation of this heightened responsiveness has been his willingness to support the Ivorians' current insistence on a greater share in and control of the economy at the expense of foreigners. The method he has used is a modern version of the old African custom of palavers. During the series of long "dialogues" held late in 1969 Houphouët gave critics in his party, student leaders, and union officials the opportunity to air their grievances, and he has subsequently made some minor concessions. That this device is only a safety valve and has failed to satisfy the opposition is indicated by the revival of the Sanwi secessionist movement in December 1969, and the abortive plot to set up an Eburnean republic at Gagnoa by disgruntled Bété tribesmen in November 1970. In both cases, the reawakening of ancient ethnic rivalries threatens to add a relatively new element to the chronic opposition of the modern elites. Consequently, Houphouët may now be more dependent than before on the loyalty of his armed forces and on the presence of a French garrison to maintain order and his authority. As yet, however, there is no indication of a military coup d'état that might topple his government in the near future.

Upper Volta

Upper Volta's economy resembles that of Niger in its dependence on a distant and foreign seaport for its non-African trade, and it is even poorer in terms of natural resources except manpower. Although its area is only a fourth that of Niger, it has well over a million more inhabitants, many of whom are forced to emigrate to earn their livelihood. Regional and tribal divisions are intense, and the splintering of the Voltaic elite between the animist-Christian Mossi majority and the largely Islamized western tribes is reflected in the jealousy that exists between the administrative capital of Ouagadougou and the commercial capital of Bobo-Dioulasso. For five years, the Catholic Mossi leader, Maurice Yameogo, managed to govern Upper Volta by adroitly maintaining a balance between the several opposing forces. He might have remained longer in power had he not alienated the civil servants, the traditional Mossi chieftaincy, and the Catholic hierarchy—groups which should logically have remained his principal supporters. When, however, he demanded that the salaried class bear the cost of his and his family's use of public funds for their personal gain, his opponents united against him.[2] The most actively hostile elements, the trade unions and student organizations, joined to overthrow Yameogo but were unable to constitute a government or even to maintain their united front vis-à-vis the military leadership which they had called upon and which soon ruled the country.

The military government which took over power in January 1966 was headed by Colonel Sangoulé Lamizana, a professional officer whose career in the French army had been mostly spent abroad. Lamizana at once suspended the constitution, dissolved the assembly and parties, and reassured the diplomatic corps and the public that order would be maintained, property safeguarded, and Upper Volta's treaty obligations honored. He then proceeded to install a government comprising seven officers and five civilian technicians, and to announce that the army would stay in power until the economy had been placed on a sound basis. Brushing aside the objections of the trade unions, which, along with the militant students, claimed credit for ousting Yameogo and demanded that he be immediately brought to trial for embezzlement, Lamizana cut the pay of the bureaucracy more drastically than Yameogo had tried to do. Furthermore, by reorganizing the local administration and associating the peasantry more closely with the regional advisory bodies, he eliminated many posts and, at the same time, some of the

[2] See V. DuBois, *The Struggle for Stability in Upper Volta,* Part III, American University Field Staff Reports, March–Aug. 1969.

perquisites that the civil servants had previously enjoyed. Then he refused to take any representatives of the unions into his government, saying firmly, "We shall consult the labor leaders later, but now we prefer to restore a healthier political situation ourselves." [3] Worse still, Lamizana announced at the end of 1966 a reduction in the civil servants' family allowances, instituted a "patriotic contribution" amounting to two weeks' salary for all wage earners, and imposed new taxes on many consumer goods.

Nevertheless, Lamizana made some concessions to the unions then, and more later. The labor leaders imprisoned by Yameogo were promptly released, and a 1962 law which forbade Voltaic unions to affiliate with international labor federations was annulled. Two years later, when the economic situation had markedly improved, steps were taken to ease the wage earners' plight. The bureaucracy, whose pay and promotions had been frozen for three years, was allowed to expand slightly, and the expenditures for personnel in the 1970 budget grew to 56.1 percent of the total, compared with 52.9 per cent in the preceding year. In February 1970, the minimum wage, which had not been raised since 1960, was increased by 7 per cent for the first zone (the geographical area where living costs were the highest) and by 17 per cent for the second zone, and concurrently taxes on essential consumer goods were reduced. Despite these improvements in their status, the wage earners of Upper Volta in general, and its civil servants in particular, continue to be among West Africa's lowest paid. Nonetheless, their unions are among the least contentious in that area. Strikes have been few and far between, no demands have been publicly made for a single wage zone, and until late 1969 the union

[3] *Le Monde,* July 1, 1966.

leaders expressed no dissatisfaction with the rate of the minimum wage.[4]

Organized labor in Upper Volta is docile mainly because its leaders are aware of its weak position. This weakness stems from the fact that thousands of the country's young men emigrate each year, some permanently, and that there are too many unions—more than 100 in Yameogo's time, and even now four federations and eleven autonomous unions. Also responsible are the small number of union members and their dispersion. Of a total population of well over 5 million Voltaics, whose active element numbers some 2.7 millions, there are only approximately 30,000 wage earners. Of these the majority either do not belong to unions or, if they belong, do not pay their dues.[5] The population is growing faster than the growth in jobs. and the number of unemployed registered at the labor bureaus of Ouagadougou and Bobo-Dioulasso alone comes to some 6,000 individuals. Such a figure is a gross underestimate of the reality, particularly as regards both the jobless educated youth and the underemployed farming class, who work, on the average, only seven months of the year. Paradoxically, the current rise in the level of employment, resulting from the creation of some new industries, has been accompanied by an increase in unsatisfied demands for jobs. For the underemployed and unskilled rural population the only answer is the time-honored one of emigration, but for the educated Voltaic youth the prospects for employment either at home or abroad are dim.

Another cause of organized labor's weakness in Upper Volta is the unions' failure to maintain their alliance with the radical students, whose number in any case is very small. This alliance did not long survive Yameogo's overthrow, be-

[4] *Jeune Afrique,* Oct. 7, 1969.   [5] *Afrique Nouvelle,* April 15, 1970.

cause the needs and aspirations of the two groups are too disparate. The students were given short shrift by Yameogo, and Lamizana has perpetuated his no-nonsense policy. The military government supported Senghor's disciplinary action against the Voltaic students at Dakar University who participated in the demonstrations protesting Nkrumah's overthrow in 1966, and in the 1968 riots, imitative of those at the Sorbonne. There are no longer any Voltaics studying at Dakar, and the country's 583 university students are scholarship-holders attending other African or French institutions.[6] Because Upper Volta had no schools above the secondary level until 1969, when an embryonic Centre des Etudes Supérieures was opened at Ouagadougou, Lamizana has had to deal directly only with *lycéens,* who have shown little propensity for militant action.

Compared with Yameogo's policy, that pursued by Lamizana toward both student and labor leaders has been remarkably tolerant of criticism. He has allowed both groups freedom of action up to a limit that is recognized and respected by both sides. While it cannot be said that their relations are cordial, they have not been marked by overt hostility. Protests by wage earners and students—thus far—have taken a passive form, such as absenteeism, for both they and the government have preferred to avoid confrontations in which the army would certainly win but which would also certainly involve bloodshed.

Although Upper Volta's military regime has won acceptance if not cooperation, from the bureaucracy and students, normally the most turbulent elements of the African elite, Lamizana's dealings with the Voltaic political parties have proved less successful. To be sure, Yameogo had banned all but his own RDA-UDV party, but the others—more cliques

[6] *Ibid.,* April 8, 1970.

around individual leaders than organized political groups—
continued a kind of shadow existence. After Yameogo's disappearance, leadership disputes in his RDA-UDV led to the
formation of two splinter parties, the Groupement d'Action
Populaire (GAP) and the Union de la Nouvelle République
(UNR); Nazi Boni returned from exile to revive his PRA in
the western region; and Joseph Ki Zerbo emerged from the
underground to transform his Mouvement de Libération
Nationale (MLN) from an organization of young radical
intellectuals into a mass party.

As soon as the military government was installed, Lamizana appealed to the old-time politicians to get together and
draft a program of national union oriented to the development of Upper Volta's economy. At the same time he warned
that he would not hesitate to use force if they troubled the
public order. Neither his appeal nor his warnings were
heeded by the parties' rank and file, and in September 1966
severe clashes occurred between members of the UDV and
MLN at Koudougou, Yameogo's stronghold. Lamizana, however, persisted in his efforts to win their leaders' cooperation,
and in the fall of 1966 he held two round-table conferences
at which vain attempts were made to draft a mutually acceptable constitution. Not only did the politicians refuse to
settle their personal quarrels, but they began to infiltrate the
army and even Lamizana's cabinet, where their propaganda
created serious divisions. Such subversive tactics convinced
Lamizana that the army must remain in power for another
four years, and in December 1966 he announced the suspension of all political activities throughout the country and the
establishment of a special court to try individuals accused of
corruption and other abuses of power. Early in 1967, Lamizana dispatched seven missions to explain his new policy to
the Voltaics and to foreign countries, whose sympathy and

aid he hoped to enlist. At the same time, he courted the customary Mossi chiefs by restoring some of the income and perquisites of which Yameogo had deprived them.

For some months thereafter Upper Volta's political front seemed quiet, despite two half-hearted attempts by Yameogo to commit suicide. However, his supporters, particularly his relatives and entourage, whose fortunes had spectacularly declined under Lamizana's rule, were plotting to overthrow the military government in hostile demonstrations scheduled for Independence Day, August 5, 1967. The conspiracy was discovered in time and thirty-three arrests were made, including those of Yameogo's wife and son, but they had so obviously failed to win popular support that Lamizana could afford to be magnanimous. The plotters were later sentenced to relatively short prison terms and Yameogo, himself, when he was finally brought to trial in May 1969, was leniently treated and was finally liberated in August 1970.[7]

By this time Lamizana felt sufficiently secure to travel extensively abroad in search of new and larger sources of foreign aid, and to promise a return to civilian rule in 1970. To explain this decision to his people and assure that there would be no return to the precoup dissensions and disorders, military emissaries began touring the country urging support for candidates who would represent national and not tribal or regional interests. By November 1969, when political campaigning was again permitted, Upper Volta's parties had undergone profound changes. The GAP had not acquired a substantial following among the conservatives, in part because its leader had failed to convince the customary chiefs

[7] For embezzling 722 million CFA francs, Yameogo was sentenced to a fine and five years of hard labor. A few months later this was reduced to three years, and he was freed in August 1970 but still deprived of his civic rights.

that their interests would be promoted by joining his party. Earlier in the year, the deaths of both the UDV and PRA leaders had weakened the oldest Voltaic political organizations to the benefit of the left-wing parties, represented by the MLN and the territorial branch of the Senegal-based Parti Africain de l'Indépendance formed by a handful of pro-Peking extremists. In brief, Upper Volta's parties were even more beset by discord than before, and their leaders were no nearer the political union which Lamizana had always insisted upon as the prerequisite for a return to civilian rule.

In March 1970, Lamizana submitted the constitution which he had drafted to an advisory committee composed of representatives from a wide range of political, labor, traditional, and religious associations. Unanimously its members rejected the proposal because it provided for an indefinite perpetuation of military rule and belied Lamizana's repeated pledge to return power to a democratically elected civilian government. This expression of dissent on the part of the Voltaic elite was so clearcut that Lamizana agreed to modify his original draft, but the terms of the compromise were not known outside Upper Volta until Lamizana announced them in a broadcast only two weeks before the constitution was submitted to a popular referendum on June 14.

On that day, the Voltaic electorate was asked to vote affirmatively or negatively on the issue of restoring parliamentary democracy in the country after a four-year period of further tutelage by the army. During that interval the head of state would be the senior ranking military officer and one-third of his fifteen ministers would be appointed members of the armed forces, but the government would share part of its power with a popularly elected legislature. Eventually the

army was to turn the government over to a civilian administration headed by a premier elected by, and responsible to,
the legislative assembly. Unenthusiastically, Upper Volta's
four parties decided to opt for an affirmative vote as the most
practical means under the circumstances of effecting a return
to civilian rule, and they began feverish preparations for the
legislative elections to be held in December 1970. On June
14, 1970, although nearly one-fourth of the registered electorate numbering 2,390,735 abstained from voting, 98.4 per
cent of those who went to the polls voted in favor of the new
constitution.

In holding the referendum, Lamizana showed either a
sensitiveness to public opinion remarkable in a professional
army officer, or his fear lest some of his younger officers, who
had acquired a taste for power, try to stage a coup d'état. In
any case, he was obviously reluctant to hand over power immediately to Upper Volta's weak and warring parties which
might jeopardize the economic progress that the country had
made during its years of military rule. The GNP had shown
a real growth averaging 1.5 per cent a year, and 60 per cent
of the program outlined in Upper Volta's first development
plan (1967–1970), which gave priority to rural production
both for food and export, had been carried out, thanks to investments by France (36 per cent), the European Common
Market (23 per cent), the United Nations (4 per cent), and
the local treasury (11 per cent).[8] By early 1970, Upper Volta
had paid all its debts, amounting to 1,300 million CFA francs,
inherited from the Yameogo regime, the deficit in its trade
balance had been reduced, and the budget even showed a
small but growing surplus. To be sure, private investors had
evinced little interest in Upper Volta's meager resources, but

[8] *Afrique Nouvelle,* March 25, 1970; *Marchés Tropicaux,* June 13,
1970.

the recently surveyed manganese deposits at Tambao gave promise of attracting them.[9] Lamizana believed he could encourage foreign capitalists only by perpetuating his policy of maintaining order and governmental stability. Even under such circumstances, however, Upper Volta's viability was far from assured, and in the meantime he insisted that the country continue to live within its very modest means.

If Upper Volta's achievements have not been so spectacular as those of Ivory Coast, they nevertheless merit being termed almost miraculous in view of the catastrophic status of the country in 1966. They have been realized not by any revolutionary changes but simply by applying the orthodox methods of reducing public expenditures and increasing taxation to restore the state's credit. The "Voltaic miracle" lies not so much in its government's concrete achievements as in its ability to persuade the population to accept stoically its austerity program. This has been made possible by the Mossi tribal traditions of hard work, acceptance of authority, and self-discipline and by the military government's willingness to share the sacrifices it imposes on the rest of the population. Lamizana's draconian measures have spared neither himself nor his ministers in terms of salary cuts and long working hours, and his own way of life exemplifies the virtues of thrift, honesty, and simplicity which he preaches. In contrast to his predecessor, Lamizana still lives in the same small villa he formerly occupied, where his wife does her own housework, and he avoids public ceremonies, at which, moreover, soft drinks are now served instead of champagne. He has successfully claimed that his position is one "above politics."

Like Lamizana, the army has remained close to the people and, even more remarkable, it has remained at least out-

[9] See Ch. 9.

wardly united under a Conseil Supérieur des Forces Armées set up in December 1966. Its officers have repeatedly stressed the "legitimacy" and disinterestedness of their regime, and the patriotism of their motives has not been belied by any evidence that they have reaped appreciable monetary rewards. Militarily speaking, Upper Volta is unique among the Entente countries in regard to its unusually large number of veterans and the absence of any defense agreement with France. The latter factor has made the Voltaic army more self-reliant than the other states' military forces, and the former has posed an exceptional politico-economic problem. Far more than has been the case in Togo, Upper Volta has failed to absorb a sizeable proportion of its veterans into the armed forces, let alone even a fraction of the young men who become eligible for military conscription each year. Furthermore, to make way for a younger generation of officers, Lamizana has had to retire many of its older soldiers prematurely,[10] or to use them for the carrying out of economic projects. Both courses of action, however, risk creating more malcontents.

As regards the older generation of veterans, the problem is not acute, because they have usually retired to their native villages on adequate pensions paid by the French government. But the younger veterans prefer to live in the towns, where their smaller pensions do not suffice and where they have become a drug on the local labor market. This is particularly true of the Ouahigouya region, whose poverty and overpopulation induced many youths to enlist in the French army. It was in Ouahigouya that the only party in francophone Black Africa composed exclusively of veterans was organized in 1958 by a French officer for the purpose of opposing the political ambitions of the Moro Naba.[11] Although

[10] *West Africa,* Sept. 24, 1966.   [11] See Ch. 1.

Yameogo also aimed at destroying the authority of the traditional Mossi chieftaincy, he would not tolerate the existence
of a full-fledged and independent political party made up
of veterans. He succeeded in bringing them under his control
by creating a Ministry of Veterans, and by commissioning
the most loyal of them he built up a personal following in
the officer corps. Partly as a result of Yameogo's policy, the
majority of Voltaic officers are not drawn from any one tribe
or region, and they are more representative of the country as
a whole than has been the case in any other Entente state
under military rule.

Divisions do exist in the army of Upper Volta, but they
are those created by differences in age, education, and political affiliations. Although Lamizana himself belongs to the
older generation and rose from the lowly status of a private
to commissioned rank in the French army, he has kept close
contact with his subordinates, and although the veterans
form a significant pressure group which is courted by all the
civilian politicians, the great majority are loyal supporters
of his government. This unity enables Lamizana to impose
his authority not by the actual use of force, but by his opponents' realization that he can do so if need be. In his
broadcast of May 30, 1970, Lamizana stated his belief that
any army which is "kept apart from society and national
realities . . . is outmoded for countries in the process of
development." Thus he served notice on the civilians elected
to the Voltaic legislature on December 20, 1970, that should
they deviate from the policies he has laid down, a "people's
army" will be waiting in the wings, ready to intervene.

With Lamizana remaining as head of state and his officers
holding the key portfolios of interior, finance, information,
youth, and agriculture, the government headed by Premier
Gérard Kanga Ouedraogo and invested by the assembly on

February 13, 1971, has only marginal room for maneuver. Its civilian element is dominated by the UDV, which won thirty-seven of the fifty-seven assembly seats and took all but two of the ministerial posts. Of the half-dozen "legal" parties, only three put forward candidates in the eleven electoral circumscriptions. The PRA (twelve seats) was assigned two minor portfolios (social affairs and telecommunications), and the MLN (six seats) has no representative in the government.

The legislative elections, which were surprisingly calm, showed that the MLN's platform of moderate socialism and opposition to the "bourgeois" UDV and the "reactionary" chieftaincy had no nation-wide appeal. They also revealed that the MLN's small constituency of intellectuals were not united behind Ki Zerbo, whom some of them regarded as not radical enough and too subservient to the Catholic hierarchy. As for the PRA, it retained its following in the west, but the splits in its leadership, which had been papered over by Nazi Boni, reappeared after his death in 1969. (The death of his successor, Diongolo Traoré, in April 1971, has further weakened the PRA.) Above all, the elections proved how well entrenched was the oldest Voltaic party, the UDV, whose leaders were well known and which reportedly received lavish support in money and gifts from neighboring RDA branches for distribution among the electorate. Even more significant was the support given the UDV covertly by Maurice Yameogo (allegedly in return for its pledge to restore his civic rights) and openly by the chiefs, to whom it promised the status of civil servants. The family of Ouedraogo chiefs now so dominates the assembly and cabinet that it appears to have become a dynasty, though one whose members are far from united. Gérard, representing the Yatenga veterans and the northern Mossi, captured the top governmental post, while Joseph, spokesman for the Ouagadougou region, perforce accepted the secondary position of assembly president. Their rivalry and the chiefs' policy of intimidation during the electoral campaign were said to have accounted for the two-month delay in forming a government and for the high rate of abstentions from voting (over half of the registered electorate).

Obviously, the UDV is far from monolithic and, although its opposition suffers even more from a divided leadership, the old-timers who still control the Voltaic branch of the RDA are too mutually competitive to benefit fully by the party's electoral victory. Upper Volta's army officers are clearly disappointed by the civilian politicians' inability to create any national unity, although Lamizana has been touring the country and preaching support for the new government. However, because the military still retains the essentials of power, Lamizana is in a position to take over the whole apparatus of government whenever he deems it necessary.

Togo

The circumstances leading to Togo's two coups d'état bore little resemblance to those that preceded the military take-over at Ouagadougou. In the coup of 1963, only the few hundred Cabrais veterans who had been demobilized from the French army the year before were involved, and their grievance against Olympio was wholly personal and not related to their country's overall political or economic situation. After the veterans asked Grunitsky to head a civilian government, he rewarded their confidence by granting more than they asked for. Not only did he absorb a majority of the veterans into the national armed services, but he also gave them representation in his government. Furthermore, he rapidly promoted Eyadema to the rank of lieutenant-colonel, and in 1965 named him head of the army's general staff. (In Togo as in Dahomey, no civilian politician by showering favors on an army officer seems able to forestall a coup d'état when the latter decides to move in.) The soldiers retired peaceably to their barracks in the Cabrais capital of Lama-Kara, to all outward appearances content to leave the country under the guidance of a government in which northerners were for the first time given responsible posts.

Just what triggered the second military coup of January 12, 1967, is not even now wholly clear, but in the interval, the advent of military governments in Ghana, Dahomey, Upper Volta, Nigeria, and the Congo was doubtless influential. In local terms, it may have been a combination of dissatisfaction with the mounting budgetary deficit, growing tension between the northern vice-president and the southern president, suspicions of the PUT's subversive activities, and, above all, Grunitsky's inability to promote national unity and a greater expansion of the economy. Even as late as November 1966, during the abortive putsch attempted by some PUT dissidents, Eyadema still hesitated between several courses of action. When he finally decided to move against the Grunitsky government, he chose the fourth anniversary of Olympio's assassination to do so.

There seems little doubt that Eyadema acted to forestall a coup d'état by the PUT, but as has become customary in such circumstances he claimed that he did so to save his country from civil war. In an interview published four months later in *Afrique Nouvelle,* on May 24, 1967, he is reported to have said: "I did everything in my power to help Grunitsky in his task of national reconciliation. . . . We wanted a government of young men, but he preferred to surround himself with his friends, although they had proved to be failures in 1956. Nothing went well, many civil servants were in prison, others had fled, foreign ambassadors assured me that Togo was losing prestige abroad, and anti-government tracts were appearing every day. I was fed up, and everyone urged me to seize power . . . so that is why I took over."

If Eyadema truly expected foreign governments to applaud his action, he must have been disillusioned by the attitude of France and Ivory Coast, neither of whose presidents was pleased by still another military coup d'état and especially by his failure to carry out elections as promised. Initially Eyadema had set up a committee composed of military officers and civilians to run the government until a new constitution could be drafted and a civilian government elected in late March 1967. During the intervening two months, he allegedly received so many petitions urging him to remain in power from spokesmen "representing a majority of the population, including the traditional northern chiefs," that he yielded to their appeals. He first canceled the elections and then on April 4 appointed a new twelve-man government comprising eight civilians and four officers, of whom seven were from northern Togo. (The omission from his cabinet of Meatchi, who was reappointed to his old post as director of the agricultural service, indicated that the latter had not, as some believed, conspired with Eyadema to oust Grunitsky.) Despite an attempt soon after to assassinate Eyadema, he proceeded to amnesty political prisoners, and of the thirty principal PUT exiles all but Kutuklui returned home. Then on May 12, after having abolished the elected municipal councils, Eyadema dissolved Togo's four political parties, again promising that, once peace and national unity had been restored, elections for a civilian government would be held and he would retire from the political scene.

By September 1967, it was high time for Eyadema to go

abroad and mend his most important political fences. By
then, however, both General de Gaulle and Houphouët had
become more inured to accepting military coups d'état, and
they promised him financial and technical aid. At the same
time he received substantial assistance from West Germany,
as well as overtures from Ghana and Dahomey, whose leaders had become increasingly worried by the deteriorating
situation in Nigeria. The next month, Eyadema named a
widely representative committee to draft a new constitution
and promised to hold a referendum that would determine
whether the Togolese wanted the army to remain in power.
Eyadema described such a plebiscite as "unique in the an-
nals of Africa," but warned that if the population rejected
military control they would have to propose a constructive
alternative. Such an alternative, he said, must obviate any
"revival of the tribalism and regionalism which have always
characterized our politics." [12]

During 1968, calm reigned in Togo, and there was no
further talk of a constitution or referendum. Eyadema's real
intentions remained obscure, for at one time he would promise a return to civilian government and then, soon after,
reverse himself, allegedly always in response to multiple
pleas for the army to stay on. In the meantime Eyadema, like
Lamizana, gave his country a comparatively honest, stable,
and competent government, improving its economy by attracting foreign investments, compressing expenditures, and
refusing to permit any opposition to raise its disorderly head.
Also like Lamizana, he pictured himself—perhaps sincerely
or for Western consumption—as the professional soldier who
had reluctantly assumed political responsibility so as to bring
about national reconciliation. In one respect, however, he
differed from his predecessors and military colleagues, in that

[12] *Afrique Nouvelle,* Nov. 22, 1967.

he frankly described "the persistent antagonism between northerners and southerners as Togo's number-one problem," and attributed it mainly to the "lack of economic equilibrium between those two regions of the country." [13]

The committee of twenty senior civil servants whom Eyadema named to study this question and propose solutions met for the first time in April 1969, but like so many other of Eyadema's projects it was never heard of thereafter. Similarly, after announcing on January 13, 1969, that the political parties could resume their activities, he banned all political demonstrations four days later because they had "immediately revived agitation" in Togo's main towns. Once more he yielded to the "people's wishes," which doubtless meant that the army and the northerners had expressed to him their fears—which he may well have shared—that a return to civilian government would lead to a revival of the power of the PUT's southern oligarchy, and consequently to reprisals against those held responsible for Olympio's assassination. No further mention was made of a constitution, elections, or a referendum, but in November 1969, to fill the political void that had lasted almost three years, Eyadema convened a congress attended by several thousand persons to approve his proposal to create a Rassemblement du Peuple Togolais (RPT). According to its author, the RPT was to be a "crucible in which all the country's vital forces would be fused," [14] a nationwide movement that was, however, to differ from the old single-party system under Olympio in significant respects. Its twenty-five member politburo, albeit dominated by Eyadema's loyal collaborators, comprised civilians as well as military men, and southerners as well as northerners. More importantly, if not surprisingly, Eyadema was elected

[13] *Marchés Tropicaux,* Dec. 28, 1968.
[14] *Jeune Afrique,* Dec. 16, 1969.

president of the RPT, thereby insuring the army's continued participation in politics and the success of the government's policies by providing it with forceful backing.

These measures showed that Eyadema now felt strong enough to dispense with the usual formalities to "legitimatize" his government. Naturally the northern chiefs and veterans were his main supporters, but he had also effectively nibbled away at the Ewe opposition, and the economy had made sufficient progress to placate the traders, including the influential market women of Lomé. In 1970, Togo's budget was balanced for the third consecutive year, progress was being made toward execution of the 1966–1970 development plan (although it was not up to schedule), and the spurt registered in phosphate exports in 1968 gave promise of substantially diversifying Togo's economy and of reversing its chronically deficitary foreign trade. Labor leaders were gratified by the establishment in July 1969 of a retirement fund for all wage earners and four weeks of paid leave, and by a twenty per cent increase in the minimum wage six months later, and in any case their membership comprised less than 5 per cent of the active population and their political influence was negligible. While the budget was burdened by an expanding bureaucracy—which by 1969 numbered over 10,000 civil servants for a total population of 1.7 million and which absorbed over half the country's revenues—its increase coincided with a decline of employment in the private sector and the return of many thousands of refugees expelled from Ghana.

Under such circumstances, the growth in Togo's bureaucracy provided a safety valve for its civil servants and students, usually the most restive segments of the elite. "Griot," writing in *West Africa* (November 15, 1969) after a visit to Lomé, noted a rapprochement between the young left-wing intellectuals and Eyadema, whom they did not even accuse of extravagance for building a costly presidential palace and a "village" to house visiting heads of the Entente states. Togolese students might still go on strike and cavil at their country's continued dependence on capitalistic western Europe, but they gave Eyadema their wholehearted support when he insisted that Togo have its own institution of higher learning and not share with Dahomey a "University of Benin" to be located at Porto Novo.

The second alleged attempt by Kutuklui to stage a coup d'état, in August 1970, failed even more lamentably than did that of December 1966, and largely for the same reasons. Not only was it poorly organized, but its leaders ignored the support given to Eyadema by his own northern tribesmen, who are the mainstay of Togo's armed forces. The plotters' conspicuous failure seemed to prove that there was no substantial desire on the part of influential elements in the population for the overthrow of a government that had brought peace and relative prosperity to Togo, and this rather ludicrous incident actually strengthened Eyadema's position.

At first, the incident's most serious aspect seemed to be its indirect involvement of Dahomey, which had given asylum to Kutuklui, and some of whose nationals had allegedly supplied him with arms and money. Hastily, Kutuklui was placed under house arrest in Cotonou by the Dahomean presidential council, whose members came in a body to Lomé to offer their apologies and disavow any responsibility for his actions. As time went on, however, some observers of the Togolese scene have come to doubt the authenticity of this "plot." Mainly responsible for their skepticism were the government's failure to close Togo's frontiers, the well-rehearsed "confessions" of the arrested conspirators, Eyadema's refusal to ask for Kutuklui's extradition (followed by his request to release Kutuklui from house arrest), and the setting up of a permanent court to try state-security cases. Speculation was reportedly rife in Lomé to the effect that the so-called coup might have been staged by the Togolese army to intimidate its opponents, notably the dissident Ewes at home and abroad.

The trial of the "conspirators" at Lomé in November 1970 produced evidence of the existence of two concurrent plots, one hatched in Dahomey and the other in Togo. The only apparent link between them was that both were instigated by members of the PUT. Eyadema has consistently played down the importance of the August incidents, claiming that they were "the affair of only about 40 mercenaries." Subsequently, in January 1971, he succeeded in calming the agitation that resulted from rumors that three of the political prisoners had died in jail under mysterious circumstances by announcing a general amnesty and an overall salary increase of 10 percent.

That most of the Ewes are not pleased by the northerners' domination of the government cannot be doubted, but by no means all of them, including expatriates, have backed Kutuklui as Olympio's heir. They still predominate in the civil service and in Togo's retail trade. Their opposition to Eyadema is increasingly weak and divided, largely because he has wooed individual Ewe leaders and promised to protect their merchants against the influx of Lebanese traders from Ghana and to maintain Togo's open-door trade policy. As yet Eyadema has not had time to give his RPT a firm national base, but he has reduced regional disparities, given the country a remarkably stable government, and promoted economic production. Probably for those reasons his regime has not been troubled by the recent changes to civilian control in neighboring countries, and Togo remains the one Entente state that is still wholly under a military government.

Dahomey

Dahomey's successive coups d'état are *sui generis,* but in minor respects they resemble those in neighboring Togo and Upper Volta. Colonel Soglo, the chief figure in the first and third coups, was, like his friend Lamizana, a middle-aged professional soldier who had spent most of his career abroad. Demobilized as a lieutenant-colonel from the French army in 1960, he had returned to Dahomey as military adviser to President Maga, who soon named him chief of staff for the country's new national army. Like his much younger colleague, Eyadema, Soglo handed over power after the first coup d'état to a civilian government. Like them, too, he became progressively dissatisfied with its performance, and displaced it in December 1965 by military rule. Unlike Lamizana and Eyadema, however, Soglo failed to restore his country's economy, to control the elite, or to promote unity among its people. Perhaps because he belonged to the dominant southern Fon tribe, he was unable to prevent Dahomey's deeprooted tribal and regional divisions from infecting the army itself. At all events, a group of young northern officers staged a revolt against Soglo's government almost exactly two years after he had ousted Apithy and Ahomadegbe.

Dahomey's armed forces comprised about 2,500 troops and 1,200 gendarmes, whose small number in relation to a population totaling 2.5 million did not prevent the development of divergencies between its members. These divergencies derived mainly from differences in age, education, and ethnic and regional origins, and they divided the recently formed company of paratroopers from the established military corps, and younger from older officers. In particular, the junior officers, many of them graduates of French military academies, were impatient at being placed under the orders of their less well educated and conservative superiors, and resented being assigned economic tasks rather than purely military duties. But even the younger generation of officers was divided between the predominant Fon "Abomey Group" and a northern faction headed by Major Maurice Kouandete, the ablest, boldest, and most ambitious of them all.[15]

The only common characteristic of the military Young Turks was their hostilty to Soglo and his clique of older, corrupt officers, against whom violently worded tracts, signed by the Organisation Secrète des Forces Armées, began to circulate in southern towns during the summer of 1966. However, it was not until December 17, 1967, when the trade unions once again struck in protest against the government's austerity measures, that the two currents of discontent fused. Some sixty young commissioned and noncommissioned officers led by Kouandete overthrew the government, and Soglo followed Maga, Apithy, and Ahomadegbe into exile.

At the time he engineered this coup, Kouandete was executive officer to Colonel Alphonse Alley, chief of staff of the Dahomean army. Both men were in their middle thirties, northerners, and professional soldiers, but they were not on good personal terms. Alley did not participate in the coup of December 17, and it was not until five days later, after being selected to succeed Soglo, that he publicly announced his support for the rebels. Alley owed his elevation as head of state to his friendly relations with General de Gaulle and Houphouët, who had expressed their disapproval of still an-

[15] R. Lemarchand, "Dahomey: Coup within a Coup," *Africa Report,* June 1968.

other Dahomean coup d'état, especially one that had occurred just after Soglo's state visit to France.

The French forthwith cut off their subsidy to Dahomey, and the financial outlook for the military revolutionary committee set up after Soglo's dismissal was bleak indeed. At the time there were only 50 million CFA francs in the treasury—not enough even to pay the civil servants' monthly salaries, which amounted to seven times that amount, much less to permit rescinding the cut in wages and family allowances that had caused the unions to strike. At the end of 1967, Dahomey was saved from a disastrous upheaval only by the army's show of firmness and the labor leaders' failure to maintain a united front in pressing their demands. There was no doubt that labor had a genuine grievance, for wages had risen only 12 per cent since independence, whereas living costs had increased by 50 per cent. But unlike the Voltaic elite, Dahomey's wage earners in general, and particularly its civil servants, simply refused to make the sacrifices needed to offset the country's decline in production and its increasingly unfavorable trade balance, especially as their rulers' way of life was hardly a model of austerity.

For the first few months of 1968, Dahomey followed the same pattern as the other Entente states under military rule. The provisional military government sought to justify its seizure of power in the eyes of its own people and of the foreign nations most likely to provide it with the funds required for its functioning. Alley's cabinet differed from those initially set up by the military authorities in Togo and Upper Volta in that it comprised officers of generally junior rank, equally divided between northerners and southerners, and only one civilian minister—Chabi Kao, an able, apolitical, and experienced administrator who was assigned the finance portfolio. Another novelty introduced by the younger

Dahomean officers was a court martial appointed to try cases of corruption, involving mainly southern civil servants but also high-ranking military men who had been members of Soglo's entourage. Soon, however, the army became embarrassed at washing so much of its own dirty linen in public, and, in April 1968, this court was disbanded after some of its military judges were proven to be as venal as the men undergoing trial.

To refute the charge that Dahomey's government was now a military dictatorship and lacked public support, Alley volunteered to hold a plebiscite, to be followed by presidential and legislative elections as soon as a new constitution could be drafted, and he also promised that the army would return to its barracks by June 17, 1968. Adhering to his self-imposed timetable, Alley appointed a committee headed by the president of the supreme court, which produced on schedule a constitution of the presidential type that institutionalized a single-party system. On March 31, it was duly submitted to a referendum, in which 82 per cent of the registered electorate gave it overwhelming approval. Almost at once, however, a snag developed in regard to the election of a president of the republic, slated for May 5, because the three exiled civilian leaders insisted on running for that office. Alley, supported by the supreme court, agreed that they had the constitutional right to do so, but the younger officers adamantly opposed their candidacy and even their return to Dahomey, and they carried the day. This issue further divided the army, notably by widening the breach between Alley and Kouandete, but it briefly united Maga, Apithy, and to a lesser degree Ahomadegbe, in protesting against that decision. Only Maga and Apithy, however, urged their followers in Dahomey to boycott the election in reprisal.

Of the five candidates permitted to run for the office of president, the army's choice was Adjou Moumouni, a Dahomean doctor then working for the World Health Organization at Brazzaville, who was virtually unknown in his home country but who benefited by Ahomadegbe's undercover support. Although Dr. Moumouni received 84 per cent of the votes cast on May 5, only 27 per cent of the total registered electorate went to the polls, and the army was forced to declare the election null and void.[16] The success of the boycott, especially in northern Dahomey, where only 3 per cent of the electorate voted, showed that neither time, absence, nor the deficiencies of their past governments had diminished the popularity of Maga and Apithy in their respective regional strongholds. The election fiasco also shattered the army's prestige and demonstrated the Dahomeans' lack of confidence in its leaders, owing to their inability to develop the economy and even to maintain unity and discipline in their own ranks. The decisions of the armed forces were reached by curiously unmilitary methods, in which the votes cast by some ninety privates and commissioned and noncommissioned officers carried equal weight.[17]

A cabinet reshuffle on May 15 did little more than reflect fresh divisions in the army, notably between the followers of President Alley and those of Premier Kouandete, and the next day the labor unions called a general strike. The treasury's liquid assets having fallen to 20 million CFA francs, there was no possibility of satisfying the wage earners' demands. It was obvious that the army could not return to its barracks on June 17 as scheduled but not clear how its leaders would resolve the political impasse that their own incompetence had created. The officers now sought advice from

16 *Marchés Tropicaux,* May 11, 1968.
17 *Le Monde Diplomatique,* June 1968.

all and sundry party, labor, and religious leaders, and even from the three exiled politicians who by that time were hovering nearby, first in Niamey and then at Lomé. Obviously, no government in Dahomey could function without their blessing, but they were unable to agree among themselves as to which one of the trio would receive their united support. The only solution to this deadlock was to find a new leader outside the established civilian and military ranks, and, if possible, acceptable to both.

By the end of June 1968, the army's choice had narrowed down to Dr. Emile Zinsou, a Fon from Ouidah who had served successive Dahomean governments as foreign minister but had never been identified with any of the country's organized parties. Dr. Zinsou being a political neutral, his leadership would not reopen old party wounds, but it had certain offsetting liabilities. He had no strong local following, and moreover he was better known abroad than at home. As a man of high patriotic principles, diplomatic skill, and experience, Zinsou had won widespread international respect, and therefore was better qualified than any other Dahomean leader to elicit the foreign aid vital for his country's economic survival.

To persuade the reluctant doctor to accept the task of governing a faction-ridden and bankrupt country was not easy, so the army officers pledged him their support for a five-year period. Nevertheless, before agreeing to serve as head of state, Dr. Zinsou insisted against their wishes on holding a referendum to confirm his mandate. In the referendum held on July 28, he won 76.3 per cent of the votes cast by 72.6 per cent of the electorate.[18] This gave him a surprisingly substantial popular endorsement considering the strength of the opposition forces arrayed against him,

[18] *Afrique Nouvelle,* July 31, 1968.

including the officers who resented his recourse to such a democratic procedure. Among his other opponents were most of the labor unions, the students, and the three exiled leaders who were then in Togo, where they had been warmly welcomed by Eyadema. None of these civilian elements could find fault with Zinsou on personal grounds, but they could never forgive him for owing his mandate to the army and not to elections held in accordance with the recently adopted constitution.

The congratulatory telegrams promptly sent by General de Gaulle and all the Entente leaders except Eyadema augured well for Zinsou's foreign financial support. The government he formed also gave promise of efficiency and national unity, for it was composed of young technicians and was representative of all the regions and political tendencies. During the first months of his administration, Zinsou was able to govern in relative tranquillity because the Dahomeans for once seemed surfeited with political quarrels, government by the army had been generally discredited, and France had resumed the payment of its subsidies. Zinsou strove diligently to restore the economy and the authority of the state, but in so doing he eventually ran afoul of the unions' habitual resistance to austerity measures and—more ominous— the deepening divisions within the officer corps. In September 1968, the rivalry between Alley and Kouandete had apparently been settled by Zinsou's upgrading the latter at the expense of the former, but soon this proved to have created additional military animosities. Strikes by secondary-school students, the airlift from Cotonou to Biafra, and intrigues by the exiled leaders operating from nearby bases— all swelled the number of malcontents and made Zinsou's tenure of office increasingly shaky.

Such a formidable growth in the opposition to Zinsou

underscored his weaknesses as a political leader. Not only did he lack a popular constituency, but he had no talent for intrigue or disposition to compromise on issues he regarded as fundamental. Although he made some minor concessions to his radical opponents, such as nationalizing the operation of Cotonou port, he was intransigent about meeting labor's demands for wage increases. Nor would he permit any group or individual to trespass on his authority as head of state, and he was particularly adamant against the army's intervention in politics. Zinsou's position was relatively safe so long as Kouandete remained his ally, but during the latter part of 1969, successive plots against the premier, in which Alley was allegedly involved, convinced Kouandete that Zinsou was planning to oust him. On December 10, Kouandete staged his second military revolt, and Dahomey underwent its sixth coup d'état since independence.

Since this coup was so poorly prepared and only Kouandete's personal followers participated in it, he failed to obtain the primary position in the military directorate installed soon afterward to govern the country. Its presidency went to a middle-aged, apolitical officer, Colonel Paul de Souza, and the third post to the head of the gendarmerie, Major Benoit Sinzogan, neither of whom had taken part in the coup. Kouandete's colleagues forced him to liberate from detention not only Zinsou but also his archenemy Alley, who had been sentenced to ten years' imprisonment the preceding October. Still another humiliation for Kouandete and the other younger officers was their forced acceptance of the return from exile of Maga, Apithy, and Ahomadegbe, all of whom promptly announced their candidacy in the elections for a civilian government which the military directorate promised soon to hold.

By early 1970 the stage was set for a rerun of the old familiar scenario. The army, after again having to acknowledge its incapacity to govern, was compelled to call on the familiar cast of civilian characters to take over the country's administration. Maga, Apithy, and Ahomadegbe had proclaimed their patriotism and unity while in exile, but—once back home—they could reach no agreement on a single candidate to support for election as the future president of Dahomey. They were now united only in their common opposition to Zinsou, who also offered his candidacy for that office. To prevent "fraud and turbulence," the military directorate decided to stagger the elections over the weeks between March 9 and 31, and to hold them successively in the different regions. This device failed to accomplish its purpose in two essential respects. Serious disorders occurred whenever a candidate tried to campaign in the electoral fief of his competitors, and none of them received a clear-cut mandate from the whole population, perhaps because each had his own clique of military supporters.[19] This election, like the one held under army auspices almost exactly two years before, was a fiasco and had to be annulled. The only certainty that emerged from so inconclusive an election was that each of the three exiles had retained intact his regional following, and that Zinsou, despite his one and a half years of honest government, still had no popular appeal for the Dahomeans.

Because no single military or civilian leader could muster the support needed to head a national government, an "original" solution was sought and found for Dahomey's political impasse. This was a coalition presidential council to be composed of the three former exiles, whose tenure of office was to be six years and to be guaranteed by the army.

[19] Kouandete supported Apithy, whereas Maga was the preferred candidate of Sinzogan because, when president of the republic, Maga had always favored the gendarmerie rather than the army.

Every two years the council's chairmanship would rotate among its members. Maga was chosen as its first chairman (or president) because he had received the largest number of votes in the abortive election and reportedly had the backing of the French government, and because the north had threatened to secede unless he became the head of state. In the temporary government formed by Maga after his investiture by the military directorate, the principle of parity between the council's membership was accurately reflected in his distribution of cabinet portfolios.

In that regime, all of Dahomey's long-standing rifts appear in sharp relief. Never before have so many discordant elements been present and active in the country at the same time. The only absentee was Zinsou, who chose to remain in Paris. Within a month of its establishment, the "troika" government was attacked in strongly worded tracts circulated in Dahomey's southern towns, and in whose authorship or distribution Major Kouandete and relatives of Dr. Zinsou were implicated. Consequently, Kouandete was sentenced to two months' imprisonment for "abuse of authority," and by the time he was freed he had been downgraded in rank, whereas all the other main army officers had been promoted. When Soglo returned to Cotonou in July 1970 after two and a half years' absence, his arrival could not but intensify the preexisting rivalries within the officer corps. In particular, it is unlikely that Kouandete will long accept his subordination to Alley, who in the summer of 1970 was named secretary-general for national defense. Nor is it probable that the army's guaranty of support for the new government will be any more operative and effective than that which it gave to Zinsou two years before.

As for the three members of the presidential council, their shared exile has obviously not reconciled them to each other.

Now that each has been reassured as to the strength of his regional support, it is improbable that any of them will renounce his ingrained habit of intriguing to acquire ascendancy over his old rivals. Currently they move as a phalanx, all three together making official visits upcountry and to Nigeria and Togo, but Apithy may not long accept his present position as odd-man-out in the triumvirate.

Already in the winter of 1970–1971, Apithy gave unmistakable evidence of disgruntlement with his partners. In December he reportedly walked out of a meeting of the presidential council following its decision to locate the new university of Dahomey at Abomey rather than in his own fief of Porto Novo. Then in March 1971, after a visit to Lagos (where Apithy's proposal a year before to the effect that Dahomey withdraw from the Entente to ally itself with Nigeria had made him more popular than any other Dahomean leader), he flew to Paris "for reasons of health." From there, he let Maga know his displeasure over certain decisions that had been made by the presidential council, notably the suspension of *La Patrie Dahoméenne,* a newspaper which always supported Apithy, and the dismissal of a high official who had been in Apithy's secretariat. In May he returned to Cotonou but was even more isolated from his colleagues than before his two months' absence. A crucial test of the government's stability will surely occur in 1972 when Ahomadegbe is scheduled to succeed Maga as council president, but it may come sooner if Apithy or Kouandete should try to seize power.

Maga, fully aware of the dangers inherent in Apithy's popular appeal and potential defection, has moved to steal some of the latter's thunder. He has taken the calculated risk of countering Apithy's electoral promise to restore the 20 per cent cut in the pay of wage earners, cultivated closer political

and economic ties with Nigeria to the detriment of Dahomey's good relations with the Entente, restricted the activities of foreign traders in the country, and implied his acceptance of the principle of nationalizing Dahomey's public
utilities. Maga has also succeeded in attracting more foreign
investments and loans to Dahomey, and he has persuaded
France to continue subsidizing his country's budget deficits.
By these devices Maga has gained time and parried the
threat of imminent bankruptcy, but he has not solved
Dahomey's basic problems.

There has been no perceptible change of heart on the part
of Dahomey's salaried class, which seems to suffer from
chronic and collective amnesia. Unlike the peasantry, which
has few contacts with its rulers and accepts poverty as its
inescapable lot, the Dahomean elite continues to believe that
any new government can be pressured into giving them the
well-paid posts to which they feel that their education and
talents entitle them. Some of them, of course, realize that
France will one day tire of rescuing Dahomey from its perennial financial morass, but the discovery of offshore petroleum
deposits in 1968 has given them hope of a new windfall that
will spare them the necessity for hard work and privations.

To be sure, some of Dahomey's sophisticated elite are embarrassed by their country's unenviable record of three constitutions, six coups d'état, twelve governments and twenty
parties in its short history as a nation. This record has made
it the laughingstock of West Africa.[20] Their cries of *mea
culpa,* however, have a hollow ring, for many Dahomeans
take an almost perverse nationalistic pride in their own
anarchic individualism and *frondeur* traditions. Extenuating
circumstances certainly exist, notably Dahomey's poverty,
history, colonial heritage, and overnumerous elite, and the

[20] *Afrique Nouvelle,* March 4, 11, 1970.

xenophobia of certain newly independent African countries is in part responsible for Dahomey's acute unemployment problem. Nevertheless, these difficulties are not peculiar to Dahomey, although they exist there to an exceptional degree. Students of contemporary Africa are fascinated by the phenomenon of Dahomey's persistent regionalism, which transcends even its marked ethnicity, and have offered various plausible explanations for the Dahomeans' singular lack of unity, ideology, and civic spirit.[21] No detailed study of its armed forces has been made, however, nor has any comparative analysis of the military governments in Dahomey, Togo, and Upper Volta been undertaken.

Not surprisingly, in view of its recent history, Dahomey seems to have perfected the technique of the military coup d'état. In that of December 1969, Kouandete, with only a handful of soldiers, one jeep, and a few machine guns, overthrew the civilian government in less than half an hour and kidnapped the president of the republic. Yet he was unable to reap the benefits he anticipated from that exploit, and subsequently he even faced the danger of being assassinated. Divisions within Dahomey's army have been the main cause of its inability to establish a stable government, but they have also neutralized each other. Its army presents a true image of Dahomey in the political domain, for just as no single officer can acquire undisputed power, so no civilian politician can triumph over his principal rivals because none has a truly national following and each of the main leaders has

[21] See M. Glélé, *Naissance d'un Etat Noir* (Paris, 1969); F. M. Oke, "Des Comités Electoraux aux Partis Politiques, *Revue Française d'Etudes Politiques Africaines,* Sept. 1969; E. Makedonsky, "Nouvelles Tentatives de Création d'un Parti Unique au Dahomey," *Revue Française d'Etudes Politiques Africaines,* Sept. 1969; and R. Lemarchand, "Dahomey: Coup within a Coup," *Africa Report,* June 1968.

approximately equal regional support. Furthermore, this remarkable balance of strength seems to characterize the relationship between the country's civilian and military forces. A curious aspect of the bitter electoral campaign in 1970 was the lack of even verbal criticism of the armed forces by any of the three candidates, who reserved their barbs for each other. Doubtless they realized that there existed at the time a grave danger of civil war, and that the only force able to prevent its outbreak was the army.

It has been almost solely in the realm of preserving order that the military governments of Dahomey bear a positive resemblance to those of Togo and Upper Volta, for in other respects the Dahomean armed forces have simply added one more element of discord and confusion to an already divided country. Whereas the Voltaic and Togolese military leaders have restored the authority and credit of the state, punished corruption, and promoted economic development, those of Dahomey have provided none of these assets. Dahomey, however, has avoided dictatorial procedures, whereas Togo and Upper Volta have lost almost all the characteristics of democratic government, although Lamizana's referendum in 1970 was a gesture of recognition of the principle of popular sovereignty. All the military governments have promptly suspended the constitution, dissolved the legislature and parties, and set up authoritarian administrations without recourse to elections, which are always promised but rarely held later.

Initially, at least, the military officers were genuinely reluctant to assume responsibility for an impoverished and divided country. They did so usually out of patriotism and at the behest of the labor and student elites who opposed the preceding government but were unable themselves to replace it. As professional soldiers, the officers were apparently convinced that the army alone could clean up the mess created by the civilian politicians, and provide an orderly and honest administration. Their takeover was facilitated by the surprising lack of resistance offered by the much touted single-parties, which collapsed like the proverbial house of cards, and by the total passivity of the mass of the population, which obviated bloodshed. The African peasantry, like that of Asia, apparently believes that the task of government is not theirs but that of the "ruling classes." That these ruling classes are no longer the traditional chieftaincy but civilian commoners seems not to have altered this attitude of submission to authority. The great majority of the electorate, even in so relatively literate a country as Dahomey, has voted according to the orders of those it accepts as its superiors—party officials, the clergy, civil servants, or chiefs—men who can inspire fear or dispense money and favors. How little the votes of the electorate seem to reflect public opinion in the western sense of the term was shown in Upper Volta when Yameogo was overwhelmingly endorsed at the polls on the eve of his downfall.

Once in the saddle, the military officers have called on young civilian technicians to handle the tasks of administration with which they felt unqualified to deal, but they have kept at arm's length the politicians and the labor and student leaders who had asked the army to throw out the former government but not to rule in its place. The young radicals have been displeased by the nonideological and ultraconservative policies of all the military governments, whose officers have sought aid from Western capitalistic nations and the Entente and have no inclination to carry out a social and cultural revolution like that of Sékou Touré in Guinea. This element of radical opposition, however, has been too small and too divided to become as troublesome to the mili-

tary rulers as are the former politicians and their parties.
Although they have given proof of an amazing vitality, it is
the inability of the old political leaders to forget personal
quarrels, as well as tribal and regional rivalries, and to unite
in the national interest that has been chiefly responsible for
the failure of all attempts by the military governments to
turn back power to civilian control. To this, of course, must
be added the "appetite for power" that has grown among the
officers who have acquired a taste for more of it.

Apart from the army's main asset, which is its monopoly
of physical force, it has others, not shared by the civilian
politicians, which are a stabilizing influence. One of these
assets, at least for effective rule, is its officers' political anony-
mity and their indifference to popular support. Before their
rise to power, the heads of state in Togo, Upper Volta, and
—formerly—Dahomey were unknown personalities, who had
no record of political involvement and who did not have to
woo the electorate by their charisma, oratory, or ideology.
They were disciplined and trained leaders of men, whose
attitude toward the business of government was thoroughly
practical and pragmatic. Tentative in their initial approach
to so novel an occupation, they soon gained self-confidence
and began to enjoy it. If, on occasion, they have resorted to
elections or a referendum, it has been more often than not
lip-service to democratic institutions with a view to making
their rule more acceptable internationally. For all practical
purposes their governments are dictatorships, and in the long
run this authoritarianism risks destroying what have been
the army's other main assets. These are its honesty, self-
discipline, and closeness to the people. Nevertheless, the fact
that the armed forces, by and large, are of peasant origin,
lack a formal education above the primary level, and come
principally from minority tribes in underprivileged regions,

may keep them more sensitive than have been the civilian politicians to the needs of the mass of their compatriots.

To date, the size of the Entente's armed forces in relation to the total population does not seem disproportionate, but as regards the role they have played in national defense their cost to the budget both in absolute and comparative terms appears excessive (see Table 1). In relation to the Entente states' gross national products and social services, impoverished Dahomey spends twice as much on its armed forces as

Table 1. Armed forces of the Entente states, military and social expenditures, and gross national product, by country, 1967

Country	Armed forces (number)	Expenditures *			GNP *
		Military	Education	Health	
Ivory Coast	4,000	4	127	20	267
Dahomey	3,000	6	3	2	72
Niger	3,500	1	1	2	79
Togo	1,500	2	2	1	119
Upper Volta	2,500	1	1	1	50

Sources: *Jeune Afrique,* Apr. 28, 1970; *Europe-France-Outremer, L'Afrique d'Expression Française et Madagascar,* June 1970.

* In US dollars, per capita of population.

on education, three times as much as on health, and far more proportionately on military expenditures than does wealthy Ivory Coast. Since none of the Entente's armies has had to defend national frontiers (nor is likely to be called upon to do so) the need for such outlays is highly questionable, although it could be argued that keeping standing armies trained and well equipped acts as an effective deterrent to aggression from a foreign source. In any case, military expenditures can be expected to grow rather than decrease in those states now ruled by the armed forces, but not necessarily in the two countries still under civilian rule. Although the Ivorian and Nigérien leaders worry lest the success of military coups d'état in neighboring nations prove contagious, they may not feel sufficiently sure of the loyalty of their own armed forces to risk enhancing their number or power.

Whether or not the military governments presently in control will eventually turn control back to elected civilian leaders or succumb permanently to the temptations of power and wealth, remains to be seen. There is no doubt, however, but that the armed forces of the Entente are no longer content to play their traditional role of *la grande muette,* and will continue, or try, to participate actively in their country's politics even when they do not actually control its government. Thus far, none of the Entente military regimes has tried to effect a social revolution, the administrative machinery continues to function much as before, and virtually the only victims of the transfer of power have been the civilian politicians.

CHAPTER 6

Foreign Relations
and Divisive Issues

Foreign Relations

Of all the Entente's foreign relations, those with France have been so much the most important that they have both overshadowed and influenced those with other nations in Africa itself and throughout the world.

Between 1958 and 1969, France's African policy was made by General de Gaulle alone. To the great majority of civilian leaders in francophone sub-Saharan Africa, de Gaulle was "the man of Brazzaville" and champion of French Black Africa's emancipation. To its military rulers, the general was a professional soldier whom they admired as the incarnation and leader of France's wartime resistance movement. With both groups, his prestige and leadership position survived intact despite the drastic changes in his policy during the eleven years he was in power. As regards Africa, these changes were mainly determined by the fluctuating situation in Algeria and the rise of nationalism and Pan-Africanism in the whole continent.

General de Gaulle's personality, flexibility, and evident affection for Africa gave him a unique influence in francophone African countries, that has been equalled by no other Western leader in any part of the Dark Continent. His relations with the Entente territories underwent a grave crisis between 1958 and 1961,[1] but his acquiescence in their desire

[1] See Ch. 2.

for independence and for leaving the Community, the while continuing to give them aid, restored a harmony that lasted throughout his remaining years in power. The general respected their national sovereignty, encouraged their organization, withdrew almost all French troops from their countries, and negotiated with each of them bilateral agreements for various types of assistance.

Other facets of de Gaulle's policy, such as his decision to recognize Communist China, sell arms to South Africa, intervene militarily in Gabon and Chad, and support Biafra's secession, did not affect the Entente as a group. Perhaps because France exerted no pressure on it in such matters, its members did not always follow the general's lead—only Dahomey exchanged diplomatic missions with Peking for a brief period, and Ivory Coast alone recognized Biafra—nor did they always vote with France in the United Nations. Even Ivory Coast, generally regarded by African "revolutionaries" as the country most subservient to France, showed its independence there by voting between 1960 and 1965 almost as often in opposition to France (twenty-one times) as on the same side (twenty-three).[2] By and large, however, they did not stray far from the French fold.

Aside from sentimental ties, which can never be discounted in Franco-African relations, it is the aid France provides to Black African states that has been and is likely to remain the primordial factor. This aid takes so many forms—subsidies, loans, investments, and technical and military assistance of various kinds—that it is impossible to calculate its total exactly. Although it has undergone significant modifications in recent years, it is larger than aid from any

[2] The comparable figures for the United States were 17 and 65, and for the Soviet Union, 29 and 52. See *Marchés Tropicaux,* March 28, 1970.

other single source and is still vital for the development of
francophone Africa's economies. Direct subsidies, except in
such "emergency cases" as that of Dahomey, have been
eliminated as a means of shoring up African budgets. French
aid has increasingly taken the form of investments and technical assistance in African projects primarily for the development of education, communications, agricultural production,
and health. The number of French *coopérants,* as well as of
residents (see Table 2), in the Entente countries has grown
steadily since independence, and beginning in 1963 its total

Table 2. Registered French residents living in the Entente states,
1969 and 1970

| | French residents | |
Country	1969	1970
Ivory Coast	24,250	25,262
Dahomey	2,600	2,752
Niger	2,269	2,834
Togo	2,063	2,090
Upper Volta	2,197	3,543

Source: *Europe-France-Outremer, L'Afrique d'Expression Française
et Madagascar,* Aug. 1970.

has been swelled by the addition of military conscripts as
teachers and members of the French peace corps, called
Volontaires du Progrès.

At the same time there is a growing tendency for the
Entente nations to diversify the sources of their foreign aid
and their trading partners, particularly among the nations
of the European Economic Community, of which they are
all associate members. They have also cultivated economic
relations with the United States, the United Nations, Israel,

Taiwan, and Eastern European states, and even Ivory Coast
traded briefly with the USSR. Concurrently Franco-Entente
trade has been steadily declining, although France remains
the principal client and provisioner of each member of that
organization.

The dwindling importance of France's role in the Entente
is largely a natural result of the latter's acquisition of national sovereignty and desire to match economic with political independence. It is also due, however, to a marked dimi-
nution in the volume of French aid to its former dependencies, and to a new orientation of that aid beginning in 1963.
Between that year and 1969, France's total aid to Africa,
which had amounted to more than 3 billion Metro. francs in
1961, declined by one-fifth. Although francophone Black
Africa continued to receive about 30 per cent of the total
amount of French overseas aid, the Entente states received
less than before in public-fund investments and fewer advantages in the French market. Furthermore, although in
terms of its national income France still grants a larger
proportion to developing countries than does any other
Western nation, its aid to the Third World is now more
widely dispersed to include Asian, Latin American, and
anglophone African nations.

The foregoing developments have had the general consequence of making the francophone Black African leaders
chart a course more independent of France than before, and
of causing France to agree to their wishes in matters of education and finance, which have always been a French *chasse
gardée*. At the semiannual meetings of the French and African ministers of public instruction, France has accepted the
Africans' proposals for a radical departure from the French
educational system as regards school curricula and the evalu-
ation of diplomas.

Similarly but to a less marked degree, the French finance minister has yielded to African criticisms of the policy of the franc zone, to which all the Entente states belong. Such criticism was particularly acute following France's unilateral devaluation of the franc in August 1969, which increased their public debt and living costs, and thus canceled out the benefits subsequently received from their exports to non-franc-zone countries. Although the members of the Entente appreciate the stability, strength, and convertibility of the CFA franc and have no intention of creating national currencies, they resent France's failure to consult them on major policy matters and to control the prices of its exports to Africa, as well as the conservative policy imposed by the Banque de France on the African Instituts d'Emission regarding the distribution of credits for development programs. At the Paris meeting of finance ministers on September 17, 1970, African pressure elicited from France a pledge to keep them better informed about contemplated financial measures affecting the franc zone and, more important, to guarantee up to 75 to 90 per cent of private French capital investments in Africa.

President Pompidou early announced his policy to be one of Gaullist "continuity" in his relations with francophone Africa, and he confirmed this during his state visit to its capitals in February 1971. In fact, the budget of the Secretariat of State for Cooperation, which has been fairly stable for the past few years, was increased by 15 per cent for 1971. Nevertheless, the handwriting on the wall clearly indicates a progressive tapering off of close Franco-African relations. Even before General de Gaulle disappeared from the political scene, a progressive disengagement was occurring on both sides, and his death has probably given the *coup de grâce* to the special relationship that has characterized the

ties between France and her former Black African colonies
since their independence.

The Entente states have always been so oriented toward
the West in general, and toward France in particular, that
only their relations with neighboring African countries have
acquired any comparable significance for them. Unlike their
generally uniform attitude of cooperation with Western industrialized nations, their attitude toward their African
neighbors (and with each other) has not been so harmonious.
To be sure, the Entente leaders hold the same general view
of the North African states, but there are nuances in the
relations of each of the five with the Arab nations. By and
large, their position has been "correct" and cautious, being
spontaneously cordial only toward Bourguiba's regime in
Tunisia. Upper Volta and Niger, for example, are more careful than the coastal countries to stay on good terms with the
Arabs, because of their proximity to North Africa and their
own larger Muslim populations, yet all but Togo also have
diplomatic relations and economic agreements with Israel.
Generally speaking, expediency, practical self-interest, and
prudence have governed the foreign policy of all five, and
Togo's tendency to diverge may be explained in part by the
recency of its membership in the Entente.

Divisive Issues

Much the same can be said for the Entente's relations with
its Black African neighbors, with whom all have historical,
ethnic and economic ties that antedated European rule. Inevitably such ties are affected by the institutions and boundaries inherited from their differing colonial pasts, and all
the Entente states have common frontiers with anglophone
West African countries. As the Entente's links with France
have been progressively loosened, each member state's rela-

tions with its immediate neighbors have taken on greater importance and also sharper differences. The recent upheavals in anglophone West Africa have only temporarily obscured Ghana's influence in Togo, Upper Volta, and Ivory Coast, and that of Nigeria in Niger and Dahomey. The return of relative stability and peace to Ghana and Nigeria has already altered relations with their Entente neighbors, and cannot but affect that organization's evolution, probably by further endangering its solidarity. Even during the Entente's formative years, when relations between its member states were of primary importance to its survival, the proximity of Ghana and Nigeria was both directly and indirectly responsible for some of the extremely serious rifts that almost tore the Entente apart.

Dual Nationality

Of all the issues that have divided the Entente, that of dual nationality has caused the deepest rift, particularly between Ivory Coast and its partners. The term "dual nationality" is misleading in that its implications seem mainly political, whereas in reality they are basically economic. They concern the perennial mobility of all the West African peoples, which takes different forms in the hinterland and in the coastal states but affects all the Entente countries. The interterritorial migration, by and large, is from the poorer hinterland to the coast, and internally from the north to the south, and it involves principally unskilled seasonal or permanent laborers in search of remunerative employment. However, there is also a countercurrent of emigration by the numerically smaller coastal elites of Togo and Dahomey. Unable to find high-salaried positions at home, they were encouraged by the colonial regime to seek posts in the hinterland, which lacks cadres, or in the more prosperous coastal territories. Among the Entente states, over the past twenty years, the main focus of both types of immigration has been Ivory Coast.

The rapid growth of the Ivorian economy dates from 1950, when cutting of the Vridi canal transformed Abidjan into a deepwater port. Ivory Coast's subsequent prosperity cannot be attributed to outstanding natural resources, for its traditional exports are not rare mineral ores but coffee, cocoa, bananas, and timber, all of which suffer from competition and fluctuating prices in world markets. What has come to be called the "Ivorian miracle" is the result of the confidence inspired in foreign investors by the stability of Houphouët's government and its active encouragement of free enterprise, liberal financial policy, employment of European experts, and the welcome it has extended to African immigrants. From the outset, Houphouët gave priority to the economic rather than to the "political kingdom," which was the ideological choice of Sékou Touré and Nkrumah. By opening Ivory Coast's doors wide to African immigration, Houphouët hoped to refute the criticism that he had sacrificed the unity of Africa to the aggrandizement of his own territory, and also to accelerate Ivory Coast's economic development. In so doing, Houphouët achieved his goal of rapid economic progress but, paradoxically, this very success aroused dangerously xenophobic tendencies among his compatriots, to the point where they now threaten to slow down their country's economic expansion and even undermine the Entente's solidarity.

Houphouët early realized that the Ivorians were too deficient numerically, educationally, and psychologically to serve as the sole instruments he required to develop and modernize his country's economy. By temperament and tradition, the Ivorian is a man of the soil and of the sea—a peasant-farmer, herder, or fisherman, but not a trader, bureaucrat, or wage earner. Furthermore, when Ivory Coast became politically independent, it lacked the educational facilities to produce an elite quantitatively and qualitatively prepared to man the civil service and business enterprises of a fully sovereign nation. Houphouët therefore moved first to fill the void at the top by employing Europeans, mainly Frenchmen, in the administrative and technical services. Then so rapidly did the Ivorian economy expand that its very prosperity spontaneously attracted an increasing number of foreign businessmen, Lebanese and Occidentals, as well as alien Africans. The 1965 census showed that the resident French population (more than 35,000) had almost doubled since independence, the Lebanese numbered about 10,000, and foreign Africans, both domiciled and seasonal residents, came to nearly one million. Foreigners then formed about one-fourth of the total population, whose annual growth rate of 3 per cent was due less to natural increase than to immigration (see Table 3).

Aliens have been the main promoters as well as the principal beneficiaries of Ivory Coast's extraordinary prosperity, but the general rise in Ivorian living standards shows that some of the wealth has filtered through to the indigenous population. The Ivorians' share, however, has not been evenly distributed, either geographically or by social classes, and they increasingly feel that their portion is disproportionately small. Those who have received the largest benefits are the southern planters, whose income derives from their coffee and cocoa export crops, which are cultivated mainly by immigrant Mossi laborers. It was these indigenous planters whom Houphouët organized during World War II into a

Table 3. Population and related data

Country	Population (millions) 1960–61	1970	Annual growth rate (%)	Density per sq. km.	Main towns (thousands)	Town dwellers (% of total)	Main tribes (thousands)	
Ivory Coast	3.2	4.5	3.0	14.1	Abidjan 500	25	Abron-Agni- Baoulé	1,000
					Bouaké 105		Krou	710
					Man- Danane 52		Lagunaires	395
							Malinké	665
					Korhogo 24		Mandé	350
							Voltaics	700
Dahomey	2.0	2.6	2.9	22.0	Cotonou 120	9	Fon	634
					Porto Novo 76		Nagot	338
					Abomey 29		Goun	303
					Ouidah 20		Bariba	285
					Parakou 16		Adja-Ouatchi	281
							Somba	73
							Peul	55
Niger	3.0	4.0	3.0	3.2	Niamey 59	5	Djerma-Songhay	733
					Zinder 31		Hausa	1,627
					Maradi 23		Touareg and Toubou	330
					Tahoua 19		Peul	457
							Beriber-Mangas	240
Togo	1.5	1.95	2.6	34.0	Lomé 120	11	Ewe-Mainas- Ouatchis	550
					Sokodé 17		Cabrais- Gourounsi	600
					Palimé 15		Paragourmas- Akposso- Adélés	60
					Anecho 13			
					Atakpamé 12			
Upper Volta	4.0	5.0	2.1	19.0	Ouaga- dougou 105	6	Mossi	2,500
					Bobo- Diou- lasso 67		Bobos	275
					Koudou-		Gourounsi	180
							Lobi	100
							Mandé	230
							Peul	200
							Touareg	220

Country	Population (millions) 1960–61	1970	Annual growth rate (%)	Density per sq. km.	Main towns (thousands)		Town dwellers (% of total)	Main tribes (thousands)
					gou	27		
					Ouahi-			
					gouya			
						10		
					Kaya	10		

Sources: Based on data in *Europe-France-Outremer, L'Afrique d'Expression Française et Madagascar,* 1960–1970 (yearly issues); *L'Afrique/70.*

Syndicat Agricole, which became the nucleus of his PDCI. Today they form a small but significant rural bourgeoisie that still serves as the main indigenous economic base of that party. Because they depend on the continued availability of cheap imported manual labor, the Ivorian planters naturally support Houphouët's policy of large-scale immigration by unskilled agricultural wage earners.

For many years, the annual influx of several hundred thousand Mossi laborers was accepted by the Ivorians because they had no inclination nor need to perform manual tasks. Moreover, the great majority of these immigrants were seasonal, coming to the coast only during the long dry period when farming was at a standstill in the hinterland. Also, at the other end of the employment scale, the Ivorians long acquiesced in the presence of European businessmen and officials because they recognized their own inability to perform occupations that required a high degree of training and experience. It was in the middle echelons of the bureaucracy and trading firms that resentment developed in the 1950's against the alien Africans, particularly the Dahomeans and Togolese, whose superior education and enterprise made

them more readily employable than Ivorians as minor civil
servants and clerks. However, toward the end of that decade,
a serious unemployment problem had been created at Abidjan, where the expansion of secondary education had greatly
increased the number of Ivorian youths qualified to hold
such positions, and where the labor market was also being
flooded by unskilled immigrants from the underdeveloped
northern region of the territory. Together they organized an
antiforeign demonstration in October 1958, which took such
an ugly turn that thousands of Togolese and Dahomeans
fled from the country.[3]

Through various devices the PDCI government tried to
cope with this problem—initiating programs to equip the
Ivorians with employable skills, starting a national school of
administration to train indigenous civil servants, and requir-
ing military conscripts to perform "civic service" that would
execute needed public works and at the same time provide
them with vocational training. More recently, it began to
promote the economic development of the north to check
the rural exodus from that region to the cities of the south—
but all to little avail. Immigrants from upcountry have
continued to pour into Abidjan at the average rate of 4,000
a month,[4] and many of the expelled Dahomeans and Togolese have returned unobtrusively to Ivory Coast. Concurrently, a steadily expanding secondary-school and even a
university system is turning out more and more graduates
unable to find the well-paid jobs to which they feel their
diplomas entitle them. Yet, for many years the government
refused to change its policy of welcoming alien African immigrants, and five years after the riots of 1958, an official

[3] See Ch. 1.
[4] V. DuBois, *Social Aspects of the Urbanization Process in Abidjan,*
American Universities Field Staff Reports, Nov. 1967.

spokesman blandly told the domiciled foreign community that "you are in a friendly country, enjoying the same rights as your Ivorian brothers." [5] The government seemed not to realize that it was caught up in the vicious circle which it had itself created: the economic prosperity which it had so successfully promoted was sufficient to attract more and more impoverished alien immigrants, but not enough to provide remunerative positions both for them and for the fast-growing number of qualified and expectant Ivorian candidates.

Houphouët's open-door policy had given birth to an Ivorian nationalism that was rapidly taking a negative and xenophobic turn. The Ivorians now looked upon all the foreigners working in their midst not as contributors to Ivory Coast's prosperity but as parasitic competitors who were draining off their country's wealth. At first their resentment was directed only against the white-collar African immigrants, but it soon spread to include aliens in all categories of employment, in both the public and the private sectors. By the end of 1965, pressure for the *africanisation des cadres* had become so insistent that Houphouët reluctantly asked for the resignation of Raphael Saller, his French finance minister since independence. Saller was generally regarded by Europeans as the architect of Ivory Coast's prosperity, but to the Ivorians he had become the symbol of France's continued domination of their economy. Then Houphouët relegated the other French officials serving in the forefront of his administration to less conspicuous posts as advisers to the young Ivorians whom he now appointed as ministers and heads of the government services, thus belatedly bringing Ivory Coast more into line with the other francophone states. Much later, he yielded to pressures of the same sort for the promotion of Ivorians as managers of small business enter-

[5] *Le Monde,* Sept. 8, 1963.

prises. Both these moves primarily affected the domiciled Europeans and Lebanese.

Quite different were the consequences of a concurrent local campaign for the "Ivorization" of other categories of employment, which had extremely adverse effects on Ivory Coast's relations with three of its Entente partners. Initially Houphouët's dual-nationality proposal had been made principally to strengthen the bonds between the Entente states and to lure Togo into their fold. When, after a year's pause —during which he was preoccupied with foreign policy—he revived the proposal in December 1965, he failed to take into consideration how rapidly Ivorian nationalism had developed in the interval.

To all outward appearances Houphouët was then in a position of unassailable internal political strength. The first PDCI national congress since independence, held the preceding September, had been attended by more than 1,000 party delegates and by observers not only from the francophone sub-Saharan countries but also from Tunisia, Ethiopia, and Nigeria. The amnesty for political prisoners and the party's structural reforms announced by Houphouët on this occasion seemed likely to promote national reconciliation and unity by giving wider representation to his former opponents and young Ivorians in the assembly and PDCI politburo. At the same time, however, he struck a false note when he promised a qualified Africanization of the cadres. "Very soon," he told the assembled delegates, "all the top posts in our administration will be occupied by our own nationals or our brothers from other African countries." [6]

Two months later, in the presidential and legislative elections held on November 7, he and his party slate of candidates received a massive popular endorsement at the polls.

[6] Abidjan radio broadcast, Sept. 24, 1965.

Such evidence of his political security, along with Ivory Coast's steady economic progress, naturally encouraged Houphouët to assume that his dual-nationality project, which he spelled out to the PDCI politburo in December, would receive its wholehearted approval. Immediately, however, he was confronted with a revolt not only by his party's top echelons, but also by the national labor federation and even by the rural bourgeoisie, upon whose loyalty he had always relied. A report on the series of votes taken secretly among the rank and file of union members was transmitted to the politburo, which alerted Houphouët, who then took soundings among the planter community. So uniformly hostile were all the active elements of Ivorian society to sharing the steadily increasing national income with non-Ivorians that within two weeks an emergency meeting of the politburo was called to reconsider the whole dual-nationality question.

As always when faced with an opposition which he could neither ignore nor negotiate away, Houphouët yielded totally and realistically. Not only did he agree to dismiss Saller and ask local foreign businessmen to recruit Ivorian rather than Dahomean or Togolese employees, but he began discreetly to curtail the influx of alien Africans. Only to the extent of promising that the Entente nationals already permanently domiciled and employed in Ivory Coast would continue to enjoy the same rights as Ivorians was he able to salvage even a small segment of his original proposal. For the immediate future, he decided to abandon his dual-nationality project in the hope that within five to ten years it would be taken up again and accepted on a far wider scale by the OCAM countries.[7]

Houphouët's retreat on dual nationality marked a turning

[7] *Marchés Tropicaux,* Jan. 24, 1966.

point in his relations with the other members of the Entente. Until then he had proceeded on the assumption that what was good for Ivory Coast was also good for the Entente, but now he felt compelled to placate Ivorian nationalist sentiment even at the cost of alienating his partners whose goodwill he had been at pains to court. Now, as before, it was primarily Upper Volta and Dahomey, and to a lesser extent Togo, that he must appease. The Togolese had suffered in the October 1958 riots at Abidjan on a much smaller scale but for the same reasons as had the Dahomeans, and only about 1,800 of them had been forced to leave Ivory Coast.[8] Togo had never had such close relations with Ivory Coast as had Dahomey, and its CUT leaders were then absorbed in organizing the government over which they had just won control, and were also preoccupied with nearerby Ghana's aggressiveness.

When Olympio, on the eve of his departure for the United Nations in New York, learned of the Abidjan riots, he merely said: "I didn't know there were so many Togolese in Abidjan . . . but the people there draw no distinction between them and the Dahomeans. . . . His Excellency, Houphouët-Boigny, has expressed to me the deep regret caused him by these events and assured me that they will not recur and that damages will be paid to the victims. . . . I have confidence in him." [9] Moreover, there was at this time no question of Togo's forming a united front with Dahomey so as to bring stronger pressure to bear on Houphouët, for the two countries were then disputing the location of a joint deepwater port, Dahomey was making one of its periodic

[8] *Afrique Nouvelle,* Nov. 14, 1958.
[9] Interview with Sylvanus Olympio, *Marchés Tropicaux,* Nov. 22, 1958.

efforts to check smuggling from Togo, and the Togolese believed—as they had long done—that Dahomeans were meddling in their local politics.

If Togo was willing to wipe the slate clean insofar as the 1958 riots were concerned, Dahomey was not. Ivory Coast cast too long a shadow over its small and weak eastern partner for the Dahomeans to feel any genuine friendship for the Ivorians. Obviously the mistrust was reciprocal. When Houphouët withdrew his dual-nationality offer late in January 1966, he added insult to injury by adding a comment critical of the Dahomeans domiciled in Ivory Coast. Although he deplored the "excesses" against them in 1958, he implied that they had only themselves to blame because they insisted on remaining peripheral to Ivorian society and refused to take root in the country as the Senegalese and Malians had done.[10] Houphouët's remarks aroused indignation in Cotonou, where a government spokesman recalled that it was Houphouët who had initiated the dual-nationality proposal, "which we accepted only in the interests of unity." [11]

To soothe the Dahomeans' ruffled feelings, Houphouët promptly sent a mission to Cotonou, but only superficially did it clear up the "misunderstanding." Perforce the Dahomeans had to forgive the affront, but they did not forget it. Consequently the atmosphere in Dahomey was hardly propitious for the success of Houphouët's efforts, a few months later, to induce first Apithy and then Maga to join the Entente late in 1959. Nevertheless, because Houphouët's goodwill was indispensable if Dahomeans were to be readmitted for employment in Ivory Coast, Maga acquiesced *faute de mieux*. Dahomey's economy simply could not provide jobs

[10] *Le Monde,* Jan. 30, 1966.
[11] Cotonou radio broadcast, Feb. 4, 1966.

for all its educated elite, and the expulsion of thousands of its nationals from Niger late in 1963 intensified the acuteness of this problem.

With good reason, the Dahomeans call themselves the "wandering Jews of Black Africa," but they have failed to learn the lessons taught by their successive expulsions from foreign countries. They began drifting back to Abidjan, often clandestinely, bringing their friends and relatives with them. A few of them gained relative job security by marrying Ivorian women, but the great majority continued to be as clannish and unassimilable as before, with the result that they reawakened Ivorian hostility at both the social and professional levels.[12] In a speech to the National Press Club at Washington on August 18, 1967, Houphouët expressed his concern over the "growing number of alien Africans seeking a security and livelihood [in Ivory Coast] which they cannot find at home." He did not, however, mention that he had already begun quietly placing obstacles in the way of Dahomean immigration, or that he was exerting greater pressure on foreign firms, as the principal employers of alien labor, to replace their Dahomean personnel by Ivorians.

By the mid-1960's, the Ivorians' resentment against the competition of foreigners in their country's labor market—without being deflected from the Dahomean white-collar employees—had extended to include the Voltaic wage earners, who have long been the largest single group of alien laborers in Ivory Coast. The current of Voltaic emigration to the coastal region antedated French rule, but it was vastly increased under the colonial regime. France's policy of military conscription and, even more, of forced labor stimulated

[12] At Abidjan in 1968, the writer learned that Dahomeans, particularly at Port-Bouet, have sometimes been accused of murdering Ivorian children as sacrifices to their fetishes.

spontaneous Mossi emigration to the Gold Coast, whereas that to Ivory Coast was mainly the result of official coercive measures, for both the Ivorian administration and the French settlers there needed abundant and cheap labor.

After forced labor was abolished in 1945, and particularly after the Gold Coast became independent as Ghana in 1957, a growing number of Mossi emigrated to Ivory Coast voluntarily, despite its long-standing reputation of poor working conditions. This growing exodus to Ivory Coast was due in part to Ghana's severe customs regulations and unfavorable currency-exchange rates, but more to the spectacular expansion of the Ivorian economy. In 1960 this trend was further encouraged by the replacement of the unpopular Ivorian employers' association, which had theretofore monopolized the recruitment and subsidized the transport of Mossi laborers to Ivory Coast, by an agency set up and controlled by the Voltaic government.

Two other factors—one psychological and the other economic—also accounted for the rapid increase in Voltaic emigration to Ivory Coast.[13] The threat of famine, which had long hung over rural Upper Volta, was becoming more ominous with the population's rapid growth, and the social pressures on Voltaic youth were building up. To the perennial necessity of paying taxes and the bride-price was added the prospect of an easier and more glamorous life in Ivory Coast. The new clothes, bicycles, and money, as well as the freer attitude toward authority brought back by the emigrants gave them prestige. They also created the legend of that country as an El Dorado where well-paid jobs were easy to find, food and diversions were plentiful, and the constraints of family and tribal customs were loosened.

The degree to which the Mossi emigrants to Ivory Coast

[13] See R. Deniel, *De la Savane à la Ville* (Paris, 1968).

became disillusioned depended on the degree to which they had accepted the myth of that country as a land of milk and honey, and on whether they went to work in the rural areas or to the towns. Dissatisfaction was greater in the lumber camps and on the plantations, where the Mossi felt isolated and were more subject to their employers' arbitrary penalties and dismissals, and where the pay was low and the work harder and more constant than that in their native villages. Promotion being based upon seniority of employment, the turnover in the rural areas was considerable, because whenever possible the Mossi moved to the towns, preferably to Abidjan's suburbs. There living costs were higher and lodging more difficult to obtain, but they earned more money and enjoyed more social life and leisure. To offset their nostalgia and sense of inferiority and insecurity as strangers in an alien capital, the Mossi of Abidjan formed many associations of a religious, social, or even quasi-political character.[14] The most important of these was the Comité Central Voltaïque, which was initially a branch of the PDCI and whose members gratefully supported Houphouët as sponsor of the French law that abolished forced labor. After independence, however, the Comité became largely apolitical and primarily a mutual-aid society, as a consequence of the growth of both Ivorian and Voltaic nationalism.

Gradually the Upper Volta government and elite began to oppose massive emigration on the ground that Mossi manpower was needed to develop their home territory, and because the emigrants were the victims of increasing social and economic discrimination in Ivory Coast. The Voltaic immigrants there came more and more to resent being treated as inferior illiterates, whose presence was tolerated simply because they were willing to perform hard manual labor. Often,

[14] *Ibid.*, pp. 126–137.

too, upon their periodic returns to Upper Volta, they found that their welcome was less cordial than they expected and that the skills they had learned abroad were unutilizable in their native villages. Furthermore, their new concepts of freedom and self-indulgence displeased the village elders, who found them insufficiently generous with their savings and gifts and disrespectful of ancient customs. Nevertheless, so meager are Upper Volta's resources and so overabundant its surplus manpower that the flow of emigration has continued, but it is being progressively curtailed by changes in Ivorian policy.

Mossi immigrants were accepted by the Ivorians as long as they remained agricultural laborers or lumberjacks, but as they became more urbanized and brought their families to settle in Ivory Coast, they aroused hostility. Of the half-million or so Mossi in Ivory Coast in 1965, only 300,000 were male wage earners, and by 1968 the Mossi had become the main labor force at Abidjan port. Well organized and cohesive as an ethnic group, the Mossi longshoremen called a strike for higher wages in 1967. In consequence 238 of them were summarily expelled, largely because of pressure on the government exerted by the growing number of unskilled and unemployed Ivorian youths in the capital, where the principal business enterprises—and consequently wage-earning opportunities—were concentrated. To be sure, new jobs were being created as the Ivorian economy flourished, but only at the rate of 8 per cent per annum, and not even one-fourth of the requests for employment received by the government labor bureau alone could be satisfied.[15]

Since that time, tension between Ivorians and Mossi in Abidjan has become more rather than less acute. According

[15] See *Afrique Nouvelle,* Sept. 20, 1967, and DuBois, "Social Aspects."

to knowledgeable informants there, the government labor bureau offers alien Africans only the most menial jobs, not those that Ivorians want to monopolize. Notwithstanding official denials, PDCI policy is now one of deliberately favoring Ivorian candidates, and the successive labor reforms of the past few years [16] have been undertaken partly in response to the labor federation's demands but even more for overall national political considerations. Immigrant alien Africans are now required to have work permits as well as visas before being admitted to the country. Between 1968 and 1970, three riots against foreign Africans by unemployed Ivorians in Abidjan led to the forcible repatriation of several hundred more Mossi, and in the latter year all the port's foreign longshoremen were replaced by Ivorians.

To be sure, not all of the official measures discriminated against foreign wage earners. Ivorian rioters were also rounded up by the police and sent to labor camps in the interior, and alien Africans were assured that there would be no wholesale expulsions such as those that occurred in Ghana late in 1969. Furthermore, some of the reforms, such as the long-overdue wage raises, benefited foreign as well as indigenous workers. It should also be noted that the national labor federation has never been strong enough to exert a decisive influence on the government. Perhaps only one-fifth of its 238,966 nominal members pay their annual dues of 500 CFA francs, and the federation is chronically and deeply in debt, despite large subsidies from the government and the party.[17] Houphouët made the decision to favor Ivorian

[16] In 1968, the pay differential between Ivory Coast's wage zones was suppressed, and the minimum wage, which had been frozen since 1963, was raised twice in rapid succession to reach 58.3 CFA francs an hour in 1970. See *Marchés Tropicaux,* Feb. 28, 1970.

[17] *Jeune Afrique,* Nov. 10, 1968.

nationals principally to prevent the growing and widespread social malaise from developing to the point where it could endanger his regime. The twenty "dialogues" he held late in 1969 with representatives of the Ivorian cadres, wage earners, and employers made him aware of how deep-seated and unanimous was the Ivorians' resentment of foreigners at all levels of the economy. Consequently he decided to undertake a census by nationality of all the unemployed and to require all employers first to submit a list of their employes and then to "Ivorianize" their personnel by stages within a specified time limit.

No final report has yet been published on that census, but it is believed that nearly half the urban labor force is employed by foreign firms and that alien Africans occupy between one-fourth and two-thirds of all the posts in the various non-European categories.[18] Late in 1969, the president of Abidjan's Chamber of Industry stated that there were then 190,000 wage earners in private enterprise and 36,000 in the public sector, and that, of the 43,500 employed in industry, 53 per cent of the skilled and 38 per cent of the unskilled were Ivorians.[19] Doubtless the proportion of Ivorians to non-Ivorians in the higher employment brackets will increase, as the University of Abidjan graduates more and more nationals and as the program to be initiated by the newly created Ministry of Technical Education trains unemployed Ivorians in vocational skills. These developments may solve the problem of Dahomean immigration from the Ivorian viewpoint, but not that of securing manual labor. Unless there is a profound change in the educational system, the Ivorian school graduate will continue to consider such

[18] E. Sigel, "Ivory Coast: Booming Economy, Political Calm," *Africa Report,* April 1970.
[19] *Marchés Tropicaux,* January 3, 1970.

work demeaning, and Ivory Coast must perforce still depend on Mossi immigrants if its agricultural and timber exports are not to decline.

In weighing the pros and cons leading to his policy of discriminating against alien Africans, Houphouët must have concluded that the risks of offending his Entente partners were slighter than those of alienating his own compatriots. There was little likelihood that Hamani Diori would take umbrage, for fewer Nigériens worked in Ivory Coast than in Ghana, and after expelling the Dahomeans from his country, he was hardly in a position to criticize Houphouët. As for the Dahomean expatriates, they were, in Houphouët's view, easily expendable, since the antagonism their growing presence aroused among the Ivorians more than offset the services they rendered. From the political angle, Houphouët would obviously have preferred not to intensify the hostility which most of the Dahomean leaders felt toward Ivory Coast to varying degrees, but none of them, not even Maga, had been a stalwart member of any alliance that he had entered, either inside or outside Dahomey. In every instance they felt compelled, because of their own or their country's weakness, to reach some kind of working agreement with others, but they felt equally free to cast their partners adrift when they no longer found them useful. The only interterritorial ties that the Dahomean leaders really desired were customs unions with their immediate neighbors, so as to win access to their markets and to abate smuggling, and so far as Ivory Coast was concerned, the Dahomeans had no need to use Abidjan's port. Houphouët realized that if Dahomey remained a member of the Entente, it was solely to benefit by the solidarity fund, whose operations would not be adversely affected by his labor policy.

The case of Upper Volta was very different from that of

Dahomey, and the risk of increasing the Voltaics' illwill was far more serious, because of that country's geographical proximity, complementary economy, and reservoir of unskilled labor. Nevertheless, Yameogo's flirtation with Ghana had not lessened Upper Volta's dependence on the port and railroad of Abidjan, and Ivory Coast still bought about half of Upper Volta's exports. Moreover, the Mossi would have to seek work on the coast regardless of the restrictions Houphouët might place on their admission to, and occupations in, Ivory Coast. Over the years, the Voltaic leaders have vainly tried to curtail the emigration of their nationals, and even during World War II, when the frontier with the Gold Coast was officially closed, large numbers of Mossi continued to emigrate there. Upper Volta's economy cannot provide a livelihood for its abundant manpower, many Voltaic families have become dependent on the remittances sent home by their expatriate sons, and all that the Ouagadougou government can hope to do is to prevent skilled workers from permanently emigrating.

Yameogo's overthrow in January 1966 was a severe blow to Houphouët, despite their disputes of five years before. So obvious was his displeasure at the time that many Voltaics believed he had massed troops along their common frontier with a view to restoring his old friend to power. Since then tempers have cooled, Yameogo has finally been released from prison, and Houphouët seems to have decided that the most he can do is to care for Yameogo's family in Ivory Coast and to actively support Yameogo's UDV party in Upper Volta. However, no solutions have yet been found for two other controversies between these neighbors. One concerns the duties Ivory Coast levies on goods in transit from Abidjan to Upper Volta, and the other is the treatment of Mossi laborers by the Ivorians. In both cases, the Voltaics insist that Ivory

Coast is not living up to the agreements made in 1961 and, worse, they feel powerless to do anything to prevent the situation from deteriorating further.

Beginning in 1967, successive anti-Mossi riots in Abidjan brought the Voltaics' longstanding resentment against Ivory Coast, and particularly its president, to the boiling point. Houphouët did dispatch an emissary along with the first batch of returnees to "explain" their repatriation to the Voltaic authorities, but in his other contacts and dealings with Ivory Coast's northern neighbor he has shown a surprising lack of tact and of sensitivity to Voltaic feelings. For example, when Lamizana went to Abidjan to attend the first Entente meeting held since Yameogo's overthrow, Houphouët failed to meet him at the airport—a courtesy which he extended to Colonel Soglo of Dahomey. Protests against this slight to their new head of state were expressed by Voltaic labor unions and student groups over the radio and in tracts distributed in Ouagadougou.[20]

Lamizana himself minimized this incident upon his return home, but since then he has shown his independence of Houphouët, notably by being the only Entente head of state to attend the Monrovia conference of April 1968 convened to form a West African Economic Community. Nevertheless, Lamizana and other politically sophisticated Voltaics know that they are bound by virtually indissoluble bonds to Ivory Coast, and they have no intention either of letting relations deteriorate beyond the point of no return or of leaving the Entente. They may strain at the Ivorian leash but cannot hope to break free, except in the unlikely event that some deus ex machina should materialize to offer them the same or greater advantages than those they derive from membership in the Entente. The possibility of finding a more accept-

[20] *Afrique Nouvelle,* June 29, 1966.

able alternative and more advantageous partnership was rendered even more remote by the expulsion of thousands of Mossi from Ghana in December 1969.

Ghana

Until Nkrumah's downfall in February 1966, Ghana's relations with all the Entente states except Dahomey were—to varying degrees—bad. Dahomey does not adjoin Ghana and hence has no frontier disputes with that country, and as its elite could not hope to find suitable employment in a former British colony, it has had no expatriate problem there. Furthermore, in the hope that Nkrumah's overtures to Dahomey might be the prelude to his joining a Benin union, and in any case provide a counterpoise to Houphouët's pressures, Maga on June 1961 seized the friendly hand offered by Nkrumah. More recently, in 1965, Apithy was the sole head of an Entente state to refuse to endorse Houphouët's campaign against Nkrumah, and he flaunted his independence by ostentatiously making an official visit to Accra, where he voiced support for the Ghanaian leader's views on African unity. To the Dahomean elite, Nkrumah's downfall came as a disagreeable surprise, for they regarded him as one of Africa's most powerful and effective spokesmen, who had brought prosperity and prestige to his country.[21] They were further disappointed when Nkrumah's successors, both military and civilian, took great pains to mend Ghana's broken fences with its Entente neighbors.

Since Houphouët was the ringleader of the Entente's opposition to Nkrumah, he was the main target for the Ghanaian leader's attempts to undermine that organization. But the ease and rapidity with which the Ghana-supported Sanwi dissidents were suppressed dashed Nkrumah's hopes of over-

[21] Talk with Paul Tevoedjre, Cotonou, Oct. 16, 1968.

throwing the Ivorian government by subversive action in that country. Such, however, was not the case with Togo, Upper Volta, and Niger, whose leaders had nothing like Houphouët's resources with which to defend themselves against Nkrumah's intrigues. As for Togo, Olympio certainly wanted Ghana's friendship, which was vital if the Ewes were ever to be reunited, highly desirable if the two countries were to become good neighbors, and necessary if the Togolese were, as he hoped, to form the link between francophone and anglophone Africa.

Of all the former territories of French Black Africa, Togo was the least attached to France, politically, economically, and culturally, and it was also the one with the closest affinities to Ghana. The totally artificial frontier that divided those countries hampered the natural contacts between the two main branches of the Ewe tribe and encouraged a contraband trade. Yet neither Olympio nor Grunitsky was willing to sacrifice Togo's independence, this being the price Nkrumah demanded for his friendship, and they succeeded in resisting the various political and economic pressures that he brought to bear on them. Olympio played a lone hand, counting on his personal authority at home and abroad, and on the weakness of his domestic adversaries. Grunitsky, learning the lessons of Olympio's overconfidence, sought protection from Ghana through closer ties with France, the OCAM, and especially the Entente.

Ironically enough, the civilian leaders of both Ghana and Togo were ultimately overthrown, not by external enemies, but by their own armed forces. The officers who instigated the successful coups d'état on the two sides of the frontier found it easy to establish cordial relations. The climax to this new era of interstate amiability was reached in May 1969 when the Ghanaian regime agreed to the repatriation of Benito Olympio, who had been charged with plotting against the Eyadema government.[22] Certainly Ghana's co-operativeness and the concurrent chilling of Togo's relations with Dahomey[23] have made Eyadema a far less ardent member of the Entente than was Grunitsky. Nevertheless, despite the determination of the Ghanaian and Togolese leaders to live henceforth in peace and harmony, certain bones of contention continue to trouble their relationship. Togo is apprehensive about Ghana's intention to stop cocoa smuggling by intensive patrolling of their frontier, and the Ghanaians—like the Dahomeans—are worried about the hospitality granted to their political dissidents in Lomé. Moreover, Ghana's expulsion in December 1969 of some hundreds of thousands of alien African residents (including about 72,000 Togolese), who used Togo as a transit route, hardly endeared the Busia regime to Eyadema. On the other hand, the prospect of Ghana's close association with the Entente, notably in joint industrial and communications projects, may well convince the Togolese leaders that it is still worth their while to remain members of that organization.

Since independence, Upper Volta's relations with Ghana —in contrast to those of Togo—have fluctuated between short periods of hostility and longer ones of cordiality. With far less cause than Togo, Upper Volta feared Nkrumah's claims to Voltaic territory and even more a stoppage of the transfrontier trade. The two keys to the Voltaic attitude toward Ghana were the massive scale of Mossi emigration there,[24] and the degree of the Voltaics' resentment at any given moment against Ivory Coast; during Yameogo's regime

[22] Later Ghana's highest court ruled that Benito Olympio could not be expelled because he had acquired Ghanaian citizenship.

[23] See Ch. 5.

[24] See E. P. Skinner, "Labor Migration among the Mossi of Upper Volta," in H. Kuper (ed.), *Urbanization and Migration in West Africa,* Berkeley, 1965.

their sentiments shifted rapidly from one extreme to the other. Although first the French administration and then Houphouët had discouraged close ties between Upper Volta and Ghana, the former territory had long supplied the latter with meat and manpower to a greater extent than it did Ivory Coast. Nearly 700,000 Voltaics were more or less permanently resident in Ghana, and only the deficient means of communication and frontier formalities prevented a marked increase in the two countries' trade. As Upper Volta's fiscal dispute with Ivory Coast grew in intensity during 1960–1961, so Yameogo's relations with Nkrumah became ever more cordial. The climax came in their meeting on June 28, 1961, at the border village of Paga, where the two presidents cut a cord symbolic of the division between their two countries and announced the abolition of all tariff barriers.[25] This gesture, coming three months after Yameogo had refused to sign a defense agreement with France and had asked for the evacuation of all French troops from his territory, earned him for the first time the solid support of the radical Voltaic youth.

The Paga agreement caused concern to Houphouët and also to the French trading firms long entrenched in Upper Volta, whose fear of Ghanaian competition had led twice, in the 1950's, to the temporary closing of the frontier with Ghana. These moves had enabled those firms to retain a quasi-monopoly of Upper Volta's import business. While it had also benefited the few existing Voltaic trucking companies, it had at the same time increased the cost of living in Voltaic towns, where yams, colas, and textiles from Ghana became costly and scarce. Yameogo had expected the 1961 trade agreement with Ghana not only to bring down living costs in his country but also to improve its revenues appre-

[25] I. M. Wallerstein, "Background to Paga," *West Africa*, July 28, Aug. 5, 1961.

ciably. Nkrumah had promised to refund to Upper Volta 90 per cent of the duties imposed by his government on Voltaic goods in transit and on the cattle exported to Ghana, and had also offered to lend Upper Volta the equivalent of 1,500 million CFA francs at a low interest rate and repayable in fifteen years. The only tangible benefit economically that Ghana was to receive in return for such exceptional generosity was a cheaper and more abundant supply of Voltaic meat, and obviously Nkrumah's main motivation in making such a deal was political. Allegedly he proposed at Paga that the two countries adopt a common constitution, presumably in the hope that Upper Volta might thereby be induced to join the Union of African States. If this was actually the case, he was doomed to disappointment, for Yameogo was careful not to burn his bridges with France, the UAM, and the Entente. Indeed, in the various press interviews Yameogo gave throughout 1962–1963, he repeatedly stressed that his agreements with Nkrumah were in no sense political, but were prompted solely by his need to increase Upper Volta's trade with Ghana and obtain the use of Accra as an alternative seaport to Abidjan.

By mid-1964, it was apparent that for some time neither party had been respecting the Paga agreements and that tension was developing between them, particularly over implementation of the currency clauses.[26] In June of that year, Nkrumah unilaterally and without explanation closed the frontier and laid claim to an area in Tenkodogo *cercle*. The Ghanaians then built a school there, which flew the Ghanaian flag. Yameogo filed a complaint against Ghana with the OAU, claiming that this was no mere border dispute but "an attack on Upper Volta's territorial integrity." [27] Although this protest was ineffectual, Nkrumah became sufficiently

[26] *West Africa,* Feb. 10, 1968.
[27] *Marchés Tropicaux,* Oct. 1' ᵔ64.

alarmed in early 1965 by the formation of the OCAM and
the Entente's threat to boycott the OAU Accra conference
that he sent his foreign minister to Ouagadougou to negotiate a reopening of the frontier. He explained to Yameogo
that Ghana had closed the border because of a plot against
Nkrumah that was being hatched in Upper Volta, but now
that that danger was past it should be reopened to trade
in their mutual interest.[28] Yameogo refused to comply, however, until he had referred the whole issue to the Entente
for consideration.

As the Entente's campaign against Ghana got underway,
Yameogo "jumped into the garbage pail," as he graphically
put it, to exchange accusations of subversion and personal
insults with both Sékou Touré and Nkrumah. About the
Ghanaian leader, Yameogo reportedly said, "I consider him
a monster because he wants to kill human beings. . . . If
he really loves Africa as he says, he should commit suicide
in the interests of its progress and happiness." [29] At one
point in his picturesque diatribes, Yameogo threatened to
deflect the waters of the Volta River to "teach Nkrumah
that he must live on good terms with his neighbors." [30] Indeed, it was partly because of Yameogo's verbal excesses that
the moderate anglophone African leaders concluded that the
Entente's charges against Nkrumah were more hysterical
than accurate. Certainly, Yameogo's all-out offensive endeared him to Houphouët, who would never himself have
used such intemperate language but perhaps secretly yearned
to do so.

Yameogo's overthrow, followed by that of Nkrumah early
in 1966, eliminated the two leaders whose personal animosity

[28] Ouagadougou radio broadcast, March 24, 1965.
[29] Cotonou radio broadcast, April 17, 1965.
[30] *Marchés Tropicaux,* April 17, 1965.

had been largely responsible for the feud between their countries. Their disappearance from the West African political scene opened the way for an era of good feeling which both of their successors were eager to promote. Soon Ghana sent a goodwill mission to all the Entente states to apologize for Nkrumah's misdeeds and promise friendly cooperation thereafter with them. At Ouagadougou, the Ghanaian emissaries were assured by Lamizana that he would firmly oppose any attempt by Guinean troops to cross Upper Volta, should Sékou Touré try to carry out his threat of restoring Nkrumah to power at Accra by armed force.[31] The Ghana–Upper Volta frontier was reopened on June 4 in a ceremony symbolically held at Paga, where officials of the two countries promised to settle their outstanding differences by negotiation.

In 1967, joint committees were named to work out agreements concerning the disputed territory, the repayment of Upper Volta's debt to Ghana, and ways of improving commercial exchanges, especially the trade in livestock. In 1968, Upper Volta was the first African nation to be officially visited by General Ankrah, and he was also the first Ghanaian head of state ever to be received at Ouagadougou. As professional soldiers, he and Lamizana found that they had much in common. "We met as brothers," General Lamizana told the writer shortly after he returned from Accra, "and we plan to consult each other frequently in the future."

This harmonious combination of official policy and personal friendship materialized in the many projects drawn up to improve and increase direct road, air, and telephonic communications between Ghana and Upper Volta. In Voltaic eyes, such projects have the great advantage of decreasing dependence on Abidjan's port and railroad, but in eco-

[31] Ouagadougou radio broadcast, March 18, 1966.

nomic terms the benefits of bypassing Ivory Coast are not certain. Asphalting of the road from Ouagadougou to the Ghana frontier, begun early in 1970, will surely facilitate interstate trucking and trade, but the improved road will not necessarily prove to be as economical as the old rail route to Abidjan. Currency difficulties still hamper the transfer of customs duties collected at the port of Tema,[32] and not all the Voltaic merchants are pleased by the prospect of giving Ghanaian traders free access to the Upper Volta markets.

Two other major obstacles which threatened the burgeoning cooperation between Ghana and Upper Volta developed at Accra late in 1969. First, the replacement of a military by a civilian government, in September, cut the ground from under the personal relationship that Lamizana had cultivated with the Ghanaian army officers. Then, the expulsion from Ghana of thousands of Mossi, some of whom had lived there for several generations, not only caused great hardship to individuals but aggravated Upper Volta's chronic unemployment problem. Significantly enough, their forced repatriation did not arouse as much resentment among the Voltaics as did that of a far smaller number from Ivory Coast.[33]

The restoration of civilian rule with Kofi Busia's election as premier, and the expulsion of Mossi laborers from Ghana, being setbacks to Ghanaian-Voltaic cooperation, were doubly gratifying to Houphouët. He had looked with a somewhat jaundiced eye on the rapid rapprochement between the Voltaic and Ghanaian military heads of state because it threatened to weaken Upper Volta's links with both Ivory Coast and the Entente. Ghana's expulsion affected only the handful of Ivorians who were resident there, and Dr. Busia's replacement of a military regime at Accra transposed to a

[32] *West Africa,* May 9, 1970.   [33] *Afrique Nouvelle,* April 15, 1970.

warmly personal level a relationship of cooperation between Ghana and Ivory Coast that had been simply official and formal since Nkrumah's overthrow. During his ten-day state visit to Abidjan in May 1970, Busia expressed his gratitude to Houphouët for "all you have been to me personally, and for the inspiration of your life and achievements." [34] Houphouët, for his part, showed Busia exceptional marks of esteem, and the two leaders on that occasion signed a treaty of friendship.

Ghana's fluctuating relationship with Upper Volta, which was a cause of deep concern to Houphouët, affected Diori to a much lesser degree, in part because of the striking lack of political contact between Ouagadougou and Niamey. Although Niger had a long common frontier with Upper Volta (far longer than that with Dahomey), border "incidents" and trade between Niger and Upper Volta had comparatively little influence on their relationship. Diori and Yameogo never exchanged official visits until 1963, despite their frequent encounters at conferences of the Entente. To be sure, in February 1960, Diori had rushed to the Voltaic capital to patch up the quarrel between Houphouët and Yameogo, but he was then mainly concerned lest Upper Volta withdraw from the Entente and thereby isolate Niger geographically from Ivory Coast. Niger's involvement with the Entente, however, was more the by-product of Diori's friendship with Houphouët than of direct economic self-interest, for although thousands of Nigériens worked in Ivory Coast, far more emigrated to Ghana, with whose government Diori was for many years on distinctly chilly terms.

Relations between Diori and Nkrumah almost reached the breaking point in 1964–1965 when the Ghana-trained Sawaba commandos tried to stir up a revolt among Niger's Hausas and then attempted to assassinate its president. On those

[34] *West Africa,* May 9, 1970.

occasions and during Niger's dispute with Dahomey, Hou-
phouët's protection and mediation were a great boon to
Diori, and the latter reciprocated by strongly supporting the
Entente's campaign against Nkrumah in 1965.

After Nkrumah's overthrow, Ghana's goodwill mission to
the surrounding Entente states naturally included Niamey,
where it poured oil on the troubled Nigérien waters. To
prove Ghana's sincerity, General Ankrah, in the spring of
1968, began expelling most of the 273 Sawaba militants cited
by Diori as having received active support from Nkrumah,
but their top leaders, including Djibo Bakary, had already
escaped from Ghana. That same year, Diori and Ankrah exchanged official visits and signed trade and transport agreements, and the presence of a Ghanaian observer at the
OCAM conference held at Niamey testified to Ghana's determination to promote interstate cooperation. Unfortunately for its development, the forced return from Ghana
in December 1969 of some 40,000 Nigériens in desperate
straits revived Niger's former hostility to the Accra authorities.

Not only was the Niamey government not equipped to
deal with the physical problems created by this unexpected
and massive influx, but it feared the economic and political
consequences of their return. Since most of the repatriates
were traders and not herders or farmers, there was no place
for so many of them in Niger's predominantly agricultural
economy. Of even more concern to Diori was the possibility
that they might upset his government's hard-won stability,
for the great majority of the Sawaba commandos responsible
for the disorders of 1964–1965 had been recruited by Djibo
Bakary among the expatriate community in Ghana.[35] Their

[35] Talk with Jean Colombani, former director of Niger's Security
Police, Niamey, Oct. 21, 1968.

presence will certainly aggravate unemployment in Niger and, it is feared, may also revive the Sawaba movement, which has been quiescent there in recent years.

It remains to be seen to what degree a rapprochement at the highest governmental level between the Busia adminis-tration and the Entente heads of state can alleviate the disastrous economic repercussions inadvertently caused by Ghana's large-scale expulsion of its alien African residents. Certainly the Ghanaian authorities will strive to repair the damage done, and Houphouët can be counted upon to do everything in his power to strengthen the nascent Abidjan-Accra axis. Prior to the expulsions, progress had been made toward associating Ghana more closely with the Entente as a whole, through the agreements reached for the distribution of the Volta dam's electric current to Togo and Dahomey, and the projects for a better coordination of their transport and telecommunications systems. Indirectly, France had given its blessing to a closer association between Ghana and the Entente states by promising Busia a loan of over £3 millions when he visited Paris during the fall of 1969.

Biafra

The third major divisive issue was Houphouët's recogni-tion of Biafra on May 14, 1968, which sharply differentiated his African policy from that of all the other francophone states except Gabon. None of his Entente partners followed his example, either because they disapproved of secession on principle or because their proximity to, and economic ties with, Nigeria made it impolitic for them to alienate the Lagos government. Houphouët's motivation was a complex of humanitarian, political, and economic considerations, most of which were not of equal concern to the other En-tente heads of state. Like Houphouët, they deplored the toll in human lives and misery occasioned by Nigeria's prolonged civil war, regretted the Africans' inability to settle it by negotiation, and resented the intervention of the great powers —especially the USSR—in an all-African conflict. They did not, however, share what may have been Houphouët's determining consideration, which was essentially personal and nationalistic. This was his wish to weaken West Africa's most populous and economically powerful state, whose influence and attraction for its neighbors constituted the greatest threat to the hegemony he was trying to establish over that area.

There is no doubt that Houphouët's support for Biafra stemmed to some degree from his sincere horror of violence, especially when its main victims were the Christian Ibos, and it also accorded with his long opposition to any form of federal government for Africa and to the spread of communist influence there. On the other hand, his Biafran policy conflicted with his equally long-standing opposition to changing inherited colonial boundaries and to the encouragement of dissident movements, which had been one of his main grievances against Nkrumah. Then, when his stand in favor of Biafra's right to self-determination boomeranged against him in the mini-revolt staged by the Sanwi autonomists in December 1969, Houphouët indignantly denied that there was any relevance between the two movements or indeed any inconsistency in his own stand.

The anti-Nigerian riots at Abidjan in March 1968, in which several hundred Nagots were injured, seem to have had no bearing on Houphouët's Biafran policy, but the state visit made by President Nyerere of Tanzania at about the same time probably did. Although Houphouët then publicly approved of Tanzania's recognition of Biafra, his long delay in officially following suit was generally attributed to the resistance put up by influential members of the PDCI politburo to such a policy. While Houphouët felt strong enough to override his own party's opposition, he did not attempt to impose his views on his partners. What prevented his recognition of Biafra from becoming a seriously divisive issue for the Entente was Houphouët's understanding and acceptance of his colleagues' reasons for supporting the Lagos government.

Both Togo and Upper Volta were too remote from Nigeria and too absorbed by more pressing concerns nearer home to feel more than an academic interest in Biafra. In principle their governments supported the policy of Lagos, but in interviews conducted during the fall of 1968 with many of their nationals, the writer was struck by their general indifference to the Nigerian drama. Among the Christians in both populations some sympathy for the Ibos was expressed, and in Upper Volta the Catholic hierarchy— presumably on orders from the Vatican—was taking a strong stand in favor of Biafra. Had the Catholic Yameogo still been in power at Ouagadougou he might have done so officially, but the Muslim Lamizana felt no such religious solidarity and, moreover, was at this time in conflict over other issues with both Houphouët and Cardinal Zoungrana of Upper Volta.[36]

The attitude of the governments and the peoples of Dahomey and Niger was markedly different and with good reason. Both those countries were contiguous with Nigeria

[36] Paul Zoungrana, the son of a Mossi mechanic and educated for the priesthood at Ouagadougou, Algiers, and Rome, was consecrated as West Africa's first cardinal by Pope Paul VI in 1965. To underscore his protest against Lamizana's reduction of official subsidies to mission schools, Zoungrana turned over responsibility for them to the state in 1969.

and consequently had close ethnic, religious, and commercial relations with the populations across their common
frontiers. In Niger, Diori's policy was molded not only by
Nigeria's geographical proximity but also by the Sawaba's
advocacy of a union with that country.[37] So porous was the
long (more than 2,000 kilometers) frontier separating them
that merchandise and individuals flowed freely across it, and
consequently a flourishing interstate trade supplemented the
existing ethnic and religious ties between the Hausas of Nigeria and those of Niger. The latter could readily sell their
food crops and animals for sterling in Nigeria's markets,
where they were able to buy rice and manufactured goods at
prices far lower than those prevailing in Niger, and the government lacked the means to control this contraband trade.
The populations of eastern Niger even bought their basic
food in Nigeria, and for the western Nigériens Maradi
served both as the distribution center for Nigerian imports
and as a commercial crossroads through which most of
Niger's peanut crop was carried to the Nigerian railroad for
export via Lagos. To be sure, Niger's exports could take an
alternative route to the Dahomean seaport of Cotonou, but
although that route had the advantage of lying wholly within
the CFA franc zone, it was slower and more costly.

By playing upon the Djerma chiefs' fear of Hausa domination, Diori succeeded in winning their allegiance and then
control of the government, and once in power he strengthened
his position by assiduously cultivating good relations with
the Lagos authorities. Nevertheless, so long as the Sawaba
found active support in Niger, the threat of a Hausa secessionist movement hung over Diori's head and influenced
both his domestic and foreign policy. As regards military
defense and moral support he could count on his agreements

[37] See Ch. 3.

with France and the moderate francophone African countries, and he used much of the financial aid he received from
both sources to develop Niger's resources, with a view to
diminishing the economic attraction of Nigeria. At the same
time, he worked to better the road communications between
the two countries and took the initiative in convening conferences to improve the navigation and utilization of the
Niger River.

Three times since independence, Niger has learned the
hard way how dependent it is on Nigeria's goodwill. In 1961,
when Nigeria broke off diplomatic relations with France as
a protest against French nuclear testing in the Sahara, Niger's
interests there were left without any official representation
in Lagos. Then the closing of Dahomey's frontier in reprisal
against Niger's expulsion of Dahomean civil servants, late in
1963, made the Lagos port and the Nigerian railroad for
some months the sole means of transporting Niger's exports
and imports. Conversely, in 1967, the outbreak of Nigeria's
civil war created currency and shipping difficulties for Niger's
transfrontier and foreign trade, and also caused the Niger-
ians to reverse the previous commercial current by seeking
their supplies in Niger.

Although warfare in Nigeria certainly diminished that
country's appeal for the Hausas of Niger and consequently
lessened the danger of their secession, there was never any
question of Diori's incurring Lagos's wrath by recognizing
Biafra. To make the Nigerian federal government overlook
his close ties with France and Ivory Coast, both of which
supported Biafra, Diori became the most zealous peacemaker
of all the francophone heads of state. He even induced
Biafra's Colonel Ojukwu to come to Niamey for talks with
the OAU's advisory committee on Nigeria, of which he was
a member. Although his efforts proved unavailing, they were

appreciated by the Lagos government, which, until then, had shown little interest in its northern neighbor. In normal times, Niger has little to offer that Nigeria really wants—a few million more people and vast stretches of unproductive land—whereas Diori cannot afford to be indifferent to events south of Niger's border. Although for the time being the dangers of annexation and secession have receded, the desire for union still exists among the Hausa tribesmen, and any revival of Sawaba militancy among the Nigérien refugees from Ghana might bring it once again to the surface.

Dahomey's attitude toward its neighbors of the Benin Gulf has been compounded of mixed, and sometimes contradictory, emotions. In that area, its leaders have consistently favored an economic union, mainly to increase legitimate trading with both Lagos and Lomé. As to their political relations with both countries, these have been consistently colored by fear and jealousy. The Dahomeans have envied their neighbors' greater prosperity and more rapid progress toward self-government and at the same time been apprehensive about their expansionist tendencies. In short, Dahomey has wanted Togo and Nigeria to accept closer economic ties that would be all to its advantage but has rejected any extension of those ties into the political domain. This ambivalent attitude, however, has been only one cause of the failure of Dahomey's successive efforts to create a Benin Union. Far more serious have been the differences in language, institutions, and tariff systems between anglophone and francophone countries and, specifically during Nkrumah's long reign, the opposition of Togo and Nigeria to the inclusion of Ghana in the Benin Union.

On the score of imperialistic ambitions, Dahomey obviously has far less to fear from little Togo than from gigantic Nigeria. As to transfrontier ties and smuggling, the relations

between Dahomey and Nigeria closely resemble those between other neighboring states of strikingly disparate strength.
Such official contacts as existed between them were excellent
if not close until, on the eve of independence in 1960, some
articles published in the party organ of Nigeria's Action
Group proposed that a referendum be held in Dahomey to
ascertain whether or not its population wanted it to become
a province of Nigeria. Although the Lagos government did
not press the issue, the suggestion was taken up by the
Nagots of eastern Dahomey, who favored unification with
their relatives across the border because they had long been
excluded from administrative and commercial posts by the
indigenous peoples of the Porto Novo region.[38]

Maga promptly refused to consider a plebiscite and denied
the Nigerian allegation that Dahomey was so isolated that
it needed Nigeria's protection. At a press conference he asserted that Dahomey was a firm member of the Entente,
which was an instrument capable of defending it against the
"neo-imperialism" of its English-speaking neighbors.[39] Then
in 1961 Dahomey, like Niger, suffered the economic consequences of Nigeria's severing diplomatic relations with
France, for much of the equipment needed to build Cotonou's deepwater port was for some time tied up at Lagos
because the Nigerian dockers refused to unload French ships.
However, relations improved after Dahomey established an
embassy at Lagos and official visits were exchanged. (In 1968,
the embassy was closed by Zinsou, but this time as an
economy measure.)

By early 1962, the prospects for an economic union with
Nigeria appeared to be at least as good as those of forming
such a union with Togo. At this point, however, Maga made

[38] *Afrique Nouvelle,* March 2, 1960.
[39] *The Economist,* May 7, 1960.

the mistake of trying to include Ghana, with a view to enhancing Dahomey's role as a transit country for Ghana's
merchandise and to opening up the Ghanaian market to
Dahomey's exports of fish and other foods. He found Olympio adamantly opposed to Ghana's inclusion, although Togo
favored a union that would comprise Dahomey and especially Nigeria. Nigeria was unenthusiastic about Ghana's admission to such a group and in fact was so generally indifferent to the whole proposition that the national sensibilities
of the Dahomeans were wounded, and their proposal for a
Benin Union died stillborn.

Dahomey has had even less real interest than Niger for
Nigeria, whereas the capital and port city of Lagos are
located so near the Dahomean frontier that they are of vital
importance to Porto Novo and Cotonou. Consequently,
during Nigeria's civil war it was imprudent for Dahomey to
show any sympathy for the Christian Ibos, as Dr. Zinsou was
to learn early in 1969 when he allowed Cotonou to be used
as a base for flying relief supplies to Biafra. Within two
months of his installation as president of Dahomey, Zinsou
had stated his opposition to secession in general, and to the
creation of African micro-states in particular. At the same
time, however, he left his own position regarding Biafra
open to doubt by asking rhetorically whether the boundaries
inherited from the colonial period were so valid that Africans should die to defend them.[40] Although he had offered
hospitality and government land near Porto Novo to some
7,000 refugees from western Nigeria and repeatedly denied
that the "mercy flights" included firearms in their cargoes,
the Lagos authorities refused to accept his affirmations of
political neutrality. This view was shared by the Nagots of
Porto Novo, and despite the badly needed revenues which the

[40] *Marchés Tropicaux,* Oct. 5, 1968.

airlift brought to Dahomey's depleted treasury, it swelled the opposition which brought about Zinsou's overthrow in December 1969.

Thus, for the first time, Nigeria became a factor in Dahomey's domestic politics, first by contributing to its fourth military coup d'état and then by influencing the northern Dahomeans to threaten secession early in 1970. The Lagos press, notably the *Daily Times,* while it condemned the northern secessionists, openly rejoiced at Zinsou's downfall. Furthermore, the federal government's victory in January 1970 encouraged Apithy to urge again that Dahomey leave the Entente to form another regional union, whose main asset would be access to the Nigerian market. In his electoral campaign for the presidency of Dahomey, Apithy contended that membership in the Entente had been not only of no tangible benefit to Dahomey, but was responsible for most of its woes. Specifically, he claimed that the expulsions of Dahomeans from Ivory Coast and Niger were at the root of his country's financial difficulties and complained that Houphouët treated Dahomey as an appendage to Ivory Coast, not as a coequal partner. The new union he proposed at that time did not include either Togo or Ghana but comprised Upper Volta and Niger, which were, along with Dahomey, Nigeria's next-door neighbors.

This attack elicited a strong reaction from Diori and Houphouët, who cited all the financial benefits that Dahomey had received from its membership in the Entente and taxed Apithy with ingratitude. They might well have added that the expulsion of alien Africans was a widespread phenomenon and not confined to the Entente. Houphouët and Diori could only be gratified that Maga, not Apithy, became head of Dahomey's presidential council, for Maga advocated the strengthening of the Entente. In mid-1970 the Dahomean embassy at Lagos was reopened, official visits between the two countries were exchanged, and a treaty of friendship was signed. Reportedly, the thousands of Nigerian refugees still in Dahomey have no wish to return home, nor does the Cotonou government seek to expel them. Although some Porto Novo merchants resent them as competitors, these Nagots are unique among alien African immigrants in that they have brought capital with them.

As before, the Entente countries seem unable to remain on good terms with both their anglophone neighbors at the same time. Currently all but Ivory Coast have cordial relations with Nigeria and feel hostile toward Ghana, but largely for geographical and economic reasons the trend now seems to be toward closer cooperation with Accra. The outlook for Ghana's formal membership is unpropitious, although closer economic ties are likely to develop.[41]

Steps were taken by both Houphouët and General Gowon of Nigeria in the autumn of 1970 to heal the rift between their two countries. At the OAU summit meetings in September 1970 at Addis Ababa, Nigeria made its peace with those African states that had recognized Biafra. Then, early in October, General Ojukwu, the Biafran leader who had taken refuge in Ivory Coast, was asked to leave that country in the wake of interviews he gave to some Western journalists. Houphouët interpreted his comments to them as a breach of the gentlemen's agreement by which the general had promised to desist from all political activities as the condition for his receiving Ivorian hospitality. This expulsion order, soon followed by arrangements for the repatriation of the several thousand Biafran children who had been flown to Abidjan during the Nigerian civil war, certainly further promoted Ivory Coast's reconciliation, if not cordial

[41] See *West Africa,* Jan. 15, 22, 1971.

relations, with its most formidable politico-economic competitor in West Africa.

South Africa

Houphouët's efforts in 1970 to improve his relations with General Gowon and Sékou Touré may well be set at naught by his initiative, in October of that year, concerning South Africa. Moved by the recent failure of the mission entrusted by the OAU to President Kaunda of Zambia to persuade the Western nations to stop selling arms to Pretoria, and by the general ineffectuality of Black Africa's attempts to pressure the white southern Africans by boycotts and liberation movements into renouncing their apartheid policy, Houphouët proposed to initiate a "dialogue" between the opposing forces. Only by such a peaceful and reasonable approach, he believed, could South Africa be persuaded to abandon its inhumane racist attitude and, at the same time, contribute to the economic development of the whole continent.

The Ivorian president could hardly have made his proposal at a more inauspicious time, for within a few weeks the Portuguese-backed invasion of Guinea had united Black Africans solidly behind Sékou Touré and reawakened their fears of, and hostility toward, any form of white neocolonialism. In the avalanche of adverse reactions to his plea, in which Houphouët was accused of seeking personal and national benefits, he found aligned against him not only the revolutionary African leaders but such moderates as Haile Selassie, Gowon, and Mobutu. Among the francophone states, only Gabon, Madagascar, and Dahomey followed his lead, and, among the anglophone nations, Ghana and Malawi. To be sure, surreptitious trade was carried on with South Africa by many of the continent's governments which either strongly dissented from Houphouët or remained prudently silent, but their spokesmen would not incur the opprobrium of majority Black African opinion by openly endorsing Houphouët's stand.

The OAU summit conference proposed by Houphouët for the purpose of discussing his proposal was not held, nor was there any public debate of that proposal at the meeting of OCAM heads of state early in 1971. Houphouët prudently allowed some months to elapse before reopening his campaign. In March, however, he was encouraged to do so by support from two new sources—President Bokassa of the Central African Republic and, more surprisingly, the Canadian government. On a visit to Abidjan, Canada's secretary of state for external affairs expressed approval of "any African efforts to achieve a realistic solution of the South African problem and offered the services of his government as intermediary in establishing contacts between black and white Africa.[42]

Heartened by these developments and still convinced that time and common sense were on his side, Houphouët held an exceptional press conference at Abidjan on April 29, 1971. He attributed so much importance to it that he invited more than 100 journalists, some of whom were flown in at his expense. To clear up misunderstandings, he explained his position at length. Africa needed peace above all, he argued, so as to counteract the underdevelopment that was its greatest obstacle to economic and social progress. If the Black African states persisted in their attempts to isolate South Africa and to encourage violent attacks on it by black nationalists, this could only lead to a war which they could not possibly win. Moreover, it would permit Peking to intensify the propagation of revolutionary communism, against which South Africa was the continent's strongest bul-

[42] *Marchés Tropicaux,* March 13, 1971.

wark. Together Africa's black and white peoples could and should settle its common problems. They were hampered in reaching this goal only by a racist doctrine which, he believed, the southern white Africans would gradually abandon as they experienced prolonged contact with their black neighbors. Without for a moment condoning apartheid, Houphouët said that he would be willing to accept the invitation proffered by the South African premier, John Vorster, if his visit would further the cause of peaceful and fruitful coexistence.

As of the present writing, Houphouët has not disarmed his critics, who continue to accuse him of sacrificing principle for material gain and, worse, of aggravating the disunity of Africa in general and of the OAU in particular. He has long been reproached by many black Africans for his pro-French attitude and for promoting the control of his country's economy by foreign capitalists, recognizing Biafra, and refusing to support the Arabs in their condemnation of Israel. Even among the African leaders who admire Houphouët's political courage and respect his integrity as a humanist and nationalist, his proposal has won no enthusiastic support. The OCAM has not committed itself, nor has the Entente as a body, although its individual members—possibly excepting Upper Volta—seem to have reconciled themselves gradually to his concept of a dialogue with Pretoria, on condition that it be conducted on the basis of equality.

Characteristically, Houphouët is not pressing for immediate action, because he realizes how widely unpopular and deeply divisive is his proposal. He also is aware that only very slowly, if ever, will the majority of black Africans concur in a policy that offends their sense of human dignity and national independence. Houphouët's initiative in the matter of South Africa has undoubtedly weakened the solidarity of the Entente, but its repercussions extend far beyond the confines of that organization. If, however, Houphouët's point of view ultimately prevails, he may well be regarded as the statesman responsible for changing the course of Africa's history in the years to come.

CHAPTER 7

Present Leadership and Traditional Authority

Heads of State

The Entente's evolution has been influenced both by economic and political issues and, perhaps to an even greater extent, by the leadership qualities of its elites. The traditional and modern elites have few contacts with each other, hence personal affinities and antagonisms between the heads of state have played an especially important role in a society so sensitive to personalities as that of Black Africa. Any analysis based wholly on quantitative data, however, would be misleading, for some member countries have had a series of heads of state, whereas others have not changed their top leaders since before independence. The biographical data in Table 4 give, despite obvious gaps, significant clues to the background of each Entente head of state, and these details throw some light on their political relationships and careers.

The age factor seems to have played almost no part in the relations between the Entente heads of state and a comparatively minor one in the coups d'état which have taken place in three of them. Olympio, Houphouët, and Soglo, the elders of the quintet, were never united by personal bonds. The longest and closest friendship, that between Houphouët and Diori, seems unrelated to their eleven-year age differential and to the stability of both their governments. In inter-Entente leadership relations, long familiarity and shared experiences—at school, in African or French political orga-

Table 4. The Entente heads of state

Country	Head of state	Birthplace	Yr. of birth	Religion	Education	Profession
Ivory Coast	Houphouët-Boigny, Félix (Nov. 27, 1960, to date)	Yamous-soukro	1905	Catholic	Medical School, Dakar	Doctor, planter, canton chief
Dahomey	Maga, Hubert (Dec. 11, 1960–Oct. 28, 1963; May 7, 1970, to date)	Parakou	1916	Catholic	Ponty School, Dakar	School-teacher
	Apithy, Sourou-Migan (Jan. 19, 1964–Nov. 27, 1965)	Porto Novo	1913	Catholic	Ecole des Sci. Pol., Paris	Accoun-tant
	Soglo, Christophe (Dec. 22, 1965–Dec. 17, 1967)	Parakou	1909	Catholic	—	Commis-sioned officer, French Army
	Alley, Alphonse (Jan. 3, 1968–June 28, 1968)	Parakou area	1930	Catholic	Military school, France	Commis-sioned officer, French Army
	Zinsou, Emile (July 17, 1968–Dec. 10, 1969)	Ouidah	1918	Catholic	Univ. of Paris	Medical doctor, jour-nalist
Niger	Diori, Hamani (Nov. 11, 1960, to date)	Soudouré, nr. Niamey	1916	Muslim	Ponty School, Dakar	School-teacher
Togo	Olympio, Sylvanus (Apr. 17, 1960–Jan. 12, 1963)	Lomé	1902	Catholic	London Sch. of Eco-nomics	Business-man
	Grunitsky, Nicolas (Jan. 17, 1963–Jan. 13, 1967)	Atakpamé	1913	Catholic	Ecole des Tra-vaux Publics, Paris	Engineer, Public Works Service
	Eyadema, Etienne (Apr. 14, 1967, to date)	Lama-Kara	1936	Protes-tant	—	Noncom. officer, French Army

Country	Head of state	Birthplace	Yr. of birth	Religion	Education	Profession
Upper Volta	Yameogo, Maurice (Dec. 8, 1960–Jan. 2, 1966)	Koudougou	1921	Catholic	Petit Séminaire, Pabré	Clerk, Public Health Service
	Lamizana, Sangoulé (Jan. 4, 1966, to date)	Tougan	1916	Muslim	—	Commissioned officer, French Army

nizations or both, and in professional occupations to a lesser degree, as well as marriages between members of the Entente's "first families"—have created the most durable ties, whereas in internal state politics the principal determinants have been tribal and regional origins.

In Dahomey, the generation gap has not been a cause of the country's successive upheavals, for Maga was replaced by Soglo, seven years his senior; Apithy, five years younger, followed Soglo; and Alley, the youngest of all Dahomean heads of state, who had the shortest tenure of office, was succeeded by Zinsou, born twelve years earlier than he. Among the Entente States, Togo's record is unique: in the course of only four years, that country had both the oldest and youngest presidents of the republic; in each of its three coups d'état, a younger man succeeded an older predecessor; and its current president is the youngest of all the Entente heads of state.

Although the age differential has not been a decisive factor in causing or preventing coups d'état in the Entente nations and has not distinguished the military from the civilian presidents of those republics, all of them have been old enough to have had direct experience of French rule. Five of them (Olympio, Houphouët, Soglo, Apithy, and Grunitsky) had been born before World War I, three (Maga,

Diori, Lamizana) in the same year during that war, and two others (Zinsou and Yameogo) very soon after it ended, thus all had spent their early years in the colonial period. Only Alley and Eyadema reached adulthood when French rule had entered a more liberal phase. No Entente head of state came to maturity after his country became independent.

The main qualifications for the civilians who have aspired to the top posts in an Entente state are a Western-type education, adherence to a world-wide religious faith, and—except for Maga—birth in their country's most developed region. These conditions are interrelated, largely because of the early introduction of Christian mission schools in some of the coastal areas. Among the Entente civilian heads of state only Diori, born in a hinterland country, is a Muslim, and none of them is a self-proclaimed animist, although animism is still the religion of the majority of Black Africans. They are all Catholic Christians, and this has given them an advantage, politically and culturally, over their compatriots who professed other creeds or lived in the less developed regions. (Togo's status as an international trust territory made it possible for Christian faiths other than Catholicism to proselytize throughout the country, so it is not surprising that the only Protestant head of an Entente state is the northern Togolese, Eyadema.)

Except in Niger, the influence of the European Catholic missionaries, which is strongest in Dahomey but is also appreciable in Upper Volta, has facilitated the political careers of such men as Apithy and Yameogo. To that influence can also be attributed the generally conservative character of the policies pursued by the civilian Entente heads of state. As to the professions they followed before taking up politics, the education they received in the mission schools was of minor importance because it rarely was locally available above the primary level. Civil-service posts in overseas French territories have usually been awarded on the basis of the diplomas held by an applicant, so attendance at a higher state educational institution has been indispensable for those seeking responsible and well-paid employment. Thus Yameogo, whose schooling did not go beyond the local Catholic seminary, qualified only for a clerkship in the Voltaic administration. Because the church was mindful of its own, however, he was encouraged to organize the Christian trade unions and through that channel achieved political prominence.

The four heads of Entente states who had graduated from universities abroad (Olympio, Zinsou, Apithy, and Grunitsky) were already high up on the professional ladder and therefore well known to the public and the administration before they sought elective office. On the other hand, the three others (Houphouët, Maga, and Diori) who had attended the best public secondary schools in French West Africa, occupied only intermediate positions in the bureaucratic hierarchy. Consequently, they had to start their upward climb from a much more restricted base, and it was through political activities supplementary to their professions that they acquired experience and exhibited outstanding leadership qualities.

Such was notably the case of Houphouët, who stands head and shoulders above all the other Entente leaders, less because of his age, education, or sponsorship by the Catholic church than because of his native abilities, experience, and prestige—in that order of importance. As the oldest head of any francophone Black African state, Houphouët is venerated by some as a "Living Buddha," but his age is a liability so far as the younger generation of Africans is concerned. Moreover, his superannuation has been compounded in their eyes by his shift in mid-career from a radical to an ultraconservative political and economic stance. At the time he reached maturity, Houphouët was able to gain political advantage from certain elements in his background. He was both a traditional chief—the only one among the Entente heads of state—and also a civil servant and prosperous planter who had had a modern scientific training at the Dakar Medical School. This unusual background enabled him to serve as a link between the old and the new Africa, and to these advantages he added flexibility, diplomatic skill, and long practice in African and French politics at high levels. Unencumbered by any doctrinaire ideology, Houphouët's approach was so realistic and pragmatic that on those crucial occasions when he was caught unawares by new trends in African opinion, he felt no hesitancy about drastically changing his course of action. Since the end of 1958, when he made Africa his permanent base, Houphouët has renewed his contact with the rural life of his country by periodic retreats to his native village and has revived the old African tradition of palavers by "endless dialogues" with various elements of the Ivorian elite, in which he encourages free discussion.

Ambitious as Houphouët is to maintain the position of leadership which he attained shortly after World War II, he is also a man of intense personal emotions. Loyalty and confidence are among the virtues he prizes most in his associates, and toward those he regards as friends he has reciprocated in kind. As for certain of his Entente colleagues toward whom he feels less warmly, Houphouët has striven to bolster their positions, for the stability of their governments is essential to the realization of his projects. It had taken him some years to convert Yameogo and Maga into devoted followers as well as helpful collaborators, and therefore it has been both emotionally and politically difficult for him to deal with the men who so unceremoniously overthrew them. With his contemporary, the amiable Soglo, Houphouët found it comparatively easy to establish friendly relations, but with Lamizana and Eyadema the process has been slower and less successful. As professional soldiers and political unknowns, neither had anything in common with Houphouët, who, moreover, deplored the means by which they had come to power. Aside from the fact that they had displaced his old friends and teammates, he feared that the easy success of their coups d'état might prove dangerously contagious in Ivory Coast.

Houphouët's leadership position has often been compared with that of Senghor, his perennial rival as standard-bearer for the moderate francophone African nations. The careers of the two men are similar with respect to their long experience in French politics, renown in Africa, and domination of their countries' political life. Both owe their domestic position to a strong party organization, mass support, and a willingness to tolerate opposition so long as it does not threaten their authority. In addition, they are about equally vulnerable to the criticism that they have sacrificed nationalist sentiments to the creation of an efficient administration and economic development. Consequently, both are now seeking new allies in their own national entrepreneurial class. In other respects, however, their leadership and their policies rest on dissimilar bases.

Senghor's prestige is higher abroad than at home because of his academic, literary, and intellectual attainments, and his power in Senegal derives from the support of the rural population, transmitted largely through the agency of party cliques and conservative Islamic leaders. The apparent contradiction between Senghor's liberal philosophy and the realities of his power base, together with his inability to appreciably improve Senegal's economy, have weakened his position. Houphouët, for his part, is less well known outside Africa than is Senghor, he has no philosophical credentials that would give him an audience among the intelligentsia at home or abroad, and his frequent drastic changes in policy have often disconcerted his most devoted followers. Ivory Coast is even more dependent on foreign capital and manpower than is Senegal. Nonetheless, Houphouët has counterbalancing assets in his flexibility and, above all, in his country's growing prosperity. Unlike Senghor, moreover, he is not the prisoner of any ideology—least of all his own—or of any traditional authority, either religious or secular, and his policy changes are made more on the basis of instinct, sentiment, and practical considerations than are those of the Senegalese president.

To be sure, Houphouët has not always read accurately or soon enough the signs of the times, either in Ivory Coast or in Africa, but he has shown a remarkable willingness to yield to opposition when he is convinced that it is at least temporarily insurmountable. In his own country and in the Entente, he has seriously underestimated the strength of economic nationalism. Belatedly, in Ivory Coast, Houphouët is coming to acquiesce in nationalist demands at the expense of foreign capitalists and alien wage earners. In the Entente, he is creating at long last a truly regional organization for the livestock industry and at the same time, widening the Entente's commercial frontiers by promoting a francophone West African free-trading zone, in which all his partners except Eyadema have accepted membership.

The tribal and regional origins of all the military heads of the Entente states except Soglo provide the key, first, to their choice of professions, and then, to the policies they have pursued since gaining control of their respective countries' governments. All of them came from minority tribes and from the least developed regions of their territory. Lamizana was born in western Upper Volta and is not a member of the dominant Mossi tribe, and Alley and Eyadema were from the backward northern tribes of, respectively, Dahomey and Togo. Enlisting in the French army offered such men a means of livelihood and, in some cases, a career that was not normally open to those who came from areas where there were few facilities for acquiring a Western-style education. Naturally these soldiers shared their kinsmen's sense of grievance against the more favored tribes and better developed areas from which virtually all the civilian politicians and civil servants derived. Added to this resentment was their scorn for the incompetence, venality, and petty quarreling characteristic of many of the civilian politicians. Furthermore, the discipline, esprit de corps, and training in the use of firearms they had acquired in the French army gave them the means of imposing their authority, and made the armed forces the only organized body capable of keeping order.

Among the older generation of officers who had risen from the ranks and fought together on the battlefields of Indochina and Algeria, there developed a kind of military fraternity. Bonds of that kind united Soglo, Lamizana, and, to a lesser extent, Alley, setting them apart from younger, better educated, but less experienced officers such as Eyadema and Kouandete, and almost totally isolating them from the civilian heads of the other Entente states. After they had consolidated their rule, the military presidents of the republics found that co-opting civilian technicians to aid them in the task of government was not enough, and increasingly they felt the need for international approval and popular cooperation. Their brief experiments with democratic procedures, before and after their coups d'état, were discouraging, yet they had to find some formula that would perpetuate the orderly development they had started, without at the same time permitting a revival of the old political intrigues.

Except in Upper Volta, the military leaders of francophone Africa seem to be returning to the African version of the single-party system, but with the essential difference that it is not usually "legitimatized" by the electorate and is headed and guaranteed by the armed forces. Such a government should benefit by more forceful backing and an inherent stability that its predecessors lacked. Nevertheless, to make such an autocratic system work, the military heads of state and of the national party will have to come to terms with, if not absorb and utilize, their country's elites. This is the same basic problem with which the colonial administration and the civilian independent African governments have had to cope.

The Traditional Chieftaincy

Initially France's colonial policy toward the traditional chiefs was the product of many complex and often contradictory attitudes. It was compounded of ignorance as to the socioreligious character of the African chieftaincy and of assimilationist theories based on the assumed superiority of French culture and the brotherhood of all mankind, as modified by France's insistence on imposing on its African colonies an authoritarian, highly centralized, secular administration, and on developing their economy so as to integrate it with, and subordinate it to, that of the Metropole.

As time went on, practical considerations tended to overshadow the ideological aspects of this policy, and they led to inconsistencies in France's attitude toward the chiefs. Direct

French administration became the order of the day in the accessible coastal areas, where export crops could be grown, where the population was more receptive to Western culture and economic practices, and where the small and scattered tribes were governed by weak chiefs. On the other hand, the more densely populated but poorer savannah and desert hinterland colonies were left largely undeveloped and under-administered by the French, who used the stronger customary chieftaincy as intermediaries with the population.

Everywhere the yardstick applied by the French administration became the usefulness of a chief as the executor of official policies and as an instrument for maintaining order. Thus village chiefs were left almost undisturbed, and the authority of the paramount chiefs was respected to the degree to which they proved cooperative with the local *commandants de cercle*. If a crisis arose, however, French officials did not hesitate to intervene in the succession of even such an important chief as the Moro Naba, either directly or by influencing the Notables in their choice of a candidate. Nevertheless, France's creation of a new administrative unit, the canton, and the appointment as canton chiefs of docile Africans who had no claim to traditional authority, were, generally speaking, the factors that most thoroughly undermined the customary chieftaincy.

In indirect ways, too, France both strengthened and weakened the chieftaincy as an institution. By being paid a salary, the chief was assured for the first time of a regular cash income, but because it was a percentage of the taxes he collected from the population and because this developed his taste for imported luxuries, the chief was tempted to abuse his power, thus enhancing the unpopularity he had acquired as a recruiter of forced laborers and of military conscripts. Then, by permitting Muslim and Catholic missionaries to proselytize freely in French Black Africa, the administration contributed to the decline of animism, from which many chiefs derived most of their religious authority. (This was primarily true of the coastal regions, where Christianity made its greatest inroads and where the chiefly power was already weak, for among the hinterland chiefs who became Muslims, Islamic theocratic concepts enhanced their power.) On the other hand, the administration's backing strengthened a cooperative chief's authority, and the development of export crops and foreign trade offered opportunities for self-enrichment that transformed the coastal chieftaincy into an embryonic rural bourgeoisie. At the same time, however, the introduction of a money economy induced many rural youths to emigrate to the fast-growing towns, where they tended to become detribalized. Their emigration had the dual consequence of lessening the chiefs' influence in the countryside and of adding to the urban elements who became increasingly hostile to the chieftaincy as an institution.

After World War II, the elective institutions and liberal legislation introduced into overseas France had similarly contradictory effects on the evolution of the traditional chieftaincy. The abolition of forced labor eliminated a major grievance of the population against the chief as a recruiter, but the new powers acquired by the modern elites who were elected to the territorial assemblies and French Parliament were often used to undermine the chiefs' residual authority. In Ivory Coast and Upper Volta, where the RDA gained a firm foothold during its radical period, the administration in the late 1940's encouraged the conservative chiefs to form their own parties and run for office. After 1951, when the franchise was expanded to include more of the rural populations, where the chiefs' influence remained strongest, this wider application of democratic practices in French West

Africa had the paradoxical effect of strengthening traditional authority at the expense of the urban modern elites. Consequently, when the francophone African territories gained independence in 1960, the authority of the customary chiefs had been weakened by their transformation into bureaucrats serving under the orders of French officials who had assumed many of their former functions, but independence had also strengthened the position of the chiefs who had adapted themselves to the new order.

Inevitably the attitude of the Entente governments toward the chieftaincy, as well as their capacity to deal with it, differs from the policy formerly followed by the French administration, but the overall repercussions on the chiefs' status are in some respects surprisingly similar. The Entente leaders are naturally more sympathetic than were the colonial officials to an institution so authentically indigenous as the chieftaincy, but they are even more adamant in their refusal to accept the chiefs as rivals to their authority and particularly as perpetuators of regionalism and tribalism among the population. Consequently, the African heads of state are even more insistent than their predecessors in their policy of molding the chiefs into agents of their administration and of curbing any impulse of the chiefs to play an independent political role. At the same time, however, the African authorities lack the means which the colonial administration had at its disposal to impose its will, either through the classical device of dividing-and-ruling or by the use of sheer force. Furthermore, the African heads of state find it traumatic to subdue their compatriots by armed force, as Houphouët learned during the Sanwi revolt. And they cannot count on the undivided loyalty of the new national armies, in which there has been a resurgence of tribalism and regionalism unrelated to chiefly influences. How damag-

ing this can be to the national government's authority has
been shown by Dahomey's military coups d'état, and on a
minor scale by the threatened mutiny of November 1963 in
the Nigérien army.

Another handicap under which the Entente governments
labor vis-à-vis the chieftaincy is the deepening of regional
and tribal divisions by politicians, who use such means to
further their personal ambitions. Since political rivalries in
the coastal countries of Togo and Dahomey are more regional than tribal, the chiefs there play a minor role in this
strategy. On the other hand, in hinterland territories such as
Niger, where the chieftaincy is much stronger, the competitive politicians address their appeals primarily to the traditional Negro chiefs. By and large, the relations between the
chiefs and the civilian governments are determined by the
size and concentration of the tribes, on the one hand, and the
comparative strength of the governing party's leadership and
of the modern elites, on the other. Since 1963, the establishment of military governments in three of the Entente states
has altered the preexisting relationship between the customary chieftaincy and the government. It has created virtually
an alliance between them in Togo and Upper Volta, but not
in Dahomey, where regional sentiment remains so strong
that in 1970 the north threatened to secede. In all the Entente countries the central authority, whether civilian or
military, is eager to enlist the cooperation of the chiefs, but
only on condition that they accept a subordinate position
politically. The modern elites, for their part, out of self-
interest or ideology, want to abolish the chieftaincy, either
on the ground that it is an "obsolete and abusive relic of
feudalism" or that it was willing to serve the colonial administration in menial capacities.

In the triangle situation represented by the government,

chiefs, and modern elites, the position of one of these elements in relation to the other two is so divergent in each of
the Entente states that few valid generalizations can be made.
The multiplicity of small tribes in the coastal countries
indicates the general absence of important chieftaincies, but
not necessarily the existence of a strong central government.
Both phenomena, however, are present in Ivory Coast and
now also in Togo, but not in Dahomey. Houphouët, as traditional chief of probably the most evolved Ivorian tribe,
the Baoulés, and as president of his party and of the republic, can cope effectively with the chieftaincy from a position
of unusual strength. This was shown both in his forceful
handling of the Sanwi and Bété secessionist movements and
also in his dealings with the Syndicat des Chefs Ivoiriens,
which has come to function as a special-interest pressure
group [1] and of which he is the honorary president. In general, his posture has been that of a benevolent despot, re-
quiring total obedience from the chiefs but also granting
them salaries and other amenities appropriate to their dignity and to the services they render to his administration.

Conversely, in Dahomey, the modern elites have largely
escaped control by the national government, and particularly
in the south they have been able for many years to vent their
spleen against the traditional chieftaincy. Descendants of the
kings of ancient Dahomey were absorbed in the French administration as canton chiefs and shorn of almost all but
their titular authority, and this made them vulnerable to the
attacks of the numerous Western-educated commoners. As a
result, none of those chiefs has even tried to create a political
party based on his traditional status, and any attempt they
make to assert themselves in such a capacity proves not only

[1] A. Zolberg, *One Party Government in the Ivory Coast* (Princeton University Press, 1964), p. 288.

futile but actually harmful to their position. This was spectacularly shown in July 1968 when King Gbefa of Porto Novo made a gesture of support for Zinsou which was so resented by Apithy's followers that they invaded his palace, and the army had to intervene.[2] In any case, the almost equal division of Dahomey's forty-odd tribes between the northern and southern regions prevents any tribal leader from forming an electoral constituency at the national level, hence Dahomey's civilian politicians have organized their parties on a regional basis regardless of their ethnic affiliations. Because Maga had acquired a following in the area where he taught school, northern regional sentiment crystallized around his person, and, albeit a commoner, he became the spokesman for the Bariba chiefs, who, however, have always kept him on a tight rein.[3]

Similarly, and for many of the same reasons, regionalism more than tribalism is the basis of Togo's parties. It is noteworthy that Olympio, the leader of the Ewes, was a "Brazilian" and that Grunitsky, his southern rival, was not even a full-blooded Togolese. Today, Eyadema seems to speak with an authentic northern voice and to express his fellow-Cabrais' fears of falling once again under Ewe domination. The wails of anguish emitted by the association of northern chiefs whenever Eyadema proposes to hold elections are probably genuine, although they reinforce his natural inclination to perpetuate his own military rule. In January 1971 Eyadema rewarded the chiefs for their support by appreciably increasing their pay.

Although a strong central authority seems to be the chiefs' best protection from the vendetta carried on against them by the Western-educated African commoners in the coastal

[2] *Jeune Afrique,* July 21, 1968.

[3] See D. Ronen, "The Two Dahomeys," *Africa Report,* June 1968.

states, this was not the case in Upper Volta under civilian rule. To be sure, the situation there was exceptional because the Moro Naba, although much of his authority had been whittled away by the French colonial administration, was still the greatest paramount chief in francophone West Africa. It was against the Moro Naba, his own tribal chief, that Yameogo carried on a personal feud, possibly because he was only a commoner and a modest clerk in the local health service, but certainly because the recently installed and French-educated Moro Naba had clearly displayed his political ambitions.[4] By 1962, Yameogo had abolished the chiefs' official salary, prohibited the wearing of any chiefly insignia, and decreed that no more traditional chiefs should be installed after the death of the incumbents. Not content with striking such devastating blows at the institution of the chieftaincy, Yameogo cut off the Moro Naba's electricity, water supply, and telephone in a fit of pique.[5] The Mossi emperor was reduced to living off the income from his own properties and a subsidy of about 7 million CFA francs a year granted him by Houphouët.[6]

Yameogo's campaign against the chieftaincy in general, and the Moro Naba in particular, was not inspired by a conviction that the chieftaincy was an anachronistic and harmful form of totalitarianism—his own rule was more autocratic and equally abusive—but by his refusal to share power with such a dangerous competitor. Lamizana, Yameogo's successor, has striven to achieve a better balanced relationship with the chiefs by restoring their official salaries and some of their former perquisites. He has been careful to show special consideration for the Moro Naba's dignity, per-

4 See Ch. 1.
5 Interview with Joseph Ouedraogo, Ouagadougou, Oct. 25, 1968.
6 Interview with François Bassolet, Ouagadougou, Oct. 24, 1968.

sonally decorating him with the National Voltaic Order, and in April 1968 he permitted him to preside over a meeting of the Syndicat des Chefs. This organization, comprising about 100 of the major Mossi chiefs, had been formed in 1953 but had become moribund under Yameogo. At this and successive meetings of the Syndicat, the chiefs expressed their gratitude to Lamizana and promised him their cooperation in developing the country.

In October 1968, Lamizana told the writer that he had no intention of abolishing the Mossi chieftaincy, preventing that tribe from selecting their future chiefs, or transforming them into bureaucrats, but that he would not let them revert to their former status in which they had formed a state-within-a-state. Apparently the Moro Naba intends to reassert himself as the chieftaincy's political spokesman, and he may even still cherish the hope of ultimately becoming the constitutional monarch for all Upper Volta, but the military government can hardly take this seriously. To begin with, it would not be acceptable to the 500 or so non-Mossi chiefs in the west, or even to the other *nabas,* whom the Moro Naba had alienated in 1958 [7] and even more recently by appointing against their wishes an unpopular candidate to the "throne" of Boulsa.[8] Undoubtedly, however, the Mossi chiefs intend to play a political role of sorts in Upper Volta, and they effectively did so in the legislative elections of December 20, 1970. Fourteen chiefs were elected to the assembly, and many observers then living in Upper Volta attributed the UDV's success in that vote to the chieftaincy's aggressive pressure on the electorate on behalf of that party.[9]

This evidence of a resurgent chieftaincy has revived the hostility of the young Voltaic intellectuals toward it, notably

[7] See Ch. 1.   [8] *Afrique Nouvelle,* Nov. 20, 1968.
[9] *West Africa,* Feb. 26, 1971; *Afrique Nouvelle,* Feb. 3, 1971.

that of the left-wing MLN which, two years before, had been persuaded by Lamizana that the chiefs were an intrinsic and valuable part of the Voltaic heritage and could become a useful instrument for promoting rural development.[10] That such a potential exists cannot be doubted. Even though the Mossi chieftaincy has dissipated much of its authority and lost its sacrosanct character by participating in politics and business ventures, it rests on so much wider and deeper a base than do the chieftaincies in the other Entente countries that it still exerts a great moral influence over the approximately 2.5 million Mossi living in Upper Volta.

Niger presents another aspect of the tricornered government–chieftaincy–modern elites relationship, which resembles the situation in Upper Volta far more than it does that in the coastal states. In both hinterland countries the chieftaincy has remained strong and the government has become increasingly so, whereas the Western-educated youth are few in number and weak in influence. Niger is the only member of the Entente that has a nomad problem and two clearly dominant Negro tribes, the Djerma-Songhai in the southwest and the Hausa in the southeast. Since the chiefs in those areas held (and still hold) the balance of political power, the two rival Black African politicians, Diori and Djibo Bakary, appealed openly for their support. Both men being commoners, neither could count fully on the loyalty of any of the chiefs, who cast the weight of their influence in favor of whichever of the two seemed more disposed to serve chiefly interests at a given time.

In the crucial trial of strength in 1958, Diori triumphed, thanks to the chiefs' backing. He rewarded his noble sponsors, mainly Djerma chiefs, with ministerial portfolios and about one-third of the seats in Niger's legislature. Diori also

[10] Talk with Joseph Ki Zerbo, Ouagadougou, Oct. 27, 1968.

kept at bay the young party militants of the PPN who wanted to follow Guinea's example and abolish the chieftaincy overnight.[11] Like Lamizana, Diori has almost convinced his youthful followers that the rural masses are so deeply attached to their chiefs that to abolish the chieftaincy would deprive the population of an essential part of its cultural heritage. He also pointed out that the chiefs were better qualified than any other agents to perform such useful functions for the government and party as those of maintaining order and collecting taxes in the rural areas. At the same time, however, he indicated that it was only a question of time before Niger's trained civil servants and party cadres would supplant the chiefs, who would then become a purely symbolic institution and merge with the local folklore.[12] Perhaps Diori actually believed that the chieftaincy would soon obligingly fade into the background, but this has certainly not proved to be the case. Even now that Diori has appreciably reinforced his party machinery throughout Niger, the influence of the chiefs seems not to have been significantly reduced. Prudently, Diori has cultivated the favors of the chiefs, both Negro and nomad, for he knows that the stability of his regime depends on their continued support.

As for the nomads, Diori's policy toward the Touareg, Peul, and Toubou chiefs has combined conciliatory positive measures with negative ones. On the positive side, he early joined the Organisation Commune des Régions Sahariennes (OCRS), appointed Mouddour Zakara, a Targui chief, to head the newly created Ministry of Saharan Affairs, and sought to reach an understanding with independent Algeria that would safeguard Niger's portion of the great desert. In

[11] Courmo Bourcogne and Hima Djibrille, "Rapports sur la Chefferie," mimeo. Niamey, Aug. 1959.

[12] As reported by A. Blanchet, *Nice-Matin,* Jan. 27, 1961.

1961, the OCRS financed so successful a well-digging program in the sahel area that its work has since been expanded by the Niamey government; the Minister of Saharan Affairs, resident at Agadès, has promoted the nomads' welfare by teaching them modern animal husbandry techniques and establishing more schools for their children; and Diori, despite the indifference of oil-rich Libya and Algeria, has set up an organization of Saharan borderland states with headquarters at Niamey. Even more effective in winning the nomads' cooperation have been his apparently negative measures, notably his refusal to encourage actively the emancipation of the nomads' Negro servitors, on whose services their traditional economy depends, and his restriction of the area cultivated by Hausa farmers so as to preserve the nomad herds' pastureland.[13] Diori hopes to stabilize the nomads in their present habitat and to discourage them from uniting with the independent Arab countries of North Africa.

To all appearances, Diori's shrewd and flexible policies have been successful, although less so among the few, scattered, and anarchic Toubou tribes than among the Peul and Touareg, who together account for some 730,000 of Niger's total population of about 4 millions. Not only have the latter tribes become more stabilized in the north and west, but Niger's laisser-faire official attitude and its prospects of large-scale uranium mining in Agadès *cercle* are increasingly attracting those alien Touareg who seek escape from the rigorous socialism practised by the governments of Mali and Algeria. Automatically this has reversed the tendency of Niger's nomads to emigrate for work in the Tamanrasset region, where Diori feared that they were being subjected to propaganda by Algerian irredentists. To be sure, Libya's flourishing oil industry now offers job opportunities that

[13] S. Kiba, "Problèmes Nigériens," *Afrique,* Jan. 1962.

have created a new migratory trend from Niger, but it has also revived the caravan trade between Libyan oases and Nigeria, which is benefiting the Nigérien Touareg nomads.[14]

There are dark spots in this otherwise encouraging picture, for the nomad herds in Niger are increasing more rapidly than the means of supporting them, and the Negro officials of their region are guilty of inflicting vexations on Touareg Notables.[15] On the whole, however, Niger has been more successful than any other Negro-dominated Saharan borderland state in integrating the nomads into the local society and convincing their chiefs that the government is solicitous of their welfare.

In modern times the fortunes of the traditional chiefs have fluctuated, but decidedly with more ebb than flow. They have had to adapt themselves first to a foreign secular regime and then to indigenous governments headed by Western-educated men, all but one of whom are commoners. These administrations have weakened the chiefs' political authority, both intentionally and inadvertently.

In the face of such assaults on its power, the chieftaincy has defended itself poorly. Withdrawal from public affairs or reluctant collaboration was the chiefs' general response to French rule, although a small minority accepted Western training and participated in the modern economic circuit. In a few countries they organized associations of chiefs, but these have been ineffectual, largely because the status of their members or their respective interests were so divergent, and sometimes so competitive, that they could never maintain a united front. By and large, in their attitude toward the chiefs the African governments have been more rigorous

[14] *Le Monde,* Aug. 12, 1969.

[15] J.-C. Froelich, *Les Musulmans d'Afrique Noire* (Paris, 1962), p. 305.

than was the colonial regime, because they have believed that the perpetuation of chiefly authority encouraged tribalism and regionalism and that the collaboration of the chiefs in the modernization of their country's economy was largely useless.

With time, however, the strongest of the Entente governments, whether civilian or military, have been showing more consideration for the chiefs, though not to the point of restoring their former authority. They now realize that the chiefs cannot be blamed for the gravest deepening of tribal or regional divisions, and that they can even become useful allies because they still wield influence in the rural areas and because they offer a counterpoise to the turbulent elements among their common adversaries, the modern elites. Even in the religious domain, where some politicians play up their alleged occult powers, there has been a curious fusion of the traditional with the modern, for in the eyes of the electorate the present heads of state in the Entente countries have assumed much of the authority that was formerly monopolized by the customary chieftaincy.

CHAPTER 8

The Modern Elites

Any study of the modern elites in francophone West Africa must give priority to the wage-earning component, including civil servants, and to the youth groups, both the young party militants and student associations. Although the members of these two main categories vary widely as to education, orientation, and pay, they have in common certain characteristics. First, these categories were created as entities by the French government wholly outside the tribal context. Secondly, their members have been integrated into their respective countries' "modern" society, and together they form a class resistant to traditional authority and also one economically privileged by comparison with the mass of the population, from which they have become progressively aloof.

Yet the modern elites cannot be regarded as completely alienated from the milieu from which they sprang, although alienation is greater among the civil servants and students than among the unskilled wage earners. A wage earner in whatever sector of the government or economy is bound by tradition to extend hospitality and aid to his kinsmen, and the higher his position the larger the number of relatives he must support. Students, on the other hand, are on the receiving end, acquiring their education through the bounty of their family or an official scholarship, hence they feel more detached from such obligations. Indeed, the higher they rise on the academic ladder, the less they identify themselves with the peasantry from which the great majority of them derives.

The case of the Western-educated civil servant who has become a prominent politician is particularly instructive, for his viewpoint has undergone a marked change at each stage in his career, reflecting the evolutive character of the modern elites.

Wage Earners

Statistics about the Entente's wage earners are woefully inadequate and inaccurate, for such official figures as are available rarely apply to the same year or to the same category of workers (see Table 5). Those pertaining to union membership are particularly unreliable because of the labor leaders' reluctance to give out information about their organizations, and their tendency to exaggerate the size of their following. Furthermore, the minimum wage (the SMIG, or *salaire minimum interprofessionnel garanti*) is not always a gauge of the workers' real income, for it must be related to successive devaluations of the CFA franc, variations in the cost of living, and what other means of livelihood, if any, the worker has at his disposal. Nevertheless, Tables 5 and 6 provide some data that are valuable for a comparative study of the populations and the status of wage earners in each Entente country.

Such a comparison makes clear the appreciable recent increase in the population, the wage-earning component, and the urban element in each of the Entente countries. Each nation in question has some distinguishing characteristic in these respects, but obviously Ivory Coast and Upper Volta represent the two extremes. Ivory Coast has the largest foreign element, urban population, and number of wage earners, the highest gross national product and per capita income, and the most rapid population growth. Upper Volta, at the other end of the scale, has the largest number of

Table 5. Wage earners and trade unions

Country	Wage earners (1,000's)		Unions *		SMIG (hourly rate, CFA francs †)		Per capita income ‡
	1960–61	1970	1960–61	1970	1960–61	1967–70	
Ivory Coast	181	250	UNTCI CNTC CASL CGC	UNTCI	40 (zone I)	58.3 (single zone)	$267
Dahomey	25	36	UGTD CNTC	UGTD CDTC UGSD CGTD	35 (zone I)	38 (zone I)	$72
Niger	18.4	27	UNTN	UNTN	24 (zone I)	30 (zone I)	$79
Togo	15	30	USCT CATC	UNTT CATC	27.5 (zone I)	35 (single zone)	$119
Upper Volta	21.5	29	UGTAN CASL CATC UNSTHV SATM SAAC	CATC CASL UGTAN UNSTHV	29 (zone I)	31 (zone I)	$50

Sources: *Europe-France-Outremer, L'Afrique d'Expression Française et Madagascar,* June 1970; *L'Afrique/70.*

* Full names of unions:

Ivory Coast
UNTCI—Union Nationale des Travailleurs de la Côte d'Ivoire
CNTC—Confédération Nationale des Travailleurs Croyants
CASL—Confédération Africaine des Syndicats Libres
CGC—Confédération Générale des Cadres

Dahomey
UGTD—Union Générale des Travailleurs du Dahomey
CDTC—Confédération Dahoméenne des Travailleurs Croyants
UGSD—Union Générale des Syndicats du Dahomey
CGTD—Confédération Générale du Travail du Dahomey
CNTC—Confédération Nationale des Travailleurs Croyants

Niger
UNTN—Union Nationale des Travailleurs du Niger

Togo
USCT—Union des Syndicats Confédéres du Togo
CATC—Confédération Africaine des Travailleurs Croyants
UNTT—Union Nationale des Travailleurs du Togo

Upper Volta
UGTAN—Union Générale des Travailleurs de l'Afrique Noire

inhabitants and of emigrants, the slowest rate of population growth, and the lowest per capita income. In both cases, massive migratory movements account for some of these differences—the immigration of foreigners into Ivory Coast, where they now make up about one-fourth of the total population, and the emigration to the coastal territories from Upper Volta, which thereby has a net annual loss of some 100,000 Mossi—for the natural rate of increase in both countries is only about 2.2 per cent per year. Niger has by far the biggest area, roughly four times that of the next largest country, Ivory Coast, and its population density and urban element are the smallest of all the five Entente states. Togo is distinguished by having the highest population density and fewest resident alien Africans, and although Dahomey is comparatively urbanized (9 per cent of the total population), Ivory Coast has more than twice the number of residents in towns of 10,000 or more inhabitants.

From the available data it is clear that the economy of all the Entente states is overwhelmingly agricultural, their populations are unevenly distributed, and their wage earners are proportionately few in number, lacking in skills, and poorly paid. In very great majority, their inhabitants, especially in the hinterland countries, are self-employed in farming, herding, and fishing, on a family—and often on a subsistence—basis. Only in the coastal territories are there appreciable numbers of paid unskilled laborers working on the coffee,

---

CASL—Confédération Africaine des Syndicats Libres
CATC—Confédération Africaine des Travailleurs Croyants
UNSTHV—Union Nationale des Syndicats des Travailleurs de la Haute-Volta
SATM—Syndicat Autonome des Travailleurs de la Mairie
SAAC—Syndicat Autonome de l'Aéronautique Civile

† 275 CFA francs = US $1; 1 CFA franc = 0.02 Metro. franc.
‡ Annual cash income, in terms of US dollars (average, 1967–1970).

cocoa, and oil-palm plantations and in the lumber camps and ports, and in Ivory Coast the great majority of these are immigrants. Remunerated employment is concentrated in the south, especially in its towns, because the rural exodus is accentuating the uneven distribution of the population and the trend toward urbanization.

By and large, the present position of the wage-earning class is related to the underdeveloped state of the economy, certain social customs, and the deficiencies in the educational system as regards both availability and orientation. The number of jobs and of schools, as well as the financial resources available, have increased in all the Entente countries since independence, but the employment opportunities have not kept pace with the demand. Wages, too, have been rising, but not so rapidly as the cost of living or as the expectations of a better life that were awakened by independence. The poverty of four of the five Entente countries, whose meager resources have been largely ignored by private capitalists, makes the payment of high wages incompatible with financing development projects and even with balancing the budget. In Ivory Coast, wages have been intentionally kept low so as to attract and retain the foreign capital investments required for its economic growth.

Niger, one of the most indigent of the Entente states, still has the lowest minimum wage, which in the decade since independence has been raised only once, and then solely for the highest category of manual workers. In the same bracket is Upper Volta, whose minimum wage was frozen from 1960 to 1969: even now it amounts to only 31 CFA francs an hour (about US 9 cents), but it is applicable to all workers throughout the country. Dahomey, no richer than Upper Volta, still has three wage zones, but it began life as an independent state with almost as high a minimum wage as Senegal and Ivory Coast, the two most industrialized territories in French West Africa. In 1964, the SMIG was raised by 3 francs an hour—far more than its economy could afford—which brought Dahomey's pay scale almost to a par with that of Ivory Coast, and, paradoxically, this comparatively privileged position has made Dahomey's wage earners among the most aggressive of all the Entente countries. Everywhere, however, the working class is becoming restive, even in Ivory Coast, where organized labor is the most tightly controlled by the government and where the minimum wage is one-third higher than in Togo, which ranks just below it. Curiously enough, Togo is the most backward of all the Entente states in regard to labor legislation. It was not until July 1969 that retired laborers were entitled to pensions and wage earners to a month's paid holiday, and workers there are still subject to the provisions of the French overseas labor code of 1952.

Throughout the Entente, the overall tendency during the past two years has been to raise the minimum wage and eliminate the differences between wage zones, but this policy cannot be specifically related to a marked improvement in general economic conditions, agitation by trade unions, or any special benevolence toward wage earners on the part of their respective governments. To be sure, all the Entente authorities are troubled by their inability to meet the population's demands for higher living standards and are genuinely eager to improve them, if only out of self-interest. They worry about urban unemployment and rural underemployment, and they have tried in various ways to remedy both. Strictly speaking, the term "unemployed" should be applied only to those jobless persons who formerly held paid positions, but the very great majority of the so-called *chomeurs* in the

Entente states are unskilled youths who have drifted to the towns, where they live parasitically at the expense of their more fortunate relatives. It is this element that has been the most vociferous in demanding not just the *africanisation des cadres* but the reservation of all forms of local employment to the indigenous population.

To meet this problem, the authorities have vainly tried coercion and persuasion—civic service, "human investment," and appeals to return to the land—as well as vocational training centers and "rural animation" programs both to improve farming techniques and to make the villages more attractive places in which to live. In Ivory Coast and Niger, the governments have gone even further and expelled or curtailed the immigration of alien Africans who have been filling the jobs that the indigenous population is neither qualified nor willing to take. Now that Ghana has adopted a similar policy, emigration—which every year has provided a livelihood for some 100,000 Togolese, 150,000 Dahomeans, 160,000 Nigérians, and 450,000 Mossi—can no longer serve as an escape hatch for such surplus populations. Difficult as it will be for the unskilled emigrants to be reabsorbed into their traditional milieu, it is the superfluity of public servants that places three of the Entente governments on the horns of their gravest dilemma.

Government Employees

Statistics concerning the bureaucracy must be viewed with caution, for more often than not they include not only civil servants but government agents, technicians under contract, clerks, and even messengers—in short, everyone on the official payroll. Clearly there has been a rapid increase in government employment in all the Entente states since independence (see Table 6). During the early 1960's all their governments dealt with the employment problem created by the rapid growth of the educated elite by multiplying the number of such posts. Each administration after its election sought to ingratiate itself with its constituents by reinstating the functionaries who had been dismissed or imprisoned by the preceding regime. Reorganizations of their local administrations also had the overall effect of increasing the number

Table 6. Government employees, as of 1969

| Country | Number of employees | | | | Salaries as share of nat'l budget (per cent) |
	African *	Technical	Cultural	Total †	
Ivory Coast	36,000	517	1,741	2,258	51
Dahomey	13,000	72	124	196	69
Niger	20,000	250	292	542	47
Togo	11,000	29	76	105	52
Upper Volta	15,000	209	268	477	56.1
Total	95,000	1,077	2,501	3,578	

Source: *Europe-France-Outremer, L'Afrique d'Expression Française et Madagascar,* June 1970.

* Approximate numbers, based on 1967–1969 data.

† In 1961, totals of French employees were as follows: Ivory Coast, 1,163; Dahomey, 258; Niger, 362; Togo, 86; Upper Volta, 369; grand total, 2,238.

of officials in the rural areas. Furthermore, government leaders found they could propitiate their opponents, declared or potential, by offering them administrative employment, such posts being graded according to the danger each such opponent was considered to represent for the party in power.

Not surprisingly, such a sudden and widespread increase in administrative operating expenses, together with the lavish use of public funds for personal advantage by many officials and politicians, brought the poorest Entente governments to the verge of bankruptcy. Their leaders, without curtailing their own extravagance, tried to cope with their financial crises by such devices as stopping any further recruitment of functionaries, freezing pay and promotions, and in some cases cutting government employees' salaries and family allowances. When such steps were carried too far, as was the case under Yameogo in Upper Volta, or when the political risk of drastically reducing the pay of government employees was taken, as in Dahomey, the result was a coup d'état. Only Ivory Coast could afford to maintain an overstaffed bureaucracy, but even there Houphouët, mindful of the revolt by civil-service unions in 1959,[1] was careful to keep its members under control and to avoid an over-rapid expansion of the government services.

Wage earners in general, and government employees in particular, feel that maintaining the state's credit is not their concern, and they are strongly opposed to the balancing of the budget at the expense of their own pay and perquisites. In justification it could be argued that the politicians are hardly models of the austerity they preach, and that the individual salaries of government employees are small even if their aggregate overburdens the country's financial resources. The employees are convinced that the money needed to meet their demands is available, either from local or foreign sources, and that the government can be pressured into granting them a larger share of the wealth, which they believe to be only their just due. This attitude was widespread during the colonial period and has not changed since independence, although it is no longer the viewpoint of the African leaders charged with the responsibilities of a sovereign government.

[1] See Ch. 2.

Both materially and psychologically, the French left a deep imprint on the African civil servants, which has now proved to be more of a liability than an asset. On the credit side of the ledger, the independent African governments inherited a strongly organized and centralized secular administration, in which the chain of command ran from the governor down to the village chief, and in which there was no separation of executive from legislative powers. That Africans were admitted to the bureaucracy, although to only a limited degree and almost wholly in the lowest echelons (except in the trust territory of Togo where the middle ranks were Africanized before World War II), was a factor of great social and economic significance. For the first time they could hold, as individuals, positions outside the tribal system, which gave them security, status, a regular salary, and—after 1950—family allowances.[2] The opportunities opened to Africans under the French administration for wage earning and government service proved to be a major solvent of tribal authority and regional loyalties. The key to entering the bureaucratic hierarchy was a knowledge of French and the three R's, and the price exacted for promotion in its ranks was docility to the colonial authority and the acceptance of a wholly new set of values. The latter automatically placed a premium on Western schooling, regular working hours, efficiency and technical expertise—all phenomena unknown in the precolonial period.

---

[2] The payment of family allowances to African functionaries had the unexpected effect of encouraging polygamy as well as increasing the birthrate. The head of a family to which the allowance was paid often used the money not for the welfare of his children but to pay the bride-price for another wife. The children resulting from such marriages also became eligible for family allowances, and so the process could be continued profitably as long as the functionary held office.

Among the liabilities inherent in the French administrative legacy was an overlarge bureaucracy, which set educational and living standards that caused a rift between the African civil servants and the mass of the population, and which also placed an unjustifiably heavy burden on the individual country's finances. Under the French system, government service became the goal of ambitious young Africans, and virtually all who held any accredited school diploma were either on the government payroll or felt themselves entitled to be. Moreover, after World War II, they could compete for elective office without sacrificing their civil-service status, and since they represented almost the totality of the African Western-educated elite, it was former bureaucrats who became the political leaders of francophone Africa.

After independence, they simply took over the top-heavy colonial administrative structure and adopted their predecessors' standards of living, which included large salaries, free housing, and various perquisites. Unfortunately, only a handful of them had the training, experience, and ideals of public service required to fill adequately the posts they inherited. Consequently, the rapid expansion of the bureaucracy was accompanied by a general decline in professional competence and integrity, but not in its numbers or its members' demands for improvement in the already privileged status. Everywhere except in Niger their pay absorbed more than half the local revenues, but only in Ivory Coast did they constitute as much as 1 per cent of the total population.

This disproportionate favoring of one very small segment of the population has reversed the preindependence relationship between the governments and their bureaucracy. When it came to dealing with their common enemy, the colonial administration, the nationalist politicians—themselves former bureaucrats—naturally supported the demands of the African civil servants for equality with French officials. Now the government leaders are asking a *quid pro quo* for such support—that is, the civil servants' help in strengthening the party in power and in modernizing the country's economy— but they find themselves faced with an uncooperative and entrenched administrative bourgeoisie. Although they have some sympathy for the plight of the great majority of underpaid government employes and find among the civil servants the few technicians indispensable for keeping the administrative machinery running, the political leaders of the Entente do not fully trust the loyalty, honesty, or professional competence of their officials. Because these governments regard the bureaucrats as an overprivileged minority and because it was easy to tax their salaries at the source, the civil servants have borne the main brunt of official austerity measures.

The Entente government leaders seem to accept embezzlement as inevitable, provided it is kept within "reasonable limits," and in any case they are often in the position of pots which call the kettle black. What they find intolerable is that the civil servants are no more than lukewarm members of the ruling party, and are frequently at loggerheads with party militants over their respective areas of competence, notably in the hinterland states. While Diori and Yameogo sometimes chided their party militants for interfering in activities that are properly administrative, they even more strongly reproached their officials for behaving like autocrats toward the people under their control and for not promoting the ruling party's interests in the rural areas. For the time being, the incumbent governments must make do with the existing bureaucracy, but in each of the Entente states there has been set up a school of national administration [3] to train a new generation of local candidates for public office, and to inculcate in them a "civic spirit" and party discipline. Ivory Coast is the only Entente state to have gone so far as to forbid civil servants to run for elective public office.

The Entente's military governments are even less indulgent than their civilian predecessors toward the civil servants' demands and toward corruption, but their commanding officers are naturally not involved in the same conflict between party and bureaucratic interests and are concerned solely with the administration's efficiency and cost. As regards efficiency, the present governments have an ever wider choice of administrators, for the number of qualified candidates has increased with the spurt in education that has followed independence and with the lack of alternative employment available in the private sector. Even in Ivory Coast, the top managerial posts are still in the hands of foreign firms which control the country's booming export-import trade, and the job opportunities open to Ivorians, albeit increasing under pressure from Houphouët, are still less attractive to the local elite than is government employment.

The Trade Unions

In their relations with the Entente governments, civilian or military, the wage earners are by no means wholly defenseless. Not only are the latter vital for the country's development, but in some categories of employment they possess organizations to represent their interests (see Table

[3] The economic aspect of this policy is very debatable. In Niger, for example, the cost of training a single civil servant at the national school of administration comes to 700,000 CFA francs—an enormous sum when compared with Niger's annual average cash income of about 24,000 CFA francs. See *Marchés Tropicaux*, Oct. 19, 1968.

5). The strongest of these are the civil-servants' unions, and the weakest those of manual laborers. But even when those organizations cannot attain their members' objectives by means of collective bargaining, demonstrations, or strikes, they still have other effective weapons, such as passive obstructionism which takes the form of inconspicuous graft, or absenteeism, or simply inertia.

In the Entente states, manual laborers in general and migrant workers in particular are the most poorly organized—for obvious reasons. Since the great majority of migrants are agricultural laborers dispersed among the coastal plantations and lumber camps, it is geographically difficult for them to organize. Moreover, both they and the migrant white-collar workers—the Dahomean and Togolese civil servants and clerks—are usually bound by verbal or written contracts, and, besides, as aliens they are either not accepted as members by the indigenous unions or are afraid to organize themselves lest they jeopardize their positions. Perhaps an exception should be made in regard to the union of the Voltaic and Ivorian *cheminots,* whose members work for the Abidjan-Niger railroad. However, this union includes the two categories of manual and clerical workers, and the liaison committee they have formed rarely meets because their respective interests are too divergent.

Probably the strongest unions of strictly manual laborers are those in the building industry and in the ports, because they are concentrated in urban centers, where, on occasion, they can make common cause with other disgruntled workers or with the unemployed. This has notably been the case in Cotonou, where there are almost no immigrant workers and where the strikes called by the unions have been more effective when supported by the floating population of unemployed youths. In Abidjan, on the other hand, the jobless nationals not only have not supported the dockers' strikes but have attacked the latter's union because its members are aliens.

At the other end of the organized labor gamut come the unions of government employees, of which the most aggressive are those of civil servants. Although the latter did not get so early a start in the Entente territories nor benefit so much by the early sponsorship of French political parties and labor federations as did those of Senegal, Soudan, and Guinea, they rapidly forged ahead owing to the homogeneity of their membership, their monopoly of technical skills, and their concentration in the capital cities.

After World War II, when the formation of trade unions was encouraged by the colonial administration, the RDA, backed by the French Communist Party, and the Christian unions, sponsored by the Catholic missionaries, organized the wage earners in their respective strongholds. Those of the RDA were in Ivory Coast, the Bobo-Dioulasso region, and Niamey, whereas the Christian unions flourished mainly in Dahomey, Togo, and the Mossi area of Upper Volta. Except for the CGT unions organized by Djibo Bakary in western Niger under the aegis of the parent labor federation in France, the decisive influences shaping trade unionism in the Entente territories have been local and African political and economic developments.

In the late 1950's, the movement toward African labor unity and autonomy in general, and the constitution of the UGTAN in particular, had important repercussions on the RDA unions of the Entente area, which had already been split by the reorientation of Houphouët's policy away from radicalism and toward cooperation with the French administration and businessmen. The only territorial RDA unions that failed to follow Houphouët's lead were those of Niger, where Djibo Bakary—so long as he held power—insisted that his followers hew to the Marxist line and that organized labor give precedence to revolutionary political goals over strictly professional ones. This policy coincided with the objectives of the UGTAN, of which the most radical unions in the Entente states became territorial branches, under various names. Then, early in 1959, after the UGTAN headquarters were moved to Conakry, its secretary-general, Sékou Touré, charged its members with the mission of destroying colonialism in francophone Africa and also of undermining those African leaders whom he considered to be neocolonialist. This directive caused alarm in the conservative ranks and another rift in the RDA labor movement, but this time at the territorial level.

In the territories where the RDA unions were strongest, governmental pressure succeeded in divorcing some of them from the orthodox UGTAN movement and, after giving them an autonomous status, brought them under the ruling party's control. At Abidjan this move was prompted by Sékou Touré's utilization of the local UGTAN branch to stir up the civil servants against Houphouët's government, and in Niger it was Diori's fear lest Djibo encourage similar unrest that induced him to follow suit. In Ivory Coast and Niger, the governments gradually united all the labor unions into a single federation, which became the executor of its economic policies and whose top officials became members of the ruling party's politburo.

The situation of organized labor in Dahomey and Togo, and to a lesser extent in Upper Volta, differed from that in the other two Entente states in several respects. In the first three mentioned, the influence of the Christian missions was stronger than that of the orthodox branches of the UGTAN and, although the Confédération Africaine des Travailleurs

Croyants (CATC) had pioneered the labor-autonomy movement in francophone Africa, its goals were strictly professional and deliberately apolitical. Since the CATC's territorial branches did not seek political power and benefited by aid from the Catholic missions and some anticommunist international labor federations, their contentious activities were confined to disputes with the government and the *patronat* over wages, hours, and labor legislation. In Dahomey, Maga's attempt to unite all the unions into a single federation did not survive his short-lived single party. In Upper Volta, Yameogo never even tried to force the numerous Voltaic unions into a single organization, although he was in almost constant conflict with the most militant of them. For different reasons, Olympio, albeit an autocrat politically, permitted the existence of two labor *centrales,* one of which was the UGTAN– oriented Union Nationale des Travailleurs Togolais. There organized labor was so weak that Olympio never bothered to draft a national labor code, as the other francophone states had done after independence.[4] Togo's current economic policy is increasingly nationalistic, but Eyadema has largely ignored the UNTT's demand for radical measures.

In all the Entente states, even those with the strongest central governments, a residue of radicalism still exists among members of the civil-servants' unions, many of which have maintained close ties, if not affiliation, with the UGTAN, international communist labor organizations, and the revolutionary All-African Trade Union Federation. Probably because these unions comprise the most literate and politically conscious elements of the wage-earning class, the resolutions passed at their congresses abound in denuncia-

[4] National labor codes were promulgated for Dahomey and Niger in 1962, for Ivory Coast in 1964, and for Upper Volta in 1967.

tions of imperialism in Africa and Asia and of nuclear testing, demands for the nationalization of public utilities, and criticism of their territorial governments' acceptance of aid from capitalistic countries, membership in the Entente, and general mismanagement of national affairs. They also share with the less militant unions more strictly local economic objectives, such as higher pay, shorter hours, larger pensions and family allowances, full employment, effective rent and price controls, and better legislative protection. The one specific issue on which they all stand united vis-à-vis both their governments and the *patronat* is their insistence upon reserving all forms of employment to nationals.

Generally speaking, the *africanisation des cadres* had been achieved in the Entente administrations by the mid-1960's. Consequently, such Europeans as are still employed in that domain are at least nominally advisers, and Houphouët's dismissal of his French finance minister in January 1966 was an outstanding victory for the proponents of Africanization. Even though, as of 1970, there were one-third more Frenchmen serving in the Entente states than ten years before, those in the cultural field were twice as numerous as the technicians (see Table 6). To be sure, many of the so-called technicians have been actually running the departments to which they are assigned as consultants. This is notably the case in Ivory Coast, where 21 per cent of all the French "agents of cooperation" serving throughout francophone Black Africa and Madagascar are employed. Indeed, the French advisers' insistence on being given a free hand is responsible for the unusual degree to which the local government institutions there are independent of the central government.[5] Because the French government pays their

[5] See M. Staniland, "Local Administration in Ivory Coast," *West Africa,* March 9, 16, 1968.

salaries and the Africans generally recognize their own inability to fill posts that require more advanced training and experience than they have yet acquired, the increase in French personnel has not aroused as much local opposition as has the employment of alien Africans, for the latter occupy the more subaltern positions which the indigenous population feels capable of holding.

As regards the civil service, the governments of Ivory Coast, Niger, and Upper Volta, while yielding to the pressure to eliminate the Dahomeans and Togolese, are reluctant to dismiss their European advisers. One reason is their fear lest an administration staffed by nationals will be less efficient, more corrupt, and unduly influenced by nepotism. In any case very few nationals are qualified to replace the incumbent foreigners. Another, more political, reason is their lack of confidence in the loyalty of their young university graduates, many of whom were radicals in their student days. Although office-holding is notably soothing to erstwhile revolutionaries and the bureaucracy has been rapidly expanded to give employment to more young people, the top leadership of the Entente states is financially and politically reluctant to give them the high-salaried and responsible posts they demand. That such apprehensions are amply justified has been shown by the number of plots and coups d'état in the Entente states which have been spearheaded or actively supported by indigenous government employees. Thus far, the Entente government leaders have tried to steer a middle course between the dangers of giving the young educated radicals a voice in policy-making decisions and those of ignoring or suppressing them.

The political role played by the civil-servants' unions in Dahomey, and to a lesser extent in Upper Volta, illustrates how easy it is for the best educated among the modern elites

to overthrow a weak government that has not been responsive to their demands, but also how difficult it is for them to
attain their objectives in so doing. In both countries they
are worse off than before as regards salary, perquisites, and
immunity to prosecution for embezzlement and for forging
their academic credentials. This failure results from the
unions' basic weaknesses—numerical, organizational, and
psychological. Although in the aggregate the unions represent only a fraction of the active population, they have not
only separate organizations for civil servants, clerks. and
skilled and unskilled laborers, but also subdivisions within
those categories, and this disunity pertains even to the two
countries where there is a single labor federation.

The Union Générale des Travailleurs de la Côte d'Ivoire
totals 100,000 members out of 220,000 wage earners, and is
composed of 190 unions which are often at loggerheads with
each other. On a much smaller scale, this is also true of the
Union Nationale des Travailleurs du Niger, which is made
up of thirty-one "autonomous" unions, more than half of
whose members are civil servants. In Dahomey and Upper
Volta, where the political leadership has felt insecure, the
multiplicity of unions has actually been encouraged by the
government with the aim of keeping labor weak and divided.
Time has proved in the Entente states that only a strong
central government, like that of Ivory Coast, can maintain
control and unity in a single national federation.

In bargaining with the government and the *patronat,* the
unions are handicapped by a lack of funds that can be traced
to their members' poverty and their mistrust of the union
officials' honesty and competence. The great majority of
union members cannot or will not pay dues, which average
only 50 CFA francs a month in the Entente states, hence
they are unable to sustain a prolonged strike in support of

their demands. So the general practice has been to call a lightning strike, often without formulating demands, as a warning not to the *patronat* but to the government, because it is the largest employer of labor, the source of legislation, and the more sensitive to such pressure. In fact, only thanks to government and party subsidies or, as in Dahomey, to aid from international organizations, do many unions survive.

The unions' dependence on external financial sources has reinforced their tendency to look to the government both for jobs and favors, and only a considerable development in the private sector of the economy offers any prospect of breaking this vicious circle. At the present writing, the general attitude of the Entente's governments toward organized labor remains ambivalent. On the one hand, the government hopes, by encouraging unionization, to appear "modern" in the eyes of the ILO and the world and, by expanding union membership on a national scale, to eliminate tribalism and regionalism. On the other hand, the government intends to keep labor on a tight rein to prevent the unions from creating trouble for it and from alienating the foreign investors on whom the country's prosperity depends.

Nevertheless, the most serious liability for a healthy development of trade unionism in each of the Entente states is less the government's attitude than that of its civil servants, who now dominate the organized labor movement. This is notably the case in Dahomey, where they have wantonly overthrown successive governments without concern for the welfare of their country or of a majority of their compatriots. Unable to bring off a coup d'état without help from the army, they are incapable either of accepting the austerity required to remedy Dahomey's dire financial plight, or of themselves taking over the government. Dahomean government employees are not ideological revolutionaries who want to carry out a specific national or foreign policy, nor do they want the responsibility of power. This is also true of the analogous unions in Upper Volta and Togo, where their leaders made no attempt to fill the political void which followed the overthrow of Yameogo and the murder of Olympio, merely hoping that the next government would prove more amenable to promoting their interests.[6] The recent decline in labor agitation in those three countries suggests a growing recognition of the futility of such negative action, particularly vis-à-vis a government controlled or backed by the army. At the same time, the increasing restiveness of the Nigérien and Ivorian labor federations indicates the path which the others may follow—that is, wresting specific concessions from the government by short-lived nonviolent demonstrations, but concurrently disclaiming any intention of conducting subversive activities.

The self-interested attitude characteristic of the Entente civil servants is in part a legacy of the colonial regime and in part derives from social customs. Because they were the employees of a foreign administration, the African bureaucrats developed no tradition of public service, and because they belong to a society in which primary loyalties are given to family and tribe, they find it natural to practice nepotism and to chisel from public funds. On a recent visit to many government offices in the Entente states, the writer was impressed by the overstaffing of the bureaucracy with men and women, many of whom were not working but simply sitting or sleeping at their desks—when they were not totally absent. This type of African government employee believes

[6] Joseph Ouedraogo, who headed the joint committee which engineered Yameogo's downfall, told the writer that the unions had had no intention of bringing about his overthrow and only aimed at making him rescind his recent antilabor measures.

that his education or relationship to an influential politician automatically entitles him to a well-paid and prestigious post for life, whose benefits he shares with his family and which requires of him no more individual effort than the irregular act of presence. This attitude is unlikely to change unless there is a radical transformation of the educational system, which breeds a generally parasitic diploma-elite and which is too costly for the state's revenues to support.

Youth and Student Organizations

If wage earners represent a very small proportion of the working population in the Entente states, the students form an even less numerically significant segment of the youthful population in countries where now nearly half of all the inhabitants are under twenty years of age. Yet what the students lack in numbers, they make up for in other respects. They are highly articulate and conscious of being an elitist group whose members inevitably—and too slowly, in their own opinion—are assuming positions of leadership in their respective nations. As regards their ideological orientation, the students naturally most closely resemble the incumbent civil servants, who in their time represented the largest educated element in French West Africa but who now appear to the younger generation of university graduates to be ignorant fossils clinging over-tenaciously to power. In principle, the students identify themselves with the working population, and on occasion they have joined forces with the wage earners and civil servants to overthrow a government regarded as inimical to their common interests, but they have never been able to maintain this solidarity or even unity among themselves. Indeed, so disparate are the interests of the rural illiterate and of the urban educated youth in general that all efforts made either by themselves or by the governments to bring them together in interterritorial or even national organizations have failed.

During the colonial period there existed only a few youth organizations in the Entente territories, the great majority of which were either of a sports, folkloric, or philanthropic type. The government sponsored the scout movement for boys and girls, and the Christian missions had their own youth associations—all of which were perforce apolitical. Few attended secondary schools and even fewer went abroad for higher education; among the latter only a handful became involved in the anticolonial organizations founded by other overseas students in France.

After World War II, a notable effort was made by the French government to increase schooling in its African federations and to offer more scholarships for study in France. Since this expansion coincided with the introduction of elective representative institutions in francophone Africa, it was inevitable that it should lead to a new phenomenon—a deliberate politicization of youth by political parties. A large proportion of the African students in France were organized into territorial associations, and these soon became members of the communist-dominated Fédération des Etudiants de l'Afrique Noire Française (FEANF). Not surprisingly, the FEANF had a strongly anti-imperialist bias, and its members acquired a Marxist vocabulary and view of international affairs. To a limited degree, this trend affected French West Africa's most advanced secondary schools, at Dakar, whose students came from all the francophone African territories, but it was not until the *loi-cadre* of 1956 that student unrest spread to the individual territories. At that time strikes occurred in widely dispersed *lycées* and colleges, noteworthy for their synchronization and their general spirit of revolt against authority.

Academically speaking, the most significant developments in the postindependence period have been the retention of the French school system with its "equivalence of diplomas," a very rapid increase in educational facilities, especially at the primary level, and a widening of the gap between the largely illiterate rural youth and those with recognized academic credentials. In the political domain, there has oc-

Table 7. School attendance and education budgets

Country	Primary schools				Secondary, normal, and technical sch. enrollment		University enrollment		Education cost in 1969 (% of national budget)
	Attendance rate *		Enrollment						
	1960–61	1969–70	1960–61	1969–70	1960–61	1969–70	1960–61	1969–70	
Ivory Coast	36.5	49.0	238,772	407,600	13,054	51,000	744	2,108	22
Dahomey	30.0	33.0	88,189	135,000	4,069	17,943	356	705	25
Niger	4.8	10.8	26,030	82,000	1,521	4,646	20	130	10
Togo	37.0	46.0	87,000	208,000	6,110	17,000	173	643	20
Upper Volta	8.0	9.5	55,598	94,500	2,955	11,400	200	583	16

Sources: *Europe-France-Outremer, L'Afrique d'Expression Française et Madagascar,* 1960–1970 (yearly issues); *L'Afrique/70.*

* Percentage of school-age children attending school.

curred a trial of strength between university and some secondary-school students on the one hand, and, on the other, the incumbent party or military leadership. This situation differs in degree rather than in kind, as between the coastal and the hinterland states of the Entente. In no Entente country do even half the school-age children attend school (see Table 7), but the percentages in towns and countryside vary widely. Nevertheless, the cost of maintaining the French system is becoming increasingly prohibitive everywhere, particularly in view of the results obtained, culturally, economically, and politically. The students resent the paternalism and authoritarianism of the national governments even more than they did that of the colonial administration, which, moreover, had fewer compunctions about suppressing their insubordination and less need of the students' cooperation.

The Entente governments are increasingly concerned by the financial burden involved in supporting an expanding school system, the majority of whose students will not or cannot be integrated into the framework of the national economic-development plans they have drawn up. There are two salient factors in this situation: the refusal of even primary-school certificate-holders to engage in manual labor and of many foreign-university graduates to return home; and the number of school drop-outs and of "failed A.B.s" who, either because they cannot find jobs or are unwilling to take those available, swell the already large ranks of urban unemployed. The aggregate result of such problems is the growing trend toward a drastic reform of the primary-school system, while the existing secondary and university systems have been left largely intact, except that greater stress has been placed in their curricula on African history, geography, and culture. It is noteworthy that such changes as have been made were initiated by the Entente governments and were not a response to the demands of African students, whose long-standing fear is that they be denied access to foreign universities and that they receive what they call a "marked-down" education. (The euphemistic phrase, "equivalence of diplomas," has been devised to disguise what will be the most unpalatable aspect of the curriculum reform—that the validity of the degrees soon to be conferred by francophone

African *lycées* and universities will no longer be on a par with that of French degrees. This means that their holders will not be automatically admitted to French institutions of higher learning.)

Because the hinterland states are faced with greater practical problems than the coastal ones, the reform movement was launched earlier in Upper Volta and Niger than in Ivory Coast. Of all the Entente states, Upper Volta and Niger, when they became independent, had the lowest school-attendance rate (8 per cent and 4.8 per cent respectively), the smallest budgetary allocations for education, and the longest-established tradition of emigration as the solution for their rural illiterate youth. Furthermore, hinterland parents were too poor to forego willingly the services of their young children so that the latter could acquire an education which they forgot after leaving school because it was so unrelated to their lives and needs. The larger Muslim component of their populations created further difficulties, for Islamic parents were reluctant to have their offspring, particularly the girls, attend secular or mission schools. In Niger, difficulties were compounded by the mobility and intractability of the numerous Touareg and Toubou nomads, who opposed a Western-type education as likely to alienate the younger generation from their traditional way of life. In Upper Volta, although the Catholic mission schools had appreciably increased the country's primary-school facilities, they met with some opposition in the animistic and Islamized western region and also from such Mossi anticlerical intellectuals as François Bassolet.[7]

The need to add rapidly and substantially to both countries' few trained elite induced their governments to spend far more than their resources justified on expanding the

[7] See his *Evolution de la Haute-Volta* (Ouagadougou, 1968).

school system. Both countries therefore undertook experiments in the early 1960's, with foreign financial and technical aid, in new and abridged forms of primary education, which stressed the three R's, basic spoken French, and improved agricultural techniques. Upper Volta began training special teachers for a new type of rural school designed for children between the ages of twelve and fifteen who had never before received any formal instruction. The cost per pupil in such schools came to 6,500 CFA francs compared with 12,000 CFA francs in a conventional primary school,[8] and by 1967 some 400 rural schools were functioning. In Niger, the experimentation took the form of televised programs for primary-school children, and it is still the only African country where television is used exclusively for educational purposes. As of 1969, the audience for its programs comprised about 800 children, and its total cost amounted to some 500 million CFA francs.[9]

In both countries, these pedagogical innovations are too recent to evaluate their worth. Their advocates maintain that they will fulfill their purpose of reintegrating the rural population into an improved version of village life, and at a cost commensurate with the country's financial resources. Some critics, however, claim that they will simply widen the gap between the manually trained rural youths and those of the towns where the old French school system still operates.[10] There is no doubt, in any case, that such experiments will be continued, for the heavy initial investment has already been made, and, in addition, more and more young people must remain at home since emigration to the coastal states is being curtailed.

Primarily because the educational facilities in Upper Volta

[8] *Jeune Afrique,* Sept. 10, 1967.   [9] *Le Figaro,* Jan. 8, 1969.
[10] Talk with Joseph Ki Zerbo, Niamey, Oct. 30, 1968.

and Niger have been so limited, the political problems posed by their youth have not become so acute as in the better-endowed coastal states. In April 1961, there was no apparent adverse reaction when Yameogo dissolved the existing ethnic and regional youth associations and transferred their members to the Jeunesse du Rassemblement Démocratique Voltaïque, which became a branch of his UDV. Much earlier, in Niger, the PPN transformed the traditional youth groups called *samarias* [11] into party cells, and in 1956 united fifteen of them into a Jeunesse du RDA. The next year, however, a new element entered the picture when the Sawaba party began infiltrating its ranks and caused a split in the PPN's youth branch. Although the Sawaba was soon banned, it contiued to exercise some influence over ambitious Nigérien youths by means of the 150 or so scholarships it offered for study in Iron Curtain countries. As of 1968, approximately half of the forty-nine communist-trained students who had returned to Niger were serving in government posts, and Abdou Moumouni,[12] the most distinguished of that group, was preparing to leave his self-imposed exile in Mali to become director of Niger's solar-energy project.[13] Although the government of Niger does not accord official recognition to the diplomas of students trained in communist countries, its need for educated men is so great that the conservative Diori has adopted a flexible policy toward their utilization for his country's economic development.

The fact that neither Volta nor Niger has had local educational facilities above the secondary-school level has spared their governments a great deal of political turmoil. Since the

[11] S. Monnier, "Les Organisations Villageoises de Jeunes," mimeo., n.d.

[12] Author of *L'Education en Afrique,* Paris, 1964.

[13] Talk with Jean Colombani, Niamey, Oct. 30, 1968.

Sawaba-inspired agitation died down, no student congresses have been held in Niger at which inflammatory antigovernment resolutions were passed. Indeed, Nigérian students are the best behaved in all the Entente, so that the government has never exercised pressure on them either to join the conservative Mouvement des Etudiants de l'OCAM (MEOCAM) or to withdraw from the radical FEANF. No student from Niger participated in the 1968 outbreaks at the universities of Paris and Dakar, and the only local echo of these disorders was a slight "incident" at Dosso provoked by a left-wing French instructor teaching there. In January 1970, a very exceptional student strike to change the curriculum and improve the equipment at the Zinder normal school spread to the *lycée* of Niamey and the *collèges* of Tillabéry and Filingué, but when the government closed those institutions the strikers quickly gave in.

Compared with the docile Nigériens—but not with their peers in Ivory Coast—the Voltaic students appear to be firebrands.[14] A few dozen of those studying at Dakar and Abidjan universities were expelled for participating in the student riots of 1966 and 1968, but at home the strikes by secondary-school students are few and far between, and often over nonpolitical issues.[15] Radicalism has taken root only at the university level and among the graduates of foreign universities who, upon their return, cannot find jobs they regard as suitable.[16] Periodically, Yameogo scolded them for criticizing his government and doing poorly in their studies "for

[14] See "Jeune Volta, Spécial IVème Congrès (Août 1968)," mimeo., Ouagadougou, 1968.
[15] See *Afrique Nouvelle*, Jan. 1, 1960, for an account of the Koudougou normal-school strike in 1959.
[16] V. Le Vine, *Political Leadership in Africa* (Stanford, 1967), pp. 26–30.

which your toiling compatriots are paying," [17] and he threatened to cancel their scholarships. Nevertheless, he regarded the Voltaic student agitation in 1961 as sufficiently significant for it to influence his policy in regard to France and Ghana [18] and his decision to include more young men in his government in 1965. Such moves, however, did not meet the demands of the "Jeunes Turbans" for a greater voice in the government at the expense of the entrenched leaders, whom they called the "Vieux Crocodiles," and it was that element that organized the demonstrations which led to Yameogo's overthrow in January 1966.

A main reason why the young Voltaic intellectuals have been so effective politically as compared with their Nigérien counterparts is that they have found a widely respected leader in the forty-eight-year-old *agrégé,* Joseph Ki Zerbo, and a readymade party in his Mouvement de Libération Nationale (MLN). Of the three territorial branches organized by the moderately socialistic and nationalistic MLN at its birth in 1958, that of Upper Volta is the only survivor (as is also the case of the formerly interterritorial PRA). The appeal of the MLN remains largely limited to urban intellectuals, despite the efforts made by its leaders since 1966 to enlarge its base, and the fact that Ki Zerbo is a Catholic and not a Mossi restricts his leadership potential. Voltaic parties in general and youth groups in particular have been handicapped by the government's ban until 1970 on political activities as well as by divisions among themselves. Small as is the number of young radical intellectuals, they are profoundly divided by their affiliations and ideologies, which range from orthodox Catholic to Maoist elements, and even the single Union Générale des Etudiants Voltaïques is split between moderate and hard-core members. Under the mili-

[17] *Marchés Tropicaux,* Aug. 8, 1959.   [18] See Ch. 2.

tary regime, Voltaic students have been allowed greater freedom of expression than under that of Yameogo, perhaps because Lamizana does not take them very seriously. In late October 1968, he told the writer that he could not regard them as valid spokesmen for Voltaic youth, "because they are only children."

In contrast to students and young intellectuals in the hinterland countries, those of the coastal states have exerted a considerable political influence. Dahomey and Togo, in particular, had a far wider literacy base when they achieved independence, and their youthful intellectuals had already acquired organizational strength and more definite objectives. Their chief demands have been greater employment opportunities and better paid, more responsible government posts, but in all the coastal countries there exist intransigent ideologists who in principle are opposed to their government's political orientation. Togo is the outstanding example of a country where all three of its main political groups early established youth branches, and its intellectuals' opposition remained within the context of an organized party. In Ivory Coast, on the other hand, the focus of youthful opposition is formed by the university students, who have refused to be integrated into that state's single party.

The Juvento party of Togo is in many ways atypical of the Entente countries in that, although from the outset it was the youth branch of the nationalistic CUT, it was not composed either of students or illiterate rural youths. It was an organization made up almost exclusively of Lomé's young intellectuals, led by Togo's most brilliant lawyer, the "Brazilian" Maître Anani Santos, whose objectives were Ewe reunification, then union with Ghana, and finally total political and economic independence within a Pan-African context. The Juvento cooperated with the older CUT leadership in appealing to the United Nations against the French administration and Grunitsky's government until 1958, when the nationalists won an oustanding victory at the polls. Olympio rewarded his youthful collaborators with some cabinet posts and assembly seats, but he ignored their pleas for a more rapid declaration of Togo's independence, Africanization of the administration, the severing of ties with France, and the application of Marxist principles to his management of the economy.

Although Santos was less of an extremist in pressing these demands than was the Juvento's co-founder, Mensah Aithson, he withdrew from Olympio's government within a year of its establishment, and by mid-1959 the Juvento had formally become an opposition party. For the next two years, however, the Juvento was so beset by internal divisions, between those who advocated and those who refused to rejoin the CUT, that it was consistently defeated at the polls and failed to exert any influence on the government's policies. As Olympio's relations with Ghana, as well as Togo's financial position, steadily worsened and he leaned ever more heavily on France, he increasingly alienated the left-wing intellectuals. Because he believed them to be "obedient to the orders of international communism," he treated their leaders with corresponding harshness. Attributing to them the inspiration for many of the plots which became a standard feature of the last years of his government, Olympio imprisoned the principal Juvento leaders in December 1961 and dissolved that party the following month.

Even after Olympio's assassination and the revival of political parties under Grunitsky's second government, the Juvento never regained its former strength. Santos, in poor health, retired to Dahomey, and Juvento's leadership passed into the hands of less dynamic men. Still divided ideologically and judging Ewe reunification and union with Ghana to be lost causes, the Juvento leaders eventually decided to join Grunitsky's administration. Consequently the torch of opposition, first to Grunitsky and then to Eyadema, was taken up by the CUT irreconcilables, and the Juvento, like all of Togo's other former parties, lapsed into political inaction.

In Ivory Coast, the story of the PDCI's relations with the youthful Ivorian radicals differs from that of the CUT in several essential respects, although during that party's early radical period the young urban intelligentsia similarly co-operated with it in combating the colonial administration. However, the PDCI failed to create a youth branch until the eve of the 1958 referendum, when it belatedly organized the Jeunesse du Rassemblement Démocratique de la Côte d'Ivoire (JRDACI) in its own image. By that time it was too late to effect a reconciliation with the youthful left-wing elements. Seven years before, the transformation of the PDCI into a conservative party had coincided with the return to Ivory Coast of the first wave of Ivorian university graduates who had been indoctrinated by the FEANF and were therefore unamenable to such an integration.[19] These highly educated Ivorian youths resisted the PDCI's efforts to divert their energies into cultural and professional organizations, and they vociferously opposed application of the *loi-cadre,* membership in the Franco-African Community and the Entente, and Western imperialism and capitalism in general. Although the non-student youths who did join the JRDACI proved to be docile instruments of government policies, the Union Générale des Etudiants de la Côte d'Ivoire (UGECI), which comprised about 1,100 of the 1,700 Ivorian students attending Dakar and French universities, became increasingly hos-

[19] A. Zolberg, *One Party Government in the Ivory Coast* (Princeton, 1964), p. 207.

tile to Houphouët personally, as well as to his domestic and foreign policies.

Houphouët, as was his wont, periodically tried to heal the breach, although at times he became so irked and alarmed by the UGECI's intransigent hostility that he clamped down on its leaders severely. After some of its spokesmen in July 1959 had called him a fascist to his face, Houphouët reacted by announcing that the scholarships of those who had participated in antigovernment activities would be canceled, and that any Ivorian who demanded independence for his country would be imprisoned. When the students persisted in their attacks, he dissolved their organization and replaced it with a more conservative one, the Union Nationale des Etudiants de la Côte d'Ivoire (UNECI). This drastic step was followed by a cooling-off period in which Houphouët wooed the students who repented by renewing their scholarships and by offering university graduates posts in his government. This strategy was reasonably successful, and by the end of 1960 Houphouët could claim that he headed the youngest government in all West Africa.[20] However, this did not effect a reconciliation with those who were ideological revolutionaries or with those who wanted a decisive voice in policy-making, for Houphouët would not change his basic course or abdicate any of his authority, nor would the entrenched PDCI leadership surrender its key positions in the party.

In July 1961, a new round of student agitation proved to Houphouët that there still existed a hard core of youthful radicals so fundamentally opposed to his regime that they could be neither seduced nor pressured into collaboration. Beginning in 1962, therefore, he began to tighten his control over Ivorian youth at all levels. For the unskilled and un-

[20] Reported by A. Blanchet, *Nice-Matin*, Jan. 19, 1961.

employed he decreed compulsory civic service, organized along the lines of Israel's Young Pioneers. As to the student element, he won France's agreement to finance a transformation of the Centre d'Enseignement Supérieur, which had been installed at Abidjan in 1959, into a university that would serve all the Entente states. In Houphouët's eyes, this project had the triple advantage of being less costly than providing scholarships for Ivorians studying abroad, keeping them under closer party control, and making Abidjan the Entente's cultural center.

Before such long-term measures could become fully effective, the discovery of plots in January and September 1963, in which former radical student leaders were deeply involved, prompted him to take more forthright steps. Scholarships were abolished for study abroad in subjects that had become available at Abidjan, and those for Ivorian secondary schools were granted only for training in fields needed to develop the country. A Ministry of Youth was established, among whose functions was the introduction of courses in civic duties and party doctrines in the local secondary schools. Houphouët next decreed that the UNECI's headquarters should be transferred from Paris to Abidjan, and that only members of that organization would receive official grants-in-aid and, upon graduation, government posts. True to his carrot-and-stick policy, Houphouët progressively opened the party doors and the civil service more widely to youth, freed students who had been imprisoned for subversive activities, and greatly increased the budgetary allocations for education. In July 1964 and again in January 1965, he held a series of meetings with thirty representatives of overseas students, but though discussion was remarkably free, the concrete results were meager. The students then voiced grievances strikingly similar to those expressed by analogous groups in all the Entente states—the slow pace of the Africanization of employment, overdependence on France, and inflexibly conservative political and economic policies. To such demands, Houphouët replied unequivocally: "Either you are for us and working inside the party to build the nation, or you are against us and we will fight you." [21]

This ultimatum, combined with other forms of pressure, was so effective that a majority of the UNECI members reportedly pledged cooperation forthwith, and for the next two years there was a notable lack of further student agitation. Early in 1967, however, and again in May 1968, the riots at Dakar University had repercussions on the students at Abidjan, who became so restive that the government dissolved the UNECI. This step was the precursor of another series of "dialogues" between Houphouët and aggrieved members of the population, including the university students, with much the same results as before. In April 1969, the government's creation of the Mouvement des Etudiants et des Elèves de la Côte d'Ivoire (MEECI) was followed by a strike, but this time there was a significant change in the scenario. When the police were called in to quell the disorders, the French rector of the university resigned in protest. The whole institution was closed and the students sent home.

Obviously the impasse between Houphouët and the Ivorian students defies solution by his standard method of palavers and minor concessions, and it has been further aggravated by a breakdown in the country's educational system at all levels. By allocating nearly a fourth of Ivory Coast's local revenues to expanding school facilities in the mid-1960's, Houphouët had hoped to place Ivorians in a more competitive position vis-à-vis the better educated Dahomeans and Togolese and therefore make them less hostile to the

[21] *West Africa,* Jan. 9, 1965.

presence of alien Africans in their midst. Far from accomplishing this, it has increased the indigenous demand for an Ivorization of all forms of employment, and concurrently the Ivorians' lamentable academic record has intensified their sense of inferiority.

The quantitative increase in attendance at secondary schools has not been matched by improvement in the quality of instruction, as shown by the failure of all but 14 per cent of the candidates for the baccalaureate in June 1968.[22] Of the 1,911 students attending Abidjan university that year, there was a larger number of foreigners (585 Metropolitan Frenchmen and 374 Voltaics, Togolese, and Dahomeans) than Ivorians (608),[23] and the latter preferred law and literature to technical studies. The inordinate proportion of failures and dropouts showed that the educational system's basic defects reached down to the primary schools, few of whose pupils earned a *certificat d'études primaires,* and even fewer of whom went on to complete their secondary studies.

Because Ivory Coast could better afford to maintain the prestigious French school system than could the hinterland countries, Houphouët was slower to reach the same conclusions as Diori and Lamizana—to wit, that a less costly and more realistic type of schooling must be devised that would prepare the great mass of young Ivorians to contribute to their own development as a united nation. Since this reform involves sacrificing the "equivalence" of Ivorian with French diplomas, which is sacrosanct in the eyes of francophone African students, it cannot but be opposed by the Ivorian elite and become still another item in the long list of student grievances against the government. As another unpalatable byproduct, it has precipitated the decline of Abidjan as the

[22] *Jeune Afrique,* July 14, 1968.
[23] *Europe–France–Outremer,* no. 485, June 1970.

Entente's cultural center, for the expulsion of alien students who had participated in the university riots of 1968 and 1969 made the governments of Upper Volta, Togo, Dahomey, and Niger intent upon having their own national universities. The cost of constructing and even of maintaining national universities is beyond the financial capacity of the hinterland states. This is especially true of Upper Volta, whose government has already assumed responsibility for the entire cost of its primary-education system. Yet Niger and Upper Volta have decided to transform their joint Center of Higher Learning into separate faculties, located respectively at Niamey and Ouagadougou. This has been made possible because France, despite its preference for a regional university to national institutions, has reluctantly agreed to finance such expenditures so as to keep its educational hegemony and to prevent a cultural balkanization of the Entente.

This decision was precipitated by the expulsion of all foreign students from Abidjan University in November 1970, following their organization of a hostile demonstration at the embassies of France, Great Britain, and the United States as a protest against the alleged support by the NATO powers of the Portuguese-backed invasion of Guinea. Togo and Dahomey were able to absorb into their joint Benin Institute most of their nationals, but Niger and Upper Volta have had great difficulty in placing their expelled students in the universities of France, Yaoundé, and Brazzaville so that they could continue their studies during the current academic year. This expulsion has further embittered the Voltaic authorities against Houphouët, for the Ivorian university students were not similarly penalized. To be sure, Abidjan University was again closed down just before the 1971 Easter holidays because its Ivorian students were then trying to organize an association in competition to the MEECI and therefore outside the PDCI framework. The dissident students were either sent home or recruited into the army or civic service, but the docile minority have been allowed to take their examinations.

This purge, which also included two high officials of the education service, has reportedly impelled Houphouët to reform drastically the school system above the primary grades. Henceforth students admitted to secondary schools and the university will be required to sign a pledge of cooperation with the party and government. Furthermore, the university curriculum is to be revised so as to eliminate most of the courses in the arts, social sciences, and law, thus compelling students to concentrate on technological studies. This new policy cannot fail to heighten the tension between the Ivorian government and the students, who have long been Houphouët's most persistent and effective adversaries in Ivory Coast.

Actually, the *dialogue des sourds* that has been carried on between the Entente governments and their students since independence relates less to ideologies, academic standards, and scholarships than to larger issues involved in the generation gap. The oldsters want credit for winning independence, coping with the problems of sovereignty, and offering to a vastly increased percentage of their compatriots an educational system that provides them with the means of upward mobility. In return, they ask what seems to them a modest but indispensable *quid pro quo*—the collaboration of youth in the task of nation-building. The youngsters, for their part, are bored with the older generation's recital of its accomplishments and resentful of its clinging to high office, and are trying to use the leverage of their superior education to wrest power for themselves. To be sure, there is an element of ideology and patriotism in some of their demands, for the idealistic youths among them sincerely believe that their country is pursuing the wrong objectives and that its leaders are worshipping false gods. The majority, however, have become so apathetic that they tend to lapse into *attentisme,* the small minority of zealous revolutionaries either resort to plotting or go into exile, and the most self-interested remain in France where their diplomas can earn for them more professional and material advantages than at home. Obviously in all the Entente states, time is on the side of youth, and the only questions that remain unanswered are whether the transfer of power will come sooner or later and whether it will be peaceful or violent.

CHAPTER 9

The Economic Base

In the economies of all the Entente states, the rural sector is by far the most important (see Table 8), for the populations' living standards and the development of all of their processing industries depend on the results of its labor. Farming, for both domestic consumption and export, predominates in the five countries, but in none of them is more than a fraction of the arable land cultivated, nor agriculture independent of climatic conditions, nor the population self-sufficient in the production of foodstuffs. The official stress is now placed on increasing the cultivation and processing of food crops, particularly rice, and of cotton, so as to reduce if not eliminate the importation of those expensive items. This trend has been accelerated since France's guaranteed market and higher than world prices for certain African tropical produce were replaced by the two agreements less favorable to the Entente states that were made with the European Economic Community in the 1960's.

Herding, generally an occupation dissociated from farming, is of almost equal importance with agriculture in the hinterland states, but not even there does it provide basic food for the population. Animal husbandry is negligible along the coast, where the prevalence of tsetse flies inhibits the rearing of all but a few breeds of livestock. Fishing, very largely for domestic consumption, is carried on in the rivers, lakes, and ponds of the interior, from which dried and smoked fish are exported in small tonnages. Only in the lagoons and off the coasts of Togo, Ivory Coast, and Da-

Table 8. Rural production *

| Country | Agriculture | | Herding (no. of head) | Fishing (tons) |
	Food crops (tons)	Industrial crops (tons)		
Ivory Coast	Yams, 1,864,000 Manioc, 1,044,000 Bananas (plantains), 1,014,000 Potatoes, sweet, 52,000 Paddy, 345,000 Corn, 205,000 Millet, 47,000 Peanuts (in shell), 29,000	Coffee, 272,000 Cocoa, 142,000 Bananas, 193,000 Cotton, unginned, 35,000 Rubber, 6,000	Cattle, 380,000 Sheep and goats, 1,600 Pigs, 120,000	72,000
Dahomey	Corn, 250,000 Sorghum, 48,700 Millet, 5,900 Paddy, 2,400 Manioc, 768,000	Palm kernels, 59,000 Palm oil, 8,860 Coffee, 450 Cotton, 12,573 Peanuts (shelled), 7,800 Karité, 6,440 Copra, 597	Cattle, 500,000 Sheep, 514,000 Goats, 531,000 Pigs, 300,000	35,600
Niger	Millet, 1,000,150 Sorghum, 342,160 Manioc, 168,000 Beans, 77,000 Potatoes, sweet, 12,100 Corn, 2,600 Wheat, 370	Peanuts (in shell), 165,000 Cotton, unginned, 6,168 Tobacco, 350 Sugarcane, 21,120	Cattle, 4,200,000 Sheep, 2,180,000 Goats, 5,600,000 Camels, 360,000 Pigs, 3,000 Horses, 170,000 Donkeys, 360,000	9,000
Togo	Manioc, 1,016,657 Corn, 112,000 Yams, 1,040,570 Paddy, 18,069 Millet, 178,147	Cocoa, 18,264 Coffee, 10,279 Cotton, unginned, 10,542	Cattle, 169,000 Sheep, 617,000 Goats, 548,000 Pigs, 224,000 Poultry, 1,300,000	14,000

Country	Agriculture		Herding (no. of head)	Fishing (tons)
	Food crops (tons)	Industrial crops (tons)		
		Peanuts (shelled), 5,775 Palm kernels, 12,000		
Upper Volta	Sorghum, 370,000 Corn, 100,000 Peanuts (in shell), 94,000 Paddy, 42,000	Cotton, un-ginned, 32,000 Sesame, 2,897 Karité, 15,300	Cattle, 2,500,000 Sheep and goats, 3,500,000 Pigs, 130,000 Donkeys, 180,000 Camels, 5,000 Horses, 70,000	(?)

Sources: *Europe-France-Outremer, L'Afrique d'Expression Française et Madagascar,* 1960–1970 (yearly issues); *L'Afrique/70; Marchés Tropicaux,* 1960–1970 (various issues).

* Production figures are those of one or another of the following years: 1966, 1967, 1968, 1969.

homey has fishing developed on a truly commercial scale.

Ivory Coast is the only member state of the Entente that has a flourishing timber industry, for the forests elsewhere have been depleted by erosion and abusive cultivation practices, such as setting bush fires to clear and fertilize the soil. Ivory Coast's forests, covering 8 million hectares and containing more than 150 species, have made that country Africa's leading exporter of logs. In 1969, wood ranked first in its exports, accounting for 30 per cent of their total value and providing a livelihood for more than 100,000 persons.[1] (A decline in wood exports by nearly 25 per cent in 1970 has led to an intensification of the official reforestation program and a revision of the policy of granting cutting permits.)

[1] *Marchés Tropicaux,* Aug. 29, 1970.

Geographic, climatic and soil conditions have disadvantaged the rural economy of the hinterland states far more than that of the coastal ones, although all the Entente countries suffer from a shortage of water and a superabundance of lateritic land. Agricultural production in the landbound states and, even more, their exports are hampered by their distance from seaports and poorer internal communications, the extent of their sahel and desert areas, their even more insufficient rainfall, and the greater dispersal of their inhabitants. Niger and Upper Volta have a narrower range of crop output, being unable to grow cocoa, coffee, oil palms, or bananas, which bring in almost all the cash income of the Togolese, Dahomeans, and Ivorians and supply the primary raw materials for their main processing industries. Niger and Upper Volta have large-scale projects to increase their rice and cotton output, but they continue to produce mainly cereals, tubers, and oilseeds.

Although Niger grows peanuts for export, it is also the largest producer of millet and sorghum in West Africa. Upper Volta, thus far, is so overwhelmingly a grower of food crops that its limited agricultural exports comprise simply such small surpluses as the local population does not itself consume. Since crop output depends on variable climatic conditions and since its increasing populations are consuming more each year, the hinterland's agricultural exports tend to stagnate or decrease, with a consequent decline in the revenues of the farmers and of their governments. Upper Volta's sole agricultural advantage over Niger is its larger number of industrious farmers, whose zeal (though not their techniques) rivals that of the Cabrais of Togo, who are reputed to be the most skillful cultivators in all the Entente states. Isolated, desperately poor, and tradition-bound, the Mossi farmers also suffer from man-made handicaps, such as archaic cultivation methods and superstitions that inhibit their farming of certain arable areas like the Yako. Niger, on the other hand, is even more subject than its neighbors to prolonged droughts—that of 1968, in particular, took a terrible toll of its livestock and crops. Because agricultural output and herding represent respectively 65 per cent and 35 per cent of Niger's rural production, it will take some time for its economy to recover from that disastrous year.

Although, numerically, Niger's herds and pastoral population are much larger than those of Upper Volta (where livestock and meat account for some 60 per cent of its total exports), the former country derives a smaller income from its livestock and animal-product exports than from peanuts. Such a paradoxical situation is due both to political circumstances and to psychological factors. Most important among the latter is the reluctance of its nomadic herders to sell their animals, which they prefer to hoard as an unproductive form of capital and a source of prestige. Furthermore, since 1967 the civil war in Nigeria has greatly reduced both the amount and sales price of Niger's livestock exports to that country, which has long been its outstanding animal market. President Diori reported in mid-1969 that the shrinkage of that market, in conjunction with the reduction of pastureland and decimation of herds caused by the 1968 drought, had already cost Niger some 5 billion CFA francs in revenues.[2] The drought having also adversely affected its cereal crops, some of the peanuts that would normally have been exported were perforce consumed at home as food. Were it not for the exploitable mineral resources of Niger and Upper Volta, the outlook for both countries' economies would be grim indeed.

Although the coastal states benefit by more favorable natural conditions than those of the hinterland, they also

[2] *Le Monde,* July 10, 1969.

suffer from circumstances beyond their control. Even though they have a more abundant rainfall and permanent streams, they have either too much water in the south or too little in the central and northern regions. The prices for their coffee, cocoa, banana, and oleaginous exports have been generally declining throughout the 1960's, and they are experiencing competition from analogous products in the Western markets. Such difficulties, of course, are not peculiar to the Entente states but are shared with other sub-Saharan nations, whose leaders have long sought to stabilize world prices for their exports at a more remunerative level.

Of all the members of the Entente, Dahomey is in the worst plight because of its insufficient production of food crops, overdependence on aging oil palms, and inability to develop alternative resources. Even its new deepwater port, on which Dahomey had counted heavily to stimulate its economy, has proved to some degree detrimental to the country's economy. Changes caused by the port in the tidal currents of Cotonou's lagoon so reduced the annual catch of some 20,000 tons that many fishermen have had to emigrate or turn to deep-sea fishing. Moreover, there has been no official confirmation of the Dahomeans' hopes that the oil strike made off its southeastern coast in 1968 will justify commercial exploitation.

Togo, like Dahomey, suffers from the restriction of a relatively dense population within a very small land area and from the imbalance between the economic development of its northern and southern regions. Nevertheless, the Togolese, who have gained greater political stability, are able to utilize a larger percentage of their arable soil for a more varied agricultural production and possess in their phosphate deposits a valuable source of export income.

Lacking even such mineral resources, and with comparable

soil and climatic conditions, albeit a larger geographical area, Ivory Coast has far outdistanced its coastal partners by the wider gamut and larger tonnages of its agricultural production and exports (see Tables 8 and 9). By consistently pursuing a policy of agricultural diversification in the north as well as the south, improving its internal and external means of communication, increasing its industrial output, and attracting foreign capital investments, Ivory Coast has appreciably reduced its imports and expanded its exports to the point where it can use an ever larger percentage of its revenues for economic equipment (44 billion CFA francs in 1969). To be sure, some of its investment funds derive from foreign aid, which between 1960 and 1969 totaled some 157 billion CFA francs (85 billion in subsidies and 72 billion in loans),[3] and three-fifths of its population still depend on coffee and cocoa exports for all or part of their livelihood. Nevertheless, during the 1960–1969 period, Ivory Coast has utilized a sizeable amount of its resources to reduce the proportion of primary products output in its gross national product from 46.8 per cent to 34.3 per cent. This situation contrasts sharply with that of Dahomey, nine-tenths of whose economy and 67 per cent of whose exports are based on oleaginous production, and also with that of Togo, where cocoa and coffee account respectively for 35 per cent and 15 per cent of its exports.

Unfortunately, accurate statistics concerning the Entente economies are unavailable, and those given in Tables 8, 9, and 10 are culled from various sources, which often give contradictory information. As a basis for comparison, however, they have a certain value in very general terms. The figures for external commerce are particularly unreliable because inevitably they cannot include the vast contraband

[3] *Marchés Tropicaux,* May 9, 1970.

Table 9. Budgets and foreign trade

	Budgets			Foreign trade		
	Total (billions of CFA francs)		Amts. allocated to investment (development), in CFA francs, 1969		Total (millions of CFA francs)	Trade with African states, 1966
Country	1960–61	1969		Country	1960–61 1968–69	(% of total)
Ivory Coast	30.8	46.5	27.2 billion	Ivory Coast		
Dahomey	6.3	15.8	—	Exports	38,808 118,233	9.1
Niger	6.3	9.9	792.6 million	Imports	32,363 86,284	10.4
Togo	6.4	6.6	450.0 million	Dahomey		
Upper Volta	5.8	9.7	900.0 million	Exports	3,579 5,507	19.2
				Imports	6,275 12,208	7.8
				Niger		
				Exports	3,103 9,350	25.8
				Imports	3,127 10,237	12.3
				Togo		
				Exports	3,588 11,477	5.0
				Imports	6,452 14,572	8.5
				Upper Volta		
				Exports	1,640 5,288	70.0
				Imports	2,027 10,122	36.3

Sources: Europe-France-Outremer, L'Afrique d'Expression Française et Madagascar, 1960–70 (yearly issues); L'Afrique/70; Marchés Tropicaux, 1960–70 (various issues).

operations in all the Entente countries, nor do they reflect the scale of their transit trade. The permeability of their frontiers and the variations in customs duties, as between Togo and its partners and as between the former French and British territories, have given rise to a very large but inde- terminate amount of smuggling in both local and imported merchandise. Cocoa, textiles, foodstuffs, cigarettes, and alco- holic beverages cross the coastal border almost uncontrolled; colas move with equal ease from south to north, and live-

Table 10. Mineral and electrical production *

Country	Minerals	Electricity (kWh.)
Ivory Coast	Diamonds, 186,483 carats Manganese, 116,700 tons	315,000,000
Dahomey	—	23,600,000
Niger	Tin, 80.6 tons	28,200,000
Togo	Phosphates, 1,356,000 tons	19,271,000
Upper Volta	—	22,540,000

Sources: *Europe-France-Outremer, L'Afrique d'Expres- sion Française et Madagascar,* June 1970; *L'Afrique/70.*
* Production in 1967 or 1968.

stock in the opposite direction. The Entente governments have been unable to stop the financial hemorrhage resulting from this contraband trade. Moreover, because smuggling has the advantages of increasing the money in circulation and of contributing to their populations' supply of consumer goods and contentment, they now only aim to keep it within reasonable bounds. As regards both illicit and legitimate commerce, landlocked Niger and Upper Volta naturally trade more with African countries than do Togo, Dahomey, and Ivory Coast.

Despite their many shortcomings, the official statistics do show unequivocally that Ivory Coast has consistently enjoyed a favorable trade balance, whereas its four partners have chronically had deficits, varying in amount from year to year. Production and most exports have generally increased in all five states since independence, but the more unfavorable terms of world trade for their output and the rising cost of their growing imports have largely canceled out any profits. In common with their neighbors, the Entente countries find themselves, like Alice in Looking-Glass Land, running ever faster to stay where they are, and since producing more does not bring in commensurate cash returns, it is no wonder that their populations are not more responsive to their leaders' appeals to increase output. Not unnaturally the Entente governments tend to seek their financial salvation by soliciting more foreign aid, and their elites by demanding an ever larger slice of the pie.

Although in fact as well as in national planning, the rural economy remains the predominant sector in each of the Entente states, all their governments aspire to a greater industrialization that will raise the masses' living standards, eliminate costly imports, and increase the value of their exports—in that order of importance. Only in Ivory Coast, however, as indicated by Tables 9 and 10, has this occurred on any considerable scale, despite its lack of indigenous fuel and mineral ores. Between 1960 and 1968, the share of industrial production in Ivory Coast's GNP rose from 15 per cent to 22 per cent, and its turnover (*chiffre d'affaires*) had grown at the annual average of 23 per cent. By 1969, investments in Ivorian industries totaled 71.1 billion CFA francs, and 23 per cent of its industrial output was exported.[4] Electric-power production more than tripled in the postindependence decade, and completion of the Kossou dam, begun

[4] *Ibid.*, July 11, 1970.

in 1969, should meet the anticipated needs of an expanding industrial production. Only mining, never on a large scale and now limited to diamond extraction, is in retrogression. On the eve of Ivory Coast's tenth anniversary of independence, Houphouët could proudly report that since 1960 per capita income had almost doubled, and the GNP had grown from 104 to 296 billion CFA francs, and that in 1969 Ivory Coast's trade had produced a surplus balance of some 32 billion CFA francs.[5]

Industrial production has also been rising in the other Entente states, especially in the late 1960's, but in none of them does it account for as much as 10 per cent of their GNP, and it consists almost wholly of processing local materials for the domestic market. Oil mills, cotton gins, brick factories, and food-processing plants have long operated on a small scale in all the Entente states, and of these the most important are those geared to the individual country's main output. Thus the processing of coffee, cocoa, and palm products and the manufacture of wood items have developed in the coastal areas, while peanut-shelling, kapok-decortication, rice-husking, tanneries, and meat industries have predominated in the hinterland regions. In recent years they have been supplemented by a few others using mainly imported materials and producing shoes, plastics, bicycles, tires, beverages, matches, and the like, exclusively for local consumers. The postindependence period has also seen the completion or initiation of several large-scale agro-industrial ventures, such as the textile complexes of Koudougou (Upper Volta) and Cotonou (Dahomey) and the cement plants of Malbaza (Niger), Cotonou and Onigbolo (Dahomey), and Aveta (Togo), all of which must find regional markets if they are to become profitable.

None of the Entente's national clienteles is numerous or

[5] *Ibid.,* August 1, 1970.

prosperous enough by itself to support sizeable industries, nor has any of them developed sufficient local power resources to operate such enterprises. Electric current now is generated by small diesel-powered plants exclusively in the main towns, and even in Ivory Coast the Abidjan region consumes 85 per cent of the electricity produced. Plans are afoot, however, to develop the hydroelectric potential of the Niger River near Niamey, the Comoé near Banfora, and the Mono River on the Dahomey-Togo border. In 1969 an agreement was signed by the governments at Lomé and Cotonou to import current from Ghana, and in 1971, Nigeria agreed to export current to Niger.

Were it not for the new prospects opened up by the mineral resources of Ivory Coast's junior partners, the expenditures required to provide them with more electric power would hardly be justified by their otherwise slight industrial development. In view of Ivory Coast's presently overwhelming economic superiority, there is poetic justice in the recent discoveries of minerals in Niger, Upper Volta, Dahomey, and Togo far richer than any found thus far in the Ivorian subsoil.

Since 1961, Togo's phosphate has been mined and concentrated at Akoupamé, and by 1969 exports had reached 1,464,000 tons, with a further rise anticipated. Two American petroleum companies drilling off the southeastern shore of Dahomey struck oil in 1968, and in 1970 the Shell Company was granted a prospecting permit, also offshore. However, the probable impact of the oil find on the country's economy cannot yet be estimated. At Tambao, in Upper Volta, near its frontiers with Mali and Niger, manganese deposits amounting to between 7 and 10 million tons of good-quality ore are being intensively studied. Because of their inaccessible location and the area's aridity, their mining and processing depend on finding more water locally and obtaining the funds to finance construction of a 353-kilometer extension of the Abidjan-Ouagadougou railroad. Should both materialize, it is planned to utilize the nearby calcareous deposits of Tin-Hrassen for a cement plant. These prospects encouraged Upper Volta, Niger, and Mali in 1970 to undertake a joint development of the Liptako-Gourma region. These enterprises would help to develop what is now a neglected and isolated area,[6] and would greatly benefit the whole region.

Much further advanced and of greater international importance is the project to mine the uranium deposits of Arlit in Niger, which are believed to contain 20,000 tons of uranium metal. Work has already begun on the building of a concentration plant and village nearby and a 1,600-kilometer road from the mine site to the Dahomean railhead at Parakou. The government of Niger anticipates that the Arlit mine, beginning in 1973, will provide additional revenues of 130 million CFA francs, rising to 698 millions two years later. French, German, Italian, and Japanese companies are already involved in developing Niger's mineral resources.

Although an expanding mining industry will be largely of indirect benefit to Niger, Upper Volta, Togo, and Dahomey, in terms of royalties and mainly temporary jobs for their unskilled laborers, any additions to their meager revenues are enthusiastically welcomed. Furthermore, their minerals have for the first time attracted private international capital to those countries, where heretofore foreign aid has been on a government-to-government basis and motivated by political rather than economic considerations. Prospecting and studies of their deposits are being undertaken and financed by United Nation agencies and foreign companies, which have

[6] *Afrique Nouvelle,* June 3, 1970.

high hopes of discovering more mineral wealth in the Entente's as yet imperfectly known subsoil. Should this materialize, it would give a new orientation to their economies,
and perhaps provide them with the first means of independent self-development.

During the 1960's, the Entente governments concentrated
almost wholly on improving their rural economies according
to national plans, none of which has been fully carried out.
In the absence of sufficient sources of indigenous capital and
skills, such planning has been subject to fitful grants of
foreign aid and consequently to a certain degree of foreign
control, as well as dependent on the services of foreign
technicians. Nor have the state organizations and companies
of "mixed" economy, devised to lessen this dependence,
proved wholly satisfactory as agents for the execution of
their plans. Although the revenues anticipated from the
development of their mineral resources should to some degree liberate the governments from the financial aspect of
their servitude, other problems of both a material and psychological order may arise. Because mineral resources are a
"wasting asset" and their processing and sale require a
technical and organizational expertise not yet present in the
Entente states, the material benefits for the country where
they are found must inevitably be short-lived and far smaller
than those accruing to the foreigners exploiting them. Furthermore, the new opportunities for the employment of
unskilled laborers created by nascent mining industries are
not only temporary but may heighten the existing disaffection of the Entente youth for agricultural occupations.

Another psychological danger is inherent in the development of mining on a national basis, for it will probably
strengthen the Entente states' established trend toward autarky. Already the competitive character of their economies,

combined with the rapid growth of nationalist sentiments, has made it difficult for the Entente to become effective as a regional economic organization, let alone to associate Ghana more closely with its operations.

At the request of the governments concerned, two experts of the African Development Bank undertook to study the feasibility of closer economic cooperation between Ghana and its neighbors. The report they submitted at the end of 1970, while admitting the advantages that would ensue from a closer coordination of the six countries' economies, stressed two major obstacles to any marked increase in interstate trade. These were the survival of the barriers between the nations erected during the colonial period and the imbalance between the economies of the coastal and hinterland countries. Together, Ivory Coast and Ghana accounted for half the total population, three-fourths of the six countries' combined GNP, and most of their existing industries. Moreover, future industrial development would probably continue to be concentrated along the coast because of its greater accessibility to foreign markets, means of distribution, and sources of raw materials and energy.

Nevertheless, some compensation for their inherent disadvantages might be given to the landlocked states in return for their serving as outlets for the coast's surplus industrial produce. They could develop more markets in the south for their agricultural and livestock output by increasing and improving their production, and by developing light industries that would find a coastal as well as a local clientele. The authors of the report listed the long- and short-term industries they considered appropriate to achieve such goals, and indicated where they could best be located. They also proposed an extension to neighboring countries of existing bilateral enterprises, such as the agreements between Ghana and three of the Entente states for utilization of the former's electric current and between Ivory Coast and Upper Volta for promoting a tire factory at Bobo-Dioulasso.

Even before receiving the bank's report, a little, though not much, progress had been made along the above-mentioned lines. Of Houphouët's initial plans for coordinating the economies of the Entente states by forming a customs union, eliminating the barriers to labor migrations, "rationalizing" their trade in manufactured goods, and creating joint industrial enterprises, virtually all have foundered on the rocks of the member countries' nascent nationalism. Only those rare schemes of obvious mutual benefit have survived, and their fewness underscores the small extent of the Entente's collective economic achievements. Only very recently has the machinery been set up for the coordination of the region's road transport (see Table 11) and telecommunications systems, the creation of a tourist association (Société de Réalisation et d'Equipement dans les Etats de l'Entente), and, above all, the organization of the interstate trade in meat and livestock (Bureau Inter-Bétail-Viande).

Significantly enough, even these projects were not officially endorsed by the heads of state until the spring of 1970, at which time they also enlisted the support of foreign capital and sought the cooperation of Ghana, Mali, and Nigeria.[7] The United States, which has been conspicuously slow about investing in the Entente states, promised in March 1971 to lend their Guaranty Fund—described below—$6 million to help finance some of these new organizations. Other Entente-based enterprises, now operating successfully at the national level, may also attract foreign funds and enlist the cooperation of neighboring states. These are the proposed extension of training facilities for mechanics at Lomé and for maritime

[7] *Marchés Tropicaux*, May 23, 1970.

fishermen at Abidjan. Such projects could well be extended beyond the borders of the Entente, and they might thus become a basis for individual cooperative ventures in west Africa that would avoid some of the obstacles encountered by a more formal and larger-scale economic grouping.

As to the development projects restricted to members of

Table 11. Surface and air communications facilities

Country	Railroads (km.)	Roads and tracks (km.)	Ocean & air cargo handled (tons)	
			Seaports	Principal airports (1967)
Ivory Coast	628 (part of "Abidjan-Niger" Ry.)	38,850 (1,137 paved)	Abidjan, 5,168,000 (1969) Sassandra, 255,938 (1967)	2,750
Dahomey	Cotonou-Parakou, 438 Cotonou-Segboroué, 34 Cotonou-Porto Novo-Pobé, 107	6,200 (692 paved)	Cotonou, 283,814 (1967); 545,000 (1969)	444
Niger	—	4,034 (259 paved)	—	1,626
Togo	Lomé-Blitta, 276 Agbonou-Atakpamé, 4 Lomé-Palimé, 116 Lomé-Anecho, 44	2,106 (204 paved)	Lomé, 315,000 (1969)	199
Upper Volta	518 (part of "Abidjan-Niger" Ry.)	4,400 (paved only in main towns)	—	261

Sources: *Europe-France-Outremer, L'Afrique d'Expression Française et Madagascar,* June 1970; *L'Afrique/70.*

the Entente, these are the province of its Mutual Aid and Loan Guaranty Fund. That fund was established in June 1966 on the same day that Togo joined the group, and it was a transformation, not an extension, of the Entente's earlier Solidarity Fund. It had the dual purpose of attracting productive foreign investments rather than subsidies, and of lightening the financial burden which the Solidarity Fund had entailed for Ivory Coast. Officially, the new fund aimed at "promoting a common economic policy and facilitating its implementation by guaranteeing loans obtained from non-member sources with a view to financing projects approved by the Entente heads of state." [8] The new fund's main source of income, like that of its predecessor, was to be the annual contributions made by member states proportionate to their national revenues.

By the time the Solidarity Fund's assets were transferred to the Loan Guaranty Fund in January 1967, Ivory Coast had contributed to it 4 billion CFA francs, compared with 84 million each from Upper Volta, Niger, and Dahomey, and 48 million from Togo.[9] Ivory Coast, to convince its partners that it was not shirking further responsibility for their financial welfare, pledged that it would not have recourse to the new fund during the first five years of its existence. Likewise France launched the Guaranty Fund with a loan of 100 million CFA francs, at the same time promising not to influence its utilization or to diminish the amount of bilateral aid it was then granting to each of the Entente states.

The Guaranty Fund, more than had been the preceding organization, has been oriented to a general development

[8] *The Mutual Aid and Loan Guaranty Fund of the Council of the Entente,* Secrétariat Administratif du Fonds d'Entr'aide et de Garantie des Emprunts du Conseil de l'Entente (Abidjan, 1967), p. 5.

[9] *Afrique Nouvelle,* Jan. 25, 1967.

program and designed to promote the economic independence of Ivory Coast's fellow members. Although still without a secretariat or any supranational bodies, it has also been more firmly structured. Its managing committee is required to reimburse the lender for any loan repayment whenever the principal borrower has failed to meet its obligations a month after they fell due. The fund's capital can be used only for the purpose of honoring its engagements with the lender. The managing committee is made up of two representatives from each member country, who are authorized by the five heads of state to make decisions on projects for which a loan is sought, and it can guarantee loans for those it approves up to ten times the total amount of its resources. These resources are deposited in three French banks, and the interest they earn is used to finance studies of projects involving two or more member states. Early in 1970, the managing committee, judging the fund's existing resources (2,006 million CFA francs) sufficient for operations in the near future, decided to suspend the states' annual payments for the next five years. Financially, the fund's position is sound, and thus far all its commitments have been honored.

If the Entente's difficulties regarding utilization of the Guaranty Fund have not derived from financial stringency, they stem mainly from the slowness and fewness of its operations. In part this is due to the time inevitably spent by committee members and the experts they employ in studying proposals that are ultimately turned down as unviable. Of the fifteen projects submitted to that committee during the first few months of its existence, all but two were rejected for that reason. Three years later, only seven had been fully approved (see Table 12) and three others accepted conditionally. By the end of 1969, the fund guaranteed loans totaling 2,125 million CFA francs, leading to a mass of investments in the four Entente states concerned which amounted to 6.5 billion CFA francs.[10] The tempo of the fund's operations speeded up during 1970, when it gave guarantees for loans to build a flour mill at Banfora and an oil mill at Bobo-Dioulasso (Upper Volta), as well as the Aveta cement plant (Togo). Among the projects still under serious consideration but which have not yet received even a qualified approval are a sugar mill at Tillabéry (Niger), a tomato-paste factory at Bobo-Dioulasso, a marketing organization for the hinterland states' leather-and-hides production, and a plan to stabilize the Entente's output of cereals.

Table 12. Mutual-Aid and Loan-Guaranty Fund, 1967–1969 inclusive

Country	Projects undertaken	Investment (millions of CFA francs)	Duration of loan (years)	Interest rate (%)
Dahomey	Kenaf Industrial I (1967)	273.6	5	4.87
	Textile plant (1968)	150.0	9	6.5
Niger	Well-digging equipment (1968)	51.5	5	7
Togo	Lomé sanitation (1968)	277.8	5	6
	Maison de l'Entente (1969)	110.0	3	10
Upper Volta	Export-goods warehouse (1967)	80.0	5	7
	Public-works equipment (1969)	65.3	5	5.85

Source: *Rapport d'Activité, Fonds d'Entr'aide et de Garantie des Emprunts, 1969,* Abidjan, Dec. 1969.

[10] *Rapport d'Activité 1969,* Fonds d'Entr'aide et de Garantie des Emprunts du Conseil de l'Entente (Abidjan, n.d.), p. 10.

Far more responsible than the technical delays for the lag
in the Entente's development as an economic region have
been the obstacles created by rival national interests. These
have made the siting of enterprises difficult and have given
rise to disputes between the five member governments as to
the type of industry to be jointly promoted. Even those states
where existing resources seem most propitious for further industrial development are now finding themselves in competition with similar and more recently founded industries.
Thus Ivory Coast is now developing on a large scale the
production of palm oil, copra, and kenaf (a fiber plant) which
will soon be strongly competitive with the longer established
vegetable oil and fiber industries of Dahomey, whose output provides the Dahomeans with virtually their sole cash
income. Similarly, the official encouragement of ranching in
northern Ivory Coast will reduce, if not eliminate, a vitally
important market for the livestock industries of Niger and
Upper Volta.

Since Ivory Coast's determination to attain self-sufficiency
is being carried out partly at the expense of its Entente
partners, this has inevitably increased their resentment of
Houphouët's ascendancy and of their own economic inferiority. The Dahomeans' feeling of frustration is so intense that
they have already announced that, if their petroleum proves
commercially exploitable, they will not ship it to Abidjan
but will build their own refinery. An even more striking
example of nationalistic intra-Entente competition is provided by its members' cement-producing programs. The
single plant that now turns out the finished product wholly
from indigenous materials is the Malbaza factory in Niger,
built in 1966 with a view to supplying the Entente's needs
in cement. But the cost of Malbaza's cement, even in Niamey,
is higher than that of the imported product, and far more so

in the other Entente markets. The Malbaza factory therefore now works to only half its capacity and is unlikely ever to show a profit. Its current failure, however, can be attributed to poor preliminary study and not to interstate competition since at present the only analogous enterprises are three clinker-crushing plants along the coast.

Of quite a different character is the rivalry between Togo and Dahomey that is shaping up in the coastal region. Initially, those two nations planned a joint venture in producing cement from local resources, but they could not agree as to which country's limestone deposits should be used, and now each has gone ahead with its own project. Both the Onigbolo plant in Dahomey, financed mainly by Spanish capital, and the Aveta enterprise in Togo, for which the World Bank has agreed to lend 12 billion CFA francs, are slated to produce far more cement than their respective domestic consumers can absorb, hence each hopes to capture the regional market.

Without a doubt, Ivory Coast has been the worst offender in selfishly promoting its own economic development and in treating its partners as suppliers of raw materials and markets for its output. In principle, its interest lies in fostering industries in the other Entente states so as to prevent their nationals from swamping the Ivorian labor market and persuading them to buy its surplus products, but in practice the reverse policy has been pursued. If the other Entente states have not effectively followed Ivory Coast's example, however, it is not because they are more philanthropically motivated or less short-sighted but because they have not the means to do so, for they are all animated by comparable ambitions. Certainly the Ivorian policy has strengthened their economic nationalism, as has that of Ghana. The large-scale repatriation of foreign Africans and the expulsion of Lebanese merchants from Ghana in 1969 to the Entente countries have now incited Togo and Dahomey to reserve certain occupations to their own nationals.

Ghana's closer association with the Entente may widen the latter's trading opportunities and lead to the launching of a few joint industrial enterprises, but it is as unlikely to prevent the wasteful and inefficient duplication of national industries as have the few common projects financed by the Guaranty Fund. Everywhere in the area the growing strength of economic nationalism has sharply narrowed the range of joint projects acceptable to all the states, as well as the employment opportunities still open to immigrants.

CHAPTER 10

A Partnership
of Inequality

The Council of the Entente still holds the record for lon-
gevity among West Africa's regional organizations. The
causes of its formation and survival are few, specific, and apparently now more or less obsolescent. Paradoxically, they
are much the same as those that make its future as an organization uncertain. The Entente was the product of a particular situation which ceased to exist within fifteen months
of its birth, and the brainchild of a single leader, to whom
its evolution has brought minimal satisfaction. Its main
organizational weakness—and one that has become more
marked with time—is its failure to pursue a constructive
policy for regional development because, on crucial issues, its
leaders refuse to accept the discipline of subordinating national interests to those of the group as a whole. To be sure,
the Entente has to some extent adapted itself to changing
internal and external circumstances during its twelve years
of existence. It has never, however, put down the deep roots
or built the institutional structure required to offset its basic
artificiality and its centrifugal tendencies, as represented by
its leaders' personal ambitions and the growing force of
territorial nationalisms.

During the Entente's formative years, its common colonial
heritage and geographical compactness were more cogent
assets in promoting its cohesion than they now are. The
natural advantages of geographical proximity have not been

fully utilized by any considerable development of the means of interstate communications. In fact, common frontiers have led to disputes, smuggling, and the harboring of political refugees from neighboring countries rather than to cooperation between Entente members. Furthermore, contacts between their respective elites have been successful only on an individual and personal basis, and the Entente functions, in effect, wholly at the summit level. (An exception could be made for the Entente students at the University of Abidjan, who on occasion have joined forces in protest against Ivorian academic or governmental policies. Such concerted action, however, has been ephemeral and will probably cease when national universities are set up in Togo, Dahomey, Niger, and Upper Volta.) As for the Entente's common colonial heritage, that, too, has become eroded. Francophone Africa's political and economic disengagement from France during the 1960's is likely, by widening the sources of its foreign aid and trading partners, to accelerate in the wake of the death of General de Gaulle, whose personal prestige and authority exerted a unifying influence on all the Entente leaders.

Nonetheless, the Entente would never have survived had its unity rested only on increasingly negative bases. Unlike the majority of West African regional bodies that were more tightly organized and ideologically oriented, the Entente has met the needs of its member states at certain times and places. Of these needs, the most pressing and perennial is that for financial aid, first in the form of disguised subsidies and, more recently, of guarantees for loans. In certain other domains, too, the Council of the Entente has scored high, if the term "entente" is construed to mean understanding rather than agreement on a positive policy of cooperation. Houphouët's leadership has never been questioned (although some of his policies have). He and his peers have had few disruptive conflicts as to their basic foreign and domestic policies, and no fundamental mutual apprehensions as to territorial aggression. Furthermore, no ideological disputes have divided them, for the heads of the Entente states are all pragmatic, conservative, and pro-Western in their outlook.

At home, the Entente governments are politically authoritarian but their economic policies are liberal, for they hope in this way to encourage the entry of capital from the industrialized nations. All of the Entente leaders have handled in much the same way the problems they encounter in their attempts to create national unity. These shared problems are derived from renascent tribalism and regionalism and from the postindependence resistance of student and labor organizations that, in each country, challenge the Entente leaders' authority to varying degrees. The Entente countries have more or less also feared the subversive activities or the irredentism of certain of their neighbors, although as a whole the Entente has been fortunate in never having been a bone of contention between the opposing world blocs. Indeed, except in the case of France (with which all of them are on cordial terms), the Entente states generally suffer from being ignored by the great powers insofar as investments are concerned.

Because of the similarity of their problems and of their backgrounds as former French dependencies, "understanding" is more highly developed among them than is agreement. Twelve years of working more or less together have made it clear to the heads of the Entente states that self-interest is the group's raison d'être and accounts for such cohesion as it possesses. Although the pledges of mutual military support in case of subversive action have never been fulfilled, and probably could not have been, and the boycott campaign against Ghana was a fiasco, the Entente leaders have derived some comfort and reassurance from belonging to an organization headed by francophone Africa's most influential leader. Had not the interests of its members been served by the existence of the Entente and, above all by its financial operations, it would never have survived so many governmental upheavals and drastic policy reorientations. That their union is based solidly on self-interest, and acknowledged as such, is shown by the candor and lack of cant in the matter-of-fact reports of the council meetings, which are in refreshing contrast to the hyperbolic phraseology used by the spokesmen of many other African organizations.

Obviously their chronic and imperative need for the funds which Ivory Coast has supplied is what has kept Upper Volta, Dahomey, Togo, and Niger members of the Entente, for as individual countries they are not economically viable. In no other grouping can they hope to obtain so many financial advantages at so little cost to themselves, as Upper Volta and Dahomey have learned from their attempts to find alternative partners and sources of income. Furthermore, restive as those countries are under the Ivorian "yoke," they cannot complain of being prevented from forming supplementary alliances or joining other organizations. All the Entente states are members of various international bodies, and they can and do make commercial treaties and exchange diplomatic missions with any country or bloc in the world.

As regards their national policies, there is no evidence to suggest that their leaders would have followed a different course had they not belonged to the Entente. No ideological or economic sacrifice has been exacted of them as the price for the benefits they receive from their membership in that group, and Houphouët did not pressure them into supporting his Biafra and South Africa policies or into adopting his anticommunist obsessions. Actually, in their relations with Ivory Coast, they have been almost wholly on the receiving end, except for the small payments they have made each year into the Entente's fund, from which, moreover, they are the sole beneficiaries. Furthermore, they have now been exempted from even such annual dues for a five-year period. It is hard to conceive of an African organization more flexible than that of the Entente, or one which leaves its members so free to choose their options.

Despite so many one-sided advantages, all of Houphouët's partners are dissatisfied to varying degrees with the tangible benefits they have received from the Entente, and all but one ask more financial aid from Ivory Coast. In the latter respect, Niger has been undemanding, not because its need is less than that of the others, but because Diori, its president, is personally devoted to Houphouët and believes his country's interests are best served by aligning Niger with Ivory Coast. Furthermore, with Houphouët's blessing, Diori is playing an outstanding international role of his own as spokesman for the OCAM, peacemaker between his Islamic neighbors, and organizer of the Niger River and Saharan borderland countries. Canada's recent decision to concentrate much of its aid to francophone Africa in Niger has given Diori greater freedom of action, but he has not used it to loosen his ties with the Entente. Nor has his loyalty to Houphouët been shaken by the dismissal of Nigérien students from Abidjan University, or to his other partners by their refusal to consider the attempt made by Chad's Toubous to stir up unrest among the nomads of Niger as a problem of concern to the Entente as a whole.

If Niger's nomad problem seems too remote and too specifically a national issue for the Entente to adopt a common policy in support of Diori (which in any case would have little impact on the anarchic Toubous), Togo's progressive disengagement from the Entente is more rooted in ideology, although it also has practical aspects. Eyadema is dissatisfied with the Entente's refusal to align itself clearly with the Pan-African movement against white imperialism and to loosen its ties with France and francophone Africa. As regards Ivory Coast, the Togolese leader opposed Houphouët's Biafra policy, and also wants some economic concessions from his government. Togo is asking for more compensation for the material damage suffered by its nationals during the 1958 riots, and also for freer access to employment opportunities in Abdijan, but its leaders have not been so insistent in their demands as have the Voltaics and Dahomeans.

Neither Houphouët's paternalism, nor his diplomatic skill in patching up their quarrels, nor his bolstering of their sagging economies can make the nationals of Upper Volta and Dahomey forgive him for reneging on his dual-nationality project or interpret his intervention in their affairs as other than meddling for his own advantage. They claim that Houphouët takes back with one hand what he gives with the other, treats them as Ivorian satellites, and uses the Entente as a captive market for Ivory Coast's industrial exports —and they may well be right. The fact that they, too, frankly pursue their own interests does not make it any more acceptable to them that Ivory Coast should do likewise. Basically, however, it is the spectacle of Ivory Coast's booming economy as contrasted with their own poverty and stagnation that arouses in them the classic love-hate emotions of admiration mixed with resentment and jealousy.

The disparity between the wealth of Ivory Coast and the indigence of its four partners would not necessarily be an impediment to the Entente's evolution as a group were

Houphouët more truly concerned to develop it as a regional organization. The coastal states need the hinterland's animal products and manual laborers, and the landlocked countries need the coast's seaports, certain of its agricultural and industrial products, and—at least for the time being—the services of its educated elite. However, the Entente has evolved in exactly the contrary direction, with each member state, led by Ivory Coast, seeking an autarky that virtually precludes mutual concessions and cooperation on a group basis.

This trend will probably be accentuated in the poorer states with the growth of mining industries on a national scale, which offer them their first prospect of greater financial independence. Doubtless they will decide to devote their growing revenues to national development, and their leaders will be even less inclined than now to make contributions on behalf of regional development. Such was Houphouët's own attitude when he co-authored the *loi-cadre* of 1956 so as to promote national autonomy and preserve Ivory Coast's revenues for its own use. Had it not been for the danger to Abidjan's ascendancy that was posed by the revival of Dakar as Mali's federal capital, or the threat to Houphouët's leadership of the RDA by the general movement toward sovereignty and an African primary federation, there probably would have been no modification of Ivory Coast's egocentric policy and no Council of the Entente.

For tactical reasons, Houphouët fashioned the Entente to be the antithesis of the Mali Federation, making it a loose economic grouping of autonomous states that would pool their resources for mutual development—but his motives in so doing were almost wholly political. However, since his partners had no illusions on that score, were not asked to surrender any of their authority, and Houphouët was willing to give the Entente a substantial dowry, they joined his organization for reasons that were as predominantly economic as his were political. The breakup of the Mali Federation, Houphouët's formation of the far larger UAM (now reincarnated as the OCAM), the unreliability and instability of his partners and of their governments, not to mention the Entente's drain on Ivorian revenues—all seemed to point to that body's early demise, and indeed at times it has been moribund. By the mid-1960's, however, the fast-changing African scene caused him to reactivate the Entente, because he saw in it a new and different dimension. As its political importance faded, after the failure of his efforts to isolate Nkrumah and of his dual-nationality proposal, its economic significance began to loom larger.

At the same time that Houphouët's motives in perpetuating the Entente acquired an economic admixture without losing their original political orientation, those of his partners became correspondingly less economic and slightly more political. To sustain and increase its prosperity, Ivory Coast needed additional markets and more unskilled labor, and one or both of these could be found in the Entente states. Then, too, the progress being made by the Organisation des Etats Riverains du Sénégal (OERS) under Senghor's guidance was again raising the specter of a West African grouping in rivalry with the Entente, and of the competition to Abidjan from Dakar, whose port traffic in 1967 began to benefit from the closing of the Suez Canal. Thus, in the late 1960's, the Entente was acquiring fresh importance in the eyes of Houphouët's partners, as well as in his own—though for different reasons. Successive military coups d'état in three of the Entente states and elsewhere in west and central Africa, the civil war in Nigeria, and later the expulsion of alien Africans from Ghana increased their feeling of dependence on Ivory Coast as a bastion of stability and prosperity.

Obviously their growing need of the security provided by Houphouët has constrained Upper Volta, Dahomey, Niger, and Togo to overlook his singleminded pursuit of his own and of Ivorian interests, as well as his inconsistencies of policy, so long as their economies depend on the modicum of funds he supplies. More complex and fluctuating are the reasons why Houphouët has been willing to perpetuate the Entente at such great cost to himself in terms of time, energy, and money, and for so few tangible advantages. To a great extent, events external to the Entente have determined the degrees of interest that Houphouët has taken in that organization, and the relative proportions of political or of economic significance that the Entente holds for him have been determined by the nature of those events.

Currently, the pendulum has swung in the political direction, for the prospect of Nigeria's resurgence since the end of its civil war has again increased its attraction for Niger and Dahomey, whereas Ghana's financial difficulties and its expulsion of African immigrants have diminished that country's importance for Togo, Niger, and Upper Volta as an outlet for their surplus nationals. This last-mentioned phenomenon, combined with the advent of the friendly Busia government at Accra, has made Ghana politically more acceptable as an Entente partner to Houphouët, although he recognizes the economic danger to Ivory Coast inherent in the addition of so populous, dynamic, and potentially rich a country. Even if Ghana's membership in the Entente were of mutual benefit economically, there are probably too many technical difficulties and too much opposition to it in both countries for Accra to become more than an "associate" of its surrounding francophone neighbors. In any case, Houphouët is likely to insist on keeping the Entente as his own personal fief, from which he can exert substantial influence over the adjacent region, and as a geographically compact base to which he can retreat whenever events elsewhere in Africa are not going his way.

It might well be asked why Houphouët has not dropped the Entente in favor of concentrating more fully on the OCAM. Albeit a far more important body, actually and potentially, the OCAM does not serve his purposes as well as does the Entente. To be sure, his is still a decisive voice in the OCAM, but that organization is too large, too dispersed, has too many competitive leaders, and is too much the object of France's "solicitude" for Houphouët to dominate it as readily as he does the Entente. Furthermore, in relation to the OCAM, the Entente has also served a useful function as a proving ground for Houphouët to experiment with organizational forms and policies which, if successful, can be transposed to the bigger group.

It is no coincidence that Houphouët founded the Entente and the OCAM as political organizations—the former to carry out his local West African objectives and the latter those relating to wider foreign-policy goals—and that both have developed into bodies with an almost wholly economic orientation. The rapid rise of African territorial nationalism in the francophone states has made any coordination of their leaders' views on political questions increasingly difficult to achieve. At the same time their common plight of underdevelopment has intensified their need to band together as the only way of inducing the investment of capital required for their equipment, without which they cannot hope to achieve economic sovereignty. Consequently, whereas an organization like the European Economic Community— composed of highly industrialized countries, each of which has a long history of nationhood—is expected to develop eventually into a political union, the Entente and the OCAM are evolving in the opposite direction.

The strength of the Entente lies in the homogeneity of

its membership in regard to background, lingua franca, and institutions; its flexibility as an organization; the primacy it accords to economic development; and the willingness of its pragmatic and realistic leaders to adapt it to changing African conditions and to shifts in the focus of their national interests. Its chief weakness lies not so much in the inequalities of its partnership, the artificiality of its boundaries, or the lack of group goals and organizational structure as in its overdependence on one man whose principal objectives are personal and national aggrandizement. Houphouët, by African standards, is old and also somewhat infirm, and he operates according to no fixed ideological guidelines. Although Ivory Coast has shown steady growth since independence, its economic future is not yet assured. On Houphouët and on him alone hangs the fate of the Entente, and should he suddenly decide that the game of maintaining that organization is no longer worth the candle, or should Ivory Coast's prosperity falter and its subsidies cease, the Entente would doubtless dissolve. In such an event, Ivory Coast's junior partners' hostility to the Ivorians would soon come to the surface, and their tribal and commercial affinities with nonmember neighbors, which Houphouët now holds partially in check, would probably reassert themselves.

No such dramatic disruption of the Entente occurred in 1970, but certain events of that year portend important changes in the organization. These, in the order of their probable significance for the future of the Entente, were the founding of the Communauté des Etats de l'Afrique Occidentale (CEAO), the end of Nigeria's civil war, a revival of the OERS, Houphouët's dissidence from the widespread African condemnation of white South Africa, and the death of General de Gaulle.

The political impact of these developments on the Entente

is likely to be less important than are their economic implications, for it seems to confirm already established trends. The process of francophone Africa's disengagement from France preceded by six years de Gaulle's retirement from politics, and Houphouët's proposal for an "accommodation" with South Africa has simply reinforced his reputation as Black Africa's number-one stooge of the West. To be sure, it has once again chilled relations between Houphouët and Sékou Touré, but this is not the first time that moves toward their reconciliation have been interrupted and, in any case, the Ivorian-Guinean relationship exerts only an indirect influence on the evolution of the Entente.

The most immediate danger for the Entente's solidarity is the resurgence of Nigeria and, to a lesser degree, Ghana's efforts to revive its economy and to repair the damage done to its neighbors by the expulsion of thousands of their nationals. If the Busia government succeeds in reasserting its attraction for Upper Volta and Togo, and if Niger and Dahomey are drawn into Nigeria's orbit, Ivory Coast may find itself relatively isolated in the region. To prevent such an eventuality, Houphouët promoted the formation of the CEAO at Bamako in May 1970. That new organization aims to create a free-trading zone among the francophone West African nations, and already it has succeeded in drawing into its membership all the Entente countries except Togo, and all the OERS states but Guinea.

Should the CEAO actually succeed in creating a common market for the franc-zone countries of West Africa, it could become a closer-knit, better balanced, and more effective economic organization than the Entente or even the OCAM. Furthermore, its wider geographic scope, more diverse resources, and larger number of producers and consumers should go far to meet some of the aspirations of Ivory

Coast's junior partners, who have been dissatisfied with the limitations of the Entente and its dependence on Houphouët. On the other hand, the Entente's main assets—its flexibility, homogeneous outlook, and relative financial stability—may well be jeopardized by the much larger membership and stronger structure of such an organization as an expanded CEAO.

The founding of the CEAO marks still another stage in Houphouët's lifelong quest for an interstate organizational vehicle suited to his leadership. Obviously it has yet to prove its worth in his eyes and in those of his fellow members, and should it fulfill their expectations and hopes, the CEAO may eventually absorb the Entente. In the meantime, Houphouët will doubtless be careful to preserve the Entente's separate identity and, as he has done so often in the past, periodically renew its lease on life. To him and to his partners the Entente has the great merit of being a going concern and one that has weathered the test of time and of successive internecine conflicts.

List of Political Parties with Abbreviations, Founding Dates, and Leaders

DAHOMEY

UPD	Union Progressiste Dahoméenne	1947	Apithy
BPA	Bloc Populaire Africain	1947	Poisson, Ahomadegbe
PRD	Parti Républicain du Dahomey	1951	Apithy
GEN	Groupement Ethnique du Nord	1951	Maga
GID	Groupement des Indépendants du Dahomey	1951	Quenum
PRD	Parti Républicain Dahoméen	1956	Apithy
MDD	Mouvement Démocratique Dahoméen	1956	Maga
UDD	Union Démocratique Dahoméenne	1956	Ahomadegbe, Zinsou, Adande
PRD	Parti Républicain Dahoméen	1957	Apithy
RDD	Rassemblement Démocratique Dahoméen	1957	Maga
PRA	Parti du Regroupement Africain	1958	Apithy, Maga
PFA	Parti de la Fédération Africaine	1959	Zinsou
PND	Parti des Nationalistes Dahoméenne	1960	Apithy, Zinsou
PDU	Parti Dahoméen de l'Unité	1961	Maga, Apithy, Zinsou, Tevoedjre
PDD	Parti Démocratique Dahoméen	1963	Apithy, Ahomadegbe, Congacou

List of Political Parties with Abbreviations, Founding Dates, and Leaders (*Continued*)

UPPER VOLTA

RDA-EV	Rassemblement Démocratique Africain–Entente Voltaïque	1946	Houphouët-Boigny
UV	Union Voltaïque	1951	Conombo
PSEMA	Parti Social d'Education des Masses Africaines	1955	Conombo, Joseph Ouedraogo
MPA	Mouvement Populaire de la Révolution Africaine	1956	Nazi Boni
RDA-UDV	Reassemblement Démocratique Africain–Union Démocratique Voltaïque	1956	Ali Barraud, Ouezzin Coulibaly, Maurice Yameogo
PDU	Parti Démocratique Unifié	1958	Ouezzin Coulibaly, Maurice Yameogo
PRA	Parti du Rassemblement Africain	1958	Nazi Boni
MLN	Mouvement de la Libération Nationale	1958	Joseph Ki Zerbo
GAP	Groupement d'Action Politique	1966	Sigué Nouhoun
UNR	Union pour la Nouvelle République	1970	Blaise Bassolet

NIGER

RDA-PPN	Rassemblement Démocratique Africain–Parti Progressiste Nigérien	1946	Hamani Diori, Boubou Hama, Djibo Bakary
UDN	Union Démocratique Nigérienne	1950	Djibo Bakary
UNI	Union Nigérienne des Indépendants	1951	Zodi Ikhia
BNA	Bloc Nigérien d'Action	1951	Issoufou Seydou Djermakoye
PRA-Sawaba	Parti du Rassemblement Africain–Freedom Party	1958	Djibo Bakary

TOGO

CUT	Comité de l'Unité Togolaise	1946	Sylvanus Olympio
PTP	Parti Togolais du Progrès	1956	Pédro Olympio, Nicolas Grunitsky
JUVENTO			
UCPN	Union des Chefs et Populations du Nord	1950	Anani Santos
UDPT	Union Démocratique des Populations Togolaises	1951	Nicolas Grunitsky
		1959	Antoine Meatchi, Nicolas Grunitsky
PUT	Parti de l'Unité Togolaise	1963	Noë Kutuklui, Théophile Mally
RPT	Rassemblement du Peuple Togolais	1969	Etienne Eyadema

IVORY COAST

PDCI	Parti Démocratique de la Côte d'Ivoire	1946	Félix Houphouët-Boigny

Bibliography

COUNCIL OF THE ENTENTE

Books and articles

Adedeji, A. "Prospects of Regional Economic Co-operation in West Africa." *Journal of Modern African Studies,* 8, no. 2, 1970.

Decraene, P. "La Politique Africaine du Général de Gaulle." *Revue Française d'Etudes Politiques Africaines,* Nov. 1969.

"Entente: Un Exemple pour les Autres Etats Africains." *Europe-France-Outremer,* no. 373, Dec. 1960.

Ewing, A. F. "Prospects for Economic Integration in Africa." *Journal of Modern African Studies,* 5, no. 1, 1967.

"Ghana and her Neighbours," *West Africa,* Jan. 15, 22, 1971.

Hazlewood, A., ed. *African Integration and Disintegration.* London, 1967.

Lampire, P. "Les Groupements d'Etats Africains." *Journal Juridique et Politique d'Outremer,* Jan.–March 1964.

Lusignan, G. de. *French-Speaking Africa since Independence.* London, 1969.

Plessz, N. *Problems and Prospects of Economic Integration in West Africa.* Montreal, 1968.

République Française. Journal Officiel, *Accords entre la République Française et les Républiques de Côte d'Ivoire, du Dahomey, du Niger, et de Haute-Volta,* no. 6220, Feb. 1962.

Welch, C. E., ed. *Soldier and State in Africa.* Chicago, 1970.

Newspapers and periodicals

Cameroun, Côte d'Ivoire, Dahomey, Haute-Volta, Madagascar, Niger, Togo. Special issue of *Europe-France-Outremer,* no. 487, Aug. 1970.

Conseil de l'Entente, Secrétariat Administratif. *Bulletin d'Information, Abidjan,* July 1970.
Entente Africaine (quarterly), Nov. 1969, May 1970.
L'Afrique / 70 (annual).
L'Afrique d'Expression Française et Madagascar (annual). June 1970.

Publications of national presses

Dahomey: *Dahomey-Information* (daily); *Aube Nouvelle* (monthly); *La Dépêche Dahoméenne* (bi-monthly).
Ivory Coast: *Fraternité-Matin* (daily); *Bulletin Quotidien de l'A.I.P.* (daily); *Bulletin de la Chambre de Commerce* (daily); *Journal Officiel* (weekly); *Fraternité* (weekly); *Eburnea* (monthly); *Réalités Ivoiriennes* (monthly); *Le Marché Ivoirien* (monthly).
Niger: *Le Temps du Niger* (daily); *Le Niger* (weekly); *Labari* (monthly); *Journal Officiel* (monthly); *Le Niger en Marche* (annual).
Togo: *Togo-Presse* (daily); *Togo-Observateur* (daily); *La Sentinelle* (fortnightly); *La Vérité Togolaise* (fortnightly); *Le National* (fortnightly); *Présence Chrétienne* (weekly); *Togo Xletivi* (weekly); *Nouvelle République* (weekly); *Journal Officiel* (monthly); *Le Lien* (monthly); *Mia Holo* (monthly); *La Réalité Togolaise* (monthly).
Upper Volta: *Bulletin d'Information* (daily); *Bulletin de la Chambre de Commerce* (daily); *Journal Officiel* (weekly); *Carrefour Africain* (weekly); *Le Courrier Consulaire* (monthly); *L'Eclair* (bi-monthly).

DAHOMEY

Adotevi, J.-B. Articles in *Afrique Nouvelle,* Feb. 14, May 1, July 10, 25, Dec. 18, 25, 1968.
Agboton, G. "Réflexions sur les Coups d'Etat Militaires au Dahomey." *Afrique Nouvelle,* March 4, 1970.
Akindele, A., and C. Aguessy. *Dahomey.* Paris, 1955.

Apithy, S.-M. *Au Service de Mon Pays (1946–1956)*. Paris, 1957.
——. *Telle est la Vérité*. Paris, 1968.
Biarnès, P. "Le Docteur Zinsou au Chevet de l'Homme Malade de l'Afrique Francophone." *Le Monde,* April 4, 1969.
Blanchet, A. "Le Dahomey." *Nice-Matin,* Feb. 2, 1961.
Brasseur, Mme. "Cotonou, Capitale Economique du Dahomey." *Encyclopédie Mensuelle d'Outre-mer,* document no. 38, June 1955.
Clerc, J. P., and C. Tardits. *Société Paysanne et Problèmes Fonciers de la Palmeraie Dahoméenne*. Paris, 1956.
Comte, G. "Une Election pour Rien." *Revue Française d'Etudes Politiques Africaines,* May 1968.
Cornevin, R. *Histoire du Dahomey*. Paris, 1962.
——. *Le Dahomey,* Paris, 1965.
——. "Les Militaires au Dahomey et au Togo." *Revue Française d'Etudes Politiques Africaines,* Dec. 1968.
Decheix, P. "La Nouvelle Constitution du Dahomey." *Revue Juridique et Politique,* July–Sept. 1968.
Decraene, P. "Dahomey: Prétoriens et Intellectuels de Gauche." *Le Monde,* June 30, 1966.
Desanti, H. *Du Danhomé au Bénin-Niger*. Paris, 1945.
Devernois, G. "L'Organisation des Administrations Publiques et Formation des Fonctionnaires." Mimeo. United Nations, May 17, 1967.
Dictionnaire Bio-Bibliographique du Dahomey. Porto Novo, 1969.
"Dr. Z. and His Enemies." *West Africa,* May 17, 1969.
Dunglas, E. *Contribution à l'Histoire du Moyen-Dahomey, Royaumes d'Abomey, de Kétou, et de Ouidah*. Etudes Dahoméennes, 19, Cotonou, 1957.
Durand, A. "Les Collectivités de Base au Dahomey: Le Village et le Commune." *Revue Juridique et Politique,* April–June 1968.
Glélé, M. *Naissance d'un Etat Noir*. Paris, 1969.
Gnonlonfoun, A. Articles in *Afrique Nouvelle:*
  1967: Jan. 18, Feb. 15, March 8, April 5, May 10, 17, June 14, July 19, Sept. 6, Nov. 29, Dec. 27.

1968: Jan. 3, 24, Feb. 26, March 13, May 1, 8, 22, July 24, 31.
"Griot." "The Dahomey Question." *West Africa,* Dec. 30, 1967.
———. "Ahomadegbe Talking." *West Africa,* June 1, 1968.
———. "The Fourth Man in Dahomey." *West Africa,* June 6, 1968.
Grivot, R. *Réactions Dahoméennes.* Paris, 1954.
Hazoumé, P. *Doguicimi.* Paris, 1938.
Herskovits, M. *Dahomey—An Ancient West African Kingdom.* 2 vols. New York, 1938.
"Dahomey." In H. Kitchen, ed. *The Educated African,* pp. 474–478. London, 1962.
Kuenstler, P. *Politiques et Problèmes Concernant la Jeunesse, Rapport sur une Visite au Dahomey du 31 octobre au 8 novembre 1965.* United Nations, March 29, 1966.
"La Conjoncture Economique et Financière." *Marchés Tropicaux,* Aug. 31, 1968.
"La Fin d'un Régime." *Le Mois en Afrique,* Jan. 1966.
"La Position des Centrales Syndicales." *Afrique Nouvelle,* May 26, 1965.
La République du Dahomey. La Documentation Française, Notes et Etudes Documentaires, no. 2629, Paris, 1959; no. 3307, Paris, 1966.
"Le Dahomey a Bougé." *Jeune Afrique,* Aug. 1, 1968.
Lemarchand, R. "Dahomey: Coup within a Coup." *Africa Report,* June 1968.
Le Marché Dahoméen. Special issue of *Marchés Tropicaux,* Nov. 27, 1965.
Le Redressement Dahoméen. Special issue of *Europe-France-Outremer,* no. 453, Oct. 1967.
Lombard, J. *Structures de Type "Féodal" en Afrique Noire.* Paris, 1965.
Makedonsky, E. "Nouvelles Tentatives de Création d'un Parti Unique au Dahomey." *Revue Française d'Etudes Politiques Africaines,* Sept. 1969.
Mendy, J. "Le Pire Evité de Justesse." *Afrique Nouvelle,* Jan. 19, 1966.

——. "Le Dahomey au Point Mort." *Afrique Nouvelle,* Feb. 16, 1966.

Mitinkpon, N. "Le Dahomey en Crise." *Afrique Nouvelle,* Oct. 12, 19, 26, 1966.

Oke, F. M. "Réflexions sur les Partis Politiques Dahoméens." *Revue Française d'Etudes Politiques Africaines,* April 1968.

——. "Des Comités Electoraux aux Partis Politiques Dahoméens." *Revue Française d'Etudes Politiques Africaines,* Sept. 1969.

——. *Chefferies Traditionnelles et Evolution Politique au Dahomey.* Paris, 1966.

Pinto, I. "Discours Prononcé lors de son Installation à la Cour Suprème." *Penant,* April–May–June 1968.

République du Dahomey, Direction de la Statistique.

——. "Annuaire Statistique, 1967." Mimeo. Cotonou, 1969.

——. "Cinq Années de Commerce Extérieur du Dahomey, 1961–1965." Mimeo. Cotonou, Dec. 1969.

——. *Enquête Démographique au Dahomey, 1961.* Paris, 1964.

Ronen, D. "The Two Dahomeys." *Africa Report,* June 1968.

Serreau, J. *Le Développement à la Base au Dahomey et au Sénégal.* Paris, 1966.

Skurnik, W. A. W. "Political Instability and Military Intervention in Dahomey and Upper Volta." Mimeo. Bloomington, Ind., Oct. 1966.

Soglo, C. "Dahomey: Le Démarrage du Plan Quinquennal." *Marchés Tropicaux,* March 19, 1966.

Tardits, C. *Porto-Novo.* Paris, 1958.

Terray, E. "Les Révolutions Congolaise et Dahoméenne." *Revue Française de Science Politique,* Oct. 5, 1964.

Vieyra, J. "Dahomey dans le Guépier." *Jeune Afrique,* Dec. 31, 1967.

——. "Le Dahomey dans la Tourmente." *Jeune Afrique,* March 24, 1970.

"A Year of Soglo." *West Africa,* Dec. 31, 1966.

IVORY COAST

Alexander, A. S., Jr. "The Ivory Coast Constitution." *Journal of Modern African Studies,* 1, no. 3, Sept. 1963.

Amon d'Aby, F. J. *La Côte d'Ivoire dans la Cité Africaine.* Paris, 1951.

——. *Le Problème des Chefferies Traditionnelles en Côte d'Ivoire.* Abidjan, 1957.

Assouan Usher, A. *La République de la Côte d'Ivoire au Service de l'Afrique et de la Paix.* Versailles, 1968.

Atger, P. *La France en Côte d'Ivoire.* Dakar, 1962.

Berg, E. "Manpower and Education in Senegal, Guinea and Ivory Coast." In F. Harbison and C. Myers, eds., *Manpower and Education: Country Studies in Economic Development.* New York, 1965.

Bernue, E. "Abidjan: Note sur l'Agglomération d'Abidjan et sa Population." Institut Français d'Afrique Noire, *Bulletin,* no. 24, 1962.

Blanchet, A. "La Côte d'Ivoire Touchée par la Grâce." *Le Monde,* Aug. 31, Sept. 1, 2, 1955.

——. "La Côte d'Ivoire." *Nice-Matin,* Jan. 19, 1961.

Chaffard, G. *Les Carnets Secrets de la Décolonisation.* Paris, 1965. Pp. 99–131.

——. "La Côte d'Ivoire et le Démarrage de l'O.E.R.S." *Le Monde Diplomatique,* May 1968.

"Cinq Années de Croissance Economique." *Marchés Tropicaux,* May 27, 1967.

Comte, G. "Fronde Universitaire et Crise Morale." *Revue Française d'Etudes Politiques Africaines,* July 1969.

Côte d'Ivoire. Special issues of *Afrique Nouvelle,* May 21, 1964, July 30, 1969.

Cys, M., and C. Zarrouk. "Où en est l'Agriculture Ivoirienne?" *Jeune Afrique,* June 8, 1969.

Decraene, P. Articles in *Le Monde,* Aug. 20, 1964; Aug. 6, 7–8, 1966; March 24, 1968.

DuBois, V. *The Quiet Revolution*. American Universities Field
Staff Reports, June 1962.

——. "The Student-Government Conflict in the Ivory Coast,"
AUFS Reports, Feb. 1965.

——. "Houphouët-Boigny: Francophone Africa's Man of the
Year," *AUFS Reports*, Dec. 1965.

——. "Social Aspects of the Urbanization Process in Abidjan,
AUFS Reports, Nov. 1967.

Due, J. N. "Agricultural Development in the Ivory Coast and
Ghana." *Journal of Modern African Studies*, 7, no. 4, 1969.

Duprez, P. *Histoire des Ivoiriens*. Abidjan, 1962.

Esperet, G. "Syndicalisme Croyant en Afrique Française." *Le
Mois en Afrique*, May 1967.

Etudes Juridiques sur la Côte d'Ivoire. Special issue of *Penant*,
no. 689, Nov. 1961.

Europe-France-Outremer. Special issues on Ivory Coast:
   *Côte d'Ivoire, Diversification des Cultures, Industrialisation,
   Grands Travaux*, no. 445, Feb. 1967.
   La Côte d'Ivoire, no. 389, July 1962.
   La Côte d'Ivoire après l'Alerte, no. 407, Dec. 1963.
   La Côte d'Ivoire Poursuit sa Progression, no. 424, May 1965.
   Une Réussite Africaine: La Côte d'Ivoire, no. 469. Feb. 1969.

Foster, P. F. "Educational Development in Ghana and the Ivory
Coast." Mimeo. New York, Nov. 2, 1967.

Gibal, M. "Sociétés Urbaines de l'Ouest Africain: L'Exemple
d'Abidjan." *Le Mois en Afrique*, May 1968.

Golan, T. K., "Themes for Korhogo," *West Africa*, April 23,
1971.

Greene, R. H. "Ghana and the Ivory Coast 1957–1967: Reflec-
tions on Economic Strategy, Structure, Implementation and
Necessity." Mimeo. New York, Nov. 2, 1967.

Hallak, J., and R. Poignant. *Les Aspects Financiers de l'Education en Côte d'Ivoire*. UNESCO, Paris, 1966.

Hamon, L. "Le Rassemblement Démocratique Africain." *Revue
Juridique et Politique*, July–Aug.–Sept. 1961.

Hoguie, C. "Structure et Organisation Communales en Côte

d'Ivoire." *Revue Juridique et Politique,* April–June 1968.

Holas, B. *Le Séparatisme Religieux en Afrique Noire: L'Exemple de la Côte d'Ivoire.* Paris 1965.

Houphouët-Boigny, F. "Black Africa and the French Union." *Foreign Affairs,* July 1957.

——. "Les Chances de l'Afrique." *Revue Politique et Parlementaire,* 63, 1961.

——. "Que les Canons se Taisent." *Jeune Afrique,* May 5, 1968.

Kobben, A. J. F. "Le Planteur Noir." *Etudes Eburnéennes,* Abidjan, 1956.

La Côte d'Ivoire en Marche. Special issue of *Afrique Magazine,* June 1967.

La Côte d'Ivoire, Pays Pilote de l'Afrique Noire. Special issue of *Combat,* Oct. 9, 1968.

Laporte, M. *La Pensée Sociale de Félix Houphouët-Boigny,* Bordeaux, 1970.

Le Marché de la Côte d'Ivoire. Special issues of *Marchés Tropicaux,* April 30, 1966; June 29, 1968.

"Le Plan 1967/1970 de la Côte d'Ivoire." *Marchés Tropicaux,* June 24, 1967.

Marchand, A. H. "La Formation des Cadres Supérieurs de l'Administration Ivoirienne." *Penant,* April–June 1968, July–Sept. 1969, Oct.–Dec. 1969.

Ministère de l'Information. *Côte d'Ivoire, Faits et Chiffres, 1966.* Abidjan, 1967.

——. *Répertoire Politique et Administratif.* Abidjan, 1969.

Ministère du Plan. *Perspectives Décennales de Développement Econimique, Social et Culturel, 1960–1970.* Abidjan, 1967.

République de la Côte d'Ivoire. *Annuaire National 1968–69.* Paris, 1969.

Rougerie, G. *La Côte d'Ivoire.* Paris, 1964.

Ruttiman, J. P. "L'Enseignement en Côte d'Ivoire." *Afrique Nouvelle,* May 21, 1964.

Samir Amin. *Le Développement du Capitalisme en Côte d'Ivoire.* Paris, 1967.

Seydou Madani Sy. *Recherches sur l'Exercice du Pouvoir Poli-*

tique en Afrique Noire (Côte d'Ivoire, Guinée, Mali). Paris, 1965.

Sigel, E. "Ivory Coast: Booming Economy, Political Calm." *Africa Report,* April 1970.

——. "Ivory Coast Education: Brake or Spur?" *Africa Report,* January 1967.

"Soviet Views on Ivory Coast." *Mizan Newsletter,* Oct. 1961.

Staniland, M. "Local Administration in Ivory Coast." *West Africa,* March 9, 16, 1968.

"The Houphouët Way." Editorial. *West Africa,* Aug. 5, 1967.

"The Ivory Coast Picture." *West Africa,* Dec. 14, 1968.

Université d'Abidjan. *Annales.* Abidjan, 1965.

Wallerstein, I. "Background to Paga." *West Africa,* July 28, Aug. 5, 1961.

——. *The Road to Independence: Ghana and the Ivory Coast.* The Hague, 1965.

Wodie, F. "Le Parti Démocratique de Côte d'Ivoire." *Revue Juridique et Politique,* Oct.–Dec. 1968.

Zolberg, A. *One Party Government in the Ivory Coast.* Princeton, 1964.

NIGER

Abadie, M. *Afrique Centrale: La Colonie du Niger.* Paris, 1926.

Anderson, P. " 'New System' in Niger." *Africa Report,* Nov. 1968.

Bernus, E. *Quelques Aspects de l'Evolution des Touareg de l'Ouest de la République du Niger.* Niamey, 1963.

Bernus, S. *Particularismes Ethniques en Milieu Urbain: L'Exemple de Niamey.* Paris, 1969.

Blanchet, A. "Le Niger." *Nice-Matin,* Jan. 27, 1961.

Bonardi, P. *La République du Niger, Naissance d'un Etat.* Paris, 1960.

Boubou Hama. *Niger, Récits Historiques.* Paris, 1967.

——. *Histoire du Gobir et de Sokoto.* Niamey, 1967.

Chaffard, G. *Les Carnets Secrets de la Décolonisation.* Paris, 1967. Pp. 269–332.

Chevalier, J. *Programmation Régionale au Niger.* Paris, 1969.

Clair, A. *Le Niger, Pays à Découvrir.* Paris, 1965.

Clifford, R. L. *Renseignements Economiques sur la République du Niger.* Niamey, 1963.

Commerce Extérieur de la République du Niger, Annuaire 1959–1969. Luxembourg, 1969.

Commissariat Général au Développement. *Programmation 1970–1973.* Niamey, 1969.

Commissariat du Plan. *"Perspectives Décennales de Développement 1965–1975."* Mimeo. 2 vols. Niamey (n.d.).

Comte, G. Three articles in *Europe-France-Outremer,* no. 430. Nov. 1965.

——. "La Difficulté d'Etre Nigérien." *Jeune Afrique,* Dec. 23, 1969.

Connaissance du Niger. Special issue of *Afrique Nouvelle,* March 13, 1968.

Development Bank of the Republic of Niger. *Activity Report 1969.* Niamey (n.d.).

Drin, F. "Niger." In H. Kitchen, ed., *The Educated African,* pp. 479–485. London, 1962.

Dupire, M. *Peuls Nomades du Sahel Nigérien.* Paris, 1962.

Froelich, J.-C. *Les Musulmans d'Afrique Noire.* Paris, 1962.

"Griot." "Peacemaker Diori." *West Africa,* July 27, 1968.

Guitton, R. "Au Niger, la Télévision Scolaire." *Le Figaro,* Jan. 8, 1969.

Kiba, Simon. "Problèmes Nigériens." *Afrique,* Jan. 1962.

Kouawo, J. E. "Le Nouveau Plan Décennal du Niger." *Afrique Nouvelle,* May 28, 1964.

"La Baisse des Cours de l'Arachide et la Guerre du Biafra Mettent en Difficulté l'Economie du Niger." *Marchés Tropicaux,* Sept. 21, 1968.

La Documentation Française. *Bibliographie Sommaire de la République du Niger.* Paris, 1969.

——. *La République du Niger.* Notes et Etudes Documentaires, no. 2638, Paris, Feb. 26, 1960.

"L'Avenir Politique au Niger." *Marchés Tropicaux,* Nov. 7, 1964.

"L'Eglise Catholique au Niger." *Afrique Nouvelle,* Sept. 12, 1963.

Le Marché Nigérien. Special issue of *Marchés Tropicaux,* Oct. 17, 1970.

"L'Industrialisation du Niger de 1960 à 1970." *Afrique Industrie,* Nov. 16, 1970.

Mendy, J. "Au Pays de la Soif." *Afrique Nouvelle,* Sept. 5, 12, 1963.

Ministère de la Coopération. *Les Budgets Familiaux Africains, Niamey, Mars 1961–Avril 1962.* Paris, 1964.

Ministére de l'Education Nationale. *Situation de l'Enseignement au 1er Janvier 1968.* Niamey (n.d.).

Monnier, A. "Les Organisations Villageoises de Jeunes." Mimeo. Niamey, 1968.

"Niger: La République a Dix Ans." *Jeune Afrique,* Jan. 6, 1969.

Niger: Stabilité Politique, Amélioration Economique. Special issue of *Europe-France-Outremer,* no. 430, Nov. 1965.

République du Niger. *Etude Démographique du Niger.* Paris, 1963.

——. *Annuaire Statistique (1963–1966).* Niamey, 1967.

Robert, G. *Le Lancement des Radio-Clubs du Niger.* Paris, 1968.

Rouch, J. *Les Sonrhay.* Paris, 1952.

Ruttiman, J. P. "Interview Exclusive du Président Hamani Diori." *Afrique Nouvelle,* June 7, 14, 1967.

Séré de Rivière, E. *Histoire du Niger.* Paris, 1965.

——. "La Chefferie au Niger." *Penant,* Oct.–Dec. 1967.

Service de l'Information. *Le Niger.* Niamey, Dec. 1969.

TOGO

Alcandre, S. *La République Autonome du Togo: de la Fiction à la Réalité.* Paris, 1957.

Brieux, J.-J. "L'Affaire Ewée." *Revue Française d'Etudes Politiques Africaines,* September 1967.

Coleman, J. M. *Togoland. International Conciliation,* no. 509, New York, 1956.

Cornevin, R. *Histoire du Togo.* Paris, 1959.

——. *Histoire de la Colonisation Allemande.* Paris, 1969.

——. *Le Togo, Nation-Pilote.* Paris, 1963.

——. "Les Militaires au Dahomey et au Togo." *Revue Française d'Etudes Africaines Politiques,* Dec. 1968.

"Des Nouvelles Structures au Togo." *AfricAsia,* no. 10, 1970.

Decraene, P. "La République du Togo Devra Livrer un Dur Combat pour Préserver son Unité." *Chroniques de la Communauté,* May 1960.

Fagla, H. "Togo An IX," *Jeune Afrique,* May 11, 1969.

Froelich, J.-C. *Cameroun-Togo.* Paris, 1956.

——. *Les Populations du Nord-Togo.* Paris, 1963.

Gonidec, P. F. "La République du Togo." *Penant,* March–April 1958.

Howe, R. W. "Togo: Four Years of Military Rule." *Africa Report,* May 1967.

Kuczynski, R. R. *The Cameroons and Togoland: A Demographic Study.* London, 1939.

La Documentation Française. *Le Togo.* Notes et Etudes Documentaires, no. 3541, Oct. 31, 1968.

Le Marché Togolais. Special issue of *Marchés Tropicaux,* Dec. 5, 1970.

Le Togo dans la Voie de la Planification. Special issue of *Europe-France-Outremer,* no. 432, Jan. 1966.

Luce, E. P. *Le Referendum du Togo (28 Octobre 1956): L'Acte de Naissance d'une République Africaine Autonome.* Paris, 1958.

Luchaire, F. *Du Togo Français sous Tutelle à la République Autonome du Togo.* Paris, 1957.

Milcent, E. "Tribalisme et Vie Politique dans les Etats du Bénin: Togo à l'Ombre d'Olympio." *Le Mois en Afrique,* June 1967.

Olympio, S. "Togo: Problems and Progress of a New Nation." *Africa Today,* April 1960.

Pauvert, J.-C. "L'Evolution Politique des Ewe." *Cahiers d'Etudes Africaines*, 1960.

Pechoux, L. *Le Mandat Français sur le Togo,* Paris, 1939.

Plan de Développement Economique et Social 1966–1970, Lomé (n.d.).

"Praetor Africanus." "Emancipations Africaines." *L'Afrique et l'Asie,* nos. 38, 39, 1957.

——. "Vers une Fédération Franco-Africaine: Naissance de la République Togolaise." *L'Afrique et l'Asie,* no. 36, 1956.

Recensement Général de la Population du Togo, 1958–1960. 2 vols. Lomé (n.d.).

Tessier du Cros, M. *Le Togo.* Paris, 1968.

Togo, Cinquième Année du Renouveau. Special issue of *Jeune Afrique,* Jan. 12, 1971.

Vlassemnko, E. *Population Active et Emploi au Togo.* Lomé, 1967.

UPPER VOLTA

"Action du Gouvernement Voltaïque en Matière Financière et Fiscale." *Afrique Nouvelle,* May 24, 31, June 7, 1967.

Balima, S. A. *Genèse de la Haute-Volta.* Ouagadougou, 1970.

——. "L'Organisation de l'Empire Mossi." *Penant,* Oct.–Dec. 1964.

——. "Notes on the Social and Labour Situation in the Republic of Upper Volta." *International Labour Review,* 82, 1960.

Bassolet, F. *Evolution de la Haute-Volta.* Ouagadougou, 1968.

Biarnès, P. "Haute-Volta: De Vigoureuses Mesures d'Austérité ont Permis le Redressement Financier." *Le Monde,* April 2, 1969.

Bichon, B. "Les Musulmans de la Subdivision de Kombissiry, Haute-Volta." In *Notes et Etudes sur l'Islam en Afrique Noire,* pp. 77–102. Paris, 1963.

Blanchet, A. "La Haute-Volta." *Nice-Matin,* Jan. 12, 1961.

——. "Yameogo et Nkrumah." *Le Monde,* March 28, 1965.

Colloques sur les Cultures Voltaïques, Ouagadougou, 1967.

Damiba, P. C. "Le Combat d'un Pays Sous-Développé." *Afrique Nouvelle,* Oct. 12, 19, 26, 1966.

Decraene, P. "Haute-Volta: Anciens d'Indochine contre Politiciens." *Le Monde,* July 1, 1966.

Deniel, R. *De la Savane à la Ville.* Paris, 1968.

Diallo Seyni Sambo. "Les Droits de Famille dans la Coutume Mossi." *Penant,* Jan.–March and April–June 1967.

Dim Delobson, A. *L'Empire du Mogho-Naba.* Paris, 1932.

DuBois, V. *The Struggle for Stability in the Upper Volta* (Parts I–V), American Universities Field Staff Reports. New York, March–Aug. 1969.

Dugue, M. "Upper Volta." in H. Kitchen, ed., *The Educated African,* pp. 486–492. London, 1962.

Givisiez, A. "Où en est les Mossi?" *Afrique Nouvelle.* Feb. 3, 1965.

Gomkoudougou, V. K. "Caractère Féodal du Système Politique Mossi." *Cahiers d'Etudes Africaines,* 2, no. 8, 1962.

Hammond, P. B. "Economic Change and Mossi Acculturation." In W. R. Bascom and M. Herskovits, eds., *Continuity and Change in African Cultures.* Chicago, 1959.

"Haute-Volta: Ferme Mise à l'Ecart des Civils." *Le Mois en Afrique,* Jan. 1967.

"Haute-Volta: Les Causes du Coup d'Etat dans le Contexte des Evènements." *Marchés Tropicaux,* Feb. 12, 1966.

"Jeune Volta, Spécial IVème Congrès (Août 1968)." Mimeo. Ouagadougou, 1968.

Ki Zerbo, J. "Fabriquer des Hommes." *Jeune Afrique,* June 30, 1968.

———. "Ce Serait plus Grave en Afrique." *Jeune Afrique,* July 14, 1968.

Kiba, S. "Comment se Porte la Haute-Volta?" *Afrique Nouvelle,* Sept. 13, 30, 1967.

———. "La Haute-Volta après Quelques Mois de Liberté." *Afrique Nouvelle,* Aug. 31, Sept. 7, 14, 1966.

——. "Quatre Années de Gouvernement Lamizana en Haute-Volta." *Afrique Nouvelle,* March 18, 25, April 1, 8, 15, 1970.

——. "Terre des Hommes." *Afrique Nouvelle,* March 21, 28, April 4, 1962.

La Documentation Française. *La République de Haute-Volta.* Notes et Etudes Documentaires, no. 2693, Aug. 19, 1960.

La Situation Démographique en Haute-Volta: Résultats Partiels de l'Enquête Démographique, 1960–1961. Paris, 1962.

Lamizana, S. "La Haute-Volta Veut Maintenir une Collaboration Constante et Sincère avec l'Entreprise Privée." *Marchés Tropicaux,* April 23, 1966.

Le Marché de la Haute-Volta. Special issue of *Marchés Tropicaux,* April 15, 1967.

"Le Pouvoir Traditionnel en Haute-Volta." *Afrique Nouvelle,* Nov. 20, 1968.

Le Redressement Voltaïque. Special issue of *Europe-France-Outremer,* no. 467, Dec. 1968.

"L'Expérience des 'Fermes-Ecoles'." *Jeune Afrique,* Sept. 10, 1967.

Marcais, M. "L'Ecole Nationale d'Administration de la République de Haute-Volta." *Penant,* July–Sept. 1964.

Ministère des Finances et du Commerce. *Commerce Extérieur et Balance Commerciale, Année 1968.* Ouagadougou, 1969.

——. *Le Commerce Intérieur de Haute-Volta, 1960–1969.* Ouagadougou, 1969.

Ministère de l'Information. *La Haute-Volta.* Ouagadougou, 1966.

Ministère du Plan. *Plan-Cadre 1967–1970.* 2 vols. Ouagadougou, 1967.

Nazi Boni. *Crépuscule des Temps Anciens.* Paris, 1962.

Skinner, E. P. "Labor Migration among the Mossi of Upper Volta." In H. Kuper, ed., *Urbanization and Migration in West Africa.* Berkeley and Los Angeles, 1965.

——. "Strangers in West African Societies." *Africa,* Oct. 1963.

——. *The Mossi of Upper Volta.* Stanford, 1964.

Skurnik, W. A. E. "Political Instability and Military Intervention in Dahomey and Upper Volta." Mimeo. Bloomington, Ind., Oct. 20, 1966.

Souleymane Konate. "Le Plan de Scolarisation en Haute-Volta. *"Afrique Nouvelle,* Nov. 19, 1964.

Sylvester, A. "Politics and Poverty." *West Africa,* June 20, 1970.

———. "Farms and Mines." *West Africa,* June 27, 1970.

"Une Innovation Voltaïque: Les Communautés Rurales." *Afrique Nouvelle,* Aug. 30, 1962.

Vieyra, J. "Dans l'Attente d'un Pouvoir Civil." *Jeune Afrique,* April 7, 1970.

Wallerstein, I. "Background to Paga." *West Africa,* July 28, Aug. 5, 1961.

Index

Library of Congress Cataloging in Publication Data
   (For library cataloging purposes only)

Thompson, Virginia McLean, date.
   West Africa's Council of the Entente.

   (Africa in the modern world)
   Bibliography: p.
   1. Conseil de l'Entente.   2. Africa, French West—Politics.
3. Houphouët-Boigny, Felix, Pres. Ivory Coast, 1905–   I. Title.
DT534.T46   320.9'66   70-171935
ISBN 0-8014-0683-8